Science Night Family Fun from A to Z

26 Activities for School or Community Family Science Events

Mickey Sarquis and Lynn Hogue

Terrific Science Press
Miami University Middletown
Middletown, Ohio

Terrific Science Press
Miami University Middletown
4200 East University Blvd.
Middletown, Ohio 45042
513/727-3269
www.terrificscience.org

ISBN 1-883822-21-1

This material is based, in part, upon work supported by the National Science Foundation under grant number ESI-9355523 and a grant under the federally funded Dwight D. Eisenhower Mathematics and Science Education Act, administered by the Ohio Board of Regents. Any opinions, findings, and conclusions or recommendations expressed in this material are those of the authors and do not necessarily reflect the views of the funding agencies.

Contents

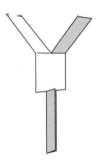

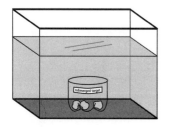

Acknowledgments

The authors wish to thank the following individuals and organizations who have contributed to the development of the activities in this book.

Contributors

Mary Jo Gardner	Fairmont Egan Elementary School	Kalispell, MT
Paula Halm	Heritage Hills Elementary School	Cincinnati, OH
Bev Kutsunai	Kamehameha Elementary School	Honolulu, HI
Phil McBride	Eastern Arizona College	Thatcher, AZ
Veronica Newman	Oakdale Elementary School	Cincinnati, OH
Mary Neises	Bauer Elementary School	Miamisburg, OH
Dwight Portman	Winton Woods High School	Cincinnati, OH
Cynthia Stanford	Norwood View Elementary School	Cincinnati, OH
Linda Woodward	Center for Chemical Education	Middletown, OH

Support for the Development of this Book

This book was developed in conjunction with the Teaching Science with TOYS program through the support of the National Science Foundation and the Ohio Board of Regents. The goals of Teaching Science with TOYS are to enhance teachers' knowledge of chemistry and physics and to encourage activity-based, discovery-oriented science through the use of toys and other everyday objects.

Terrific Science Press Design and Production Team

Document Production Manager: Susan Gertz

Technical Coordinator: Lisa Taylor

Technical Writing: Lisa Taylor, Susan Gertz, Christine Mulvin, Amy Hudepohl

Technical Editing: Amy Stander, Lisa Taylor, Christine Mulvin

Book Illustration: Carole Katz

Table Tent Art: Cynthia Stanford

Photo Editing: Brian Fair

Design/Layout: Susan Gertz

Production: Christine Mulvin, Becky Franklin, Stephen Gentle, Amy Hudepohl, Lisa Taylor, Jennifer Stencil, Brian Fair

Laboratory Testing: Eric Buck

Reviewers

Frank Cardulla	Niles North High School (retired)	Skokie, IL
Herman Keith	The Kinkaid School/Univ. of Houston	Houston, TX
Dwight Portman	Winton Woods High School	Cincinnati, OH
J. Timothy Perry	Mt. Hebron High School	Ellicott City, MD
Jerry Sarquis	Miami University	Oxford, OH
Beverley A.P. Taylor	Miami University Hamilton	Hamilton, OH

Testers

Family teams at Kamehameha School, Honolulu, Hawaii

Family teams at Central Academy, Middletown, OH

Teaching Science with TOYS Participants, 1998–1999

Chad Agnes	Lorin Andrews Middle School	Massillon, OH
Briana Ainsworth	MonDay Community Correctional Institute	Dayton, OH
Susan Alexander	Washington Elementary	Hillsboro, OH
Deborah Arndts	Twin Valley Local	West Alexandria, OH
Jennifer Arnold	Willowville Elementary	Batavia, OH
Joanne Ashworth	Monroe Elementary	Monroe, OH
Dianna Bartles	W.M. Sellman School	Madeira, OH
Pam Bennington	Vernon Primary	Wheelersburg, OH
Sheri Benton	Maineville Elementary	Maineville, OH
Karen Blackmon	Van Buren Elementary	Hamilton, OH
Sister M. Joletta Boellner	St. Wendelin Elementary	Fostoria, OH
Gerri Bolin	C.O. Harrison Elementary	Cincinnati, OH
Sheryl Borger	Laura Farrell School	Franklin, OH
Ladonna Boyd	Alexander Elementary School	Albany, OH
Rita Brown	Union Furnace Elementary	Union Furnace, OH
Virginia Browne	Lemoyne Elementary	Lemoyne, OH
Jennifer Brunka	Roselawn-Condon	Cincinnati, OH
Linda Campbell	Lynchburg Elementary/Junior High	Lynchburg, OH
Kathleen Carpenter	Ada Exempted Village Schools	Ada, OH
Toni Cary	Valley Elementary	Beavercreek, OH
Peg Cassaro	Our Lady of Lourdes	Cincinnati, OH
Holly Chakeres	Groveport Madison Middle School-North	Columbus, OH
Bonita Cochran	Valley Elementary	Beavercreek, OH
Mandy Cole	Struble Elementary	Cincinnati, OH
Tanya Cordes	Swifron Primary	Cincinnati, OH
E. Lee Cornett	Three Rivers Middle School	Cleves, OH
Julie Cowan	Van Buren Elementary	Hamilton, OH
Kelly Craig	Clearcreek Elementary	Stoutsville, OH
Jocelyn Crawford	Main Elementary School	Beavercreek, OH
Kathy Damron	College Hill Fundamental Academy	Cincinnati, OH
Diana Davis	Amelia Middle School	Batavia, OH
Barbara DeBolt	Green Elementary Logan	Logan, OH
Anne Demmel	Ann Weigel Elementary	Cincinnati, OH
Joanne DeTomaso	Bellcreek Elementary	Bellbrook, OH
Karen Develen	St. Bernard Elementary	St. Bernard, OH
Erica Devol	Central Elementary Logan	Logan, OH
Drew Dilley	Three Rivers Middle School	Cleves, OH
JoAnna Dorman	Hartwell Elementary	Cincinnati, OH
Lonnie Dusch	Mt. Healthy High School	Cincinnati, OH
Deborah Dye	New Miami Elementary	Hamilton, OH
Janice Eberle	Evamere Primary School	Hudson, OH
Kimberly Eibel	South Amherst M.S.	South Amherst, OH
Susan Eichel	C.O. Harrison Elementary	Cincinnati, OH
Mary Etter	Our Lady of Lourdes	Cincinnati, OH
Connie Fleming	East Elementary School	Logan, OH
Diana Flood	Green Elementary School	Logan, OH
Vicki Floyd	Green Elementary School	Franklin Furnace, OH
Catherine Frazier	Wm. H. Taft Elementary School	Cincinnati, OH
Jan French	Cincinnati Country Day	Cincinnati, OH
Susan Freund	Monroe Elementary	Monroe, OH
David Fugate	Heritage Elementary	West Chester, OH
Nancy Galusha	J.E. Prass Elementary	Kettering, OH
Janice Gault	Logan-Hocking Middle School	Logan, OH
John Gilpin	Conneaut High School	Conneaut, OH
Elke Gies	C.O. Harrison Elementary	Cincinnati, OH

Paige Gipson	Norwood Middle School	Norwood, OH
Cathy Girard	St. Rita School for the Deaf	Cincinnati, OH
Joanna Goldslager	Mason Heights Elementary School	Mason, OH
Roderick Gray	Meadowdale H.S.	Dayton, OH
Ginger Hamm	St. Cecilia School	Cincinnati, OH
Sheila Harris	Harrisonville Elementary	Pomeroy, OH
Tamiko Hatcher	Lehman Middle School	Canton, OH
Kimberly Hayes	East Elementary School	Logan, OH
Delores Heffner	St. Cecilia School	Cincinnati, OH
Lee Hieber	Fairfield City Schools, East Elementary	Hamilton, OH
Steven Hoffman	Clearcreek Elementary	Springboro, OH
Sheila Holbrock	Monroe Elementary	Monroe, OH
Cynthia Hopkins	Madeira City Schools	Cincinnati, OH
Deborah Howard	Adams Elementary School	Hamilton, OH
Kimberly Howard	Vernon Primary	Wheelersburg, OH
Randall Hoying	St. Henry High School	St. Henry, OH
Mary Ann Hughes	Union Furnace Elementary	Union Furnace, OH
Anbela Isaacs	Lincoln Elementary School	Hamilton, OH
Marcie Janey	Central Elementary Logan	Logan, OH
Sandra Kalisewicz	Middletown/Monroe School District	Monroe, OH
Sharon Keplar	Green Elementary Logan	Logan, OH
Linda Kraus	East Elementary	Greenville, OH
Ann Krentz	Mason Heights Elementary School	Mason, OH
Brenda Kurtz	J. F. Dulles Elementary/Oak Hills S.D.	Cincinnati, OH
Marianne Ladenburger	Clough Pike Elementary	Cincinnati, OH
Timmiera Lawrence	Lloyd Mann Primary	Loveland, OH
Gena Leisten	Hamilton-Maineville Elementary	Maineville, OH
Margaret Libecap	Westbrook Elementary	Brookville, OH
Vivian Liette	Ansonia High School	Ansonia, OH
Patricia Lillibridge	Lincoln Elementary School	Hamilton, OH
Mary Malone	McKinley Kindergarden Center-Hamilton	Hamilton, OH
Suzanne Martin	Lemoyne Elementary	Lemoyne, OH
Amy Mayer	Cherokee Elementary	Hamilton, OH
Holly McElwee	South Elementary School	Greenville, OH
Lorrie McGuire	Trimble Elementary	Glouster, OH
Sharon Meek	Green Elementary	Franklin Furnace, OH
Cheryl Miller	Pennyroyal Elementary	Franklin, OH
Lisa Miller	Harrisonville Elementary	Pomeroy, OH
Michelle Miller	New Miami Elementary	Hamilton, OH
Phyllis Miller	Twin Valley Schools	West Alexandria, OH
Charlotte Moore	Vernon Primary	Wheelersburg, OH
Sheryl Morrison	Garfield Jr. High	Hamilton, OH
Patricia Neyer	C.O. Harrison Elementary	Cincinnati, OH
Daniel Nieman	Ursuline Academy	Cincinnati, OH
Sharon Orsi	Westbrook Elementary	Brookville, OH
Rebecca Osburn	Union Furnace Elementary	Union Furnace, OH
Melissa Parsons	Norwood Middle School	Norwood, OH
Joan Pierce	MonDay Community Correctional Institute	Dayton, OH
Gwen Pleiman	West Carrollton Junior High School	West Carrollton, OH
Stephanie Quiett	Garfield Jr. High	Hamilton, OH
Marsha Radabaugh	Middleport Elementary	Middleport, OH
Teresa Reynolds	Willowville Elementary	Batavia, OH
Jo Ann Rigano	Valley Elementary	Beavercreek, OH
Julie Rush	McAuley High School	Cincinnati, OH
Patricia Scherff	Spaulding Middle School	Goshen, OH
Diana Schwartz	J.A. Garfield Middle School	Garrettsville, OH
Mary Scott	Evamere Primary School	Hudson, OH 44236
Candace Sharp	Vandalia-Butler City Schools	Vandalia, OH
Karen Sides	Fairfield City Schools- East Elementary	Hamilton, OH
Sandra Slobodzian-Zipes	E.D. Smith Elementary School	Dayton, OH
Jamee Sprengard	Bridgetown Jr. High School	Cincinnati, OH
Robert Starkey	Conneaut Area School	Conneaut, OH

Joan Stidham	Indian Hill Elementary	Cincinnati, OH
Kathy Stotts	Green Elementary Logan	Logan, OH
Elizabeth Stratman	Hartwell School	Cincinnati, OH
Julie Stueve	Kitty Hawk	Huber Heights, OH
Ken Sturgill	Wilson Jr. High School	Hamilton, OH
Patty Sutton	Indian Hill Elementary	Cincinnati, OH
Sonya Tennant	Allensville Elementary	McArthur, OH
Cheryl Turner	Amelia Middle School	Batavia, OH
Kelly Turner	Fillmore Elementary	Hamilton, OH
Carol Umberg	St. Bernard Elementary	St. Bernard, OH
Janice Vanderplough	St. Jospeh Orphanage	Cincinnati, OH
Karen Veidt	Green Elementary Logan	Logan, OH
Kelli Wagner	J.F. Dulles Elementary	Cincinnati, OH
Kathy Wallen	Washington Elementary	Hillsboro, OH
Patricia Ward	Monroe Elementary	Monroe, OH
Rebecca Ward	Jefferson Elementary	Middletown, OH
Darlene West	Delhi Junior High School	Cincinnati, OH
Amy White	Hamilton-Maineville Elementary	Maineville, OH
Linda Willard	Green Elementary Logan	Logan, OH
Wilson Willard III	R.E. Lucas Intermediate School	Cincinnati, OH
Peggy Williams	Bellcreek Elementary	Bellbrook, OH
Robin Willis	Swifton Primary	Cincinnati, OH
Jo Ann Wingereid	Mason Heights Elementary	Mason, OH
Kathleen Wirsch	St. John The Baptist School	Harrison, OH
Patricia Witson	Shroder Paideia Middle School	Cincinnati, OH
Leslie Yinger	Coolville Elementary	Coolville, OH
Karen Zearbaugh	Batavia Middle School	Batavia, OH

Foreword

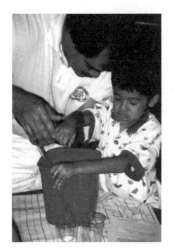

Have you been looking for a way to get families involved in your students' education? Try a Family Science event and provide a wonderful opportunity for family teams to enjoy the fun of doing and learning science together. This book is designed to help you plan and carry out a fun, successful event that will benefit your students, school, and community.

Family Science events can vary greatly in size, scope, and duration depending on your school's needs and the resources available. To provide flexibility, this book includes 26 simple, fun, and safe family science challenges from which to choose as you plan your event. To ensure accuracy, doability, and appropriateness, all the activities in this book have been extensively tested by teachers from across the nation and have been externally reviewed by expert science educators.

The information and ideas in this book stem from our own experience with conducting Family Science events and that of our large network of teachers who have successfully hosted such events. We've provided you with lots of planning details to help eliminate as much of the guesswork as possible from the process. In addition to complete instructions for planning and conducting the event, you'll find Shopping/Gathering Lists, Setup Checklists, guides for calculating quantities needed for your event, and reproducible masters for handouts, table tents, and labels. While we hope that you'll tailor the setup and structure of your Family Science event to your own needs, this book provides tips, templates, and 26 tested activities to help your event run smoothly and be lots of fun for all involved.

You can carry the momentum of your Family Science event into the classroom with the companion to this book, *Classroom Science from A to Z*. The activities in *Classroom Science from A to Z* coordinate by science topic and alphabetical letter with the activities in this book, but they are designed specifically for a classroom setting. Each lesson includes assessment plans and suggestions for cross-curricular integration to extend the learning throughout the curriculum.

We think you'll find that a Family Science event boosts your students' science learning and helps families become more involved in education. Good luck, and have fun!

Mickey Sarquis, Director
Center for Chemical Education

Why Host a Family Science Event?

Science Night Family Fun from A to Z is a resource book that enables you to easily plan and host a Family Science event: an opportunity for children and their adult partners to explore science concepts through a variety of fun and exciting activities that we call family science challenges. Getting families involved in their children's education in positive ways, such as through a Family Science event, is one of the best ways to improve student performance in school. Over 30 years of studies conclude that positive family involvement leads to these benefits for students:

- higher grades and test scores,
- better attendance at school,
- completion of more homework,
- more positive attitudes and behavior,
- higher graduation rates, and
- greater enrollment in higher education.

Both educators and parents recognize the value of greater family involvement in children's learning. In a 1993 Harris poll, teachers cited strengthening parents' roles in their children's learning as the goal that should receive the highest priority in public education policy during the next few years. Parents agree; according to a 1995 survey by Bayer Corporation, almost all parents think it is very important to keep their children interested in and enthusiastic about science and agreed that they would spend some time each week at home helping their children with science if the schools asked and provided suggestions. However, only three in ten parents feel very well equipped to teach their children science.

How can educators help parents become more involved in their children's science learning? The informal setting of a Family Science event provides a fun, comfortable environment for family involvement. The clearly written and illustrated Family Science Challenge handouts in this book will help parents feel more confident about exploring science with their children, both during the family event and later at home where they may want to repeat the science activities.

References

Henderson, A., Berla, N., Eds. *A new generation of evidence: The family is critical to student achievement;* National Committee for Citizens in Education, Center for Law and Education: Washington, D.C., 1994.

Metropolitan Life Survey of the American Teacher 1993: Violence in American Public Schools; Louis Harris & Associates: New York, 1993.

The Bayer Facts of Science Education: An Assessment of Elementary School Parent and Teacher Attitudes Toward Science Education; Research Communications: Dedham, MA, 1995.

Planning Your Event

The heart of any good Family Science event is fun, simple science activities that everyone enjoys and learns from, and *Science Night Family Fun from A to Z* contains clear, simple, step-by-step instructions for 26 great family science challenges. However, hosting a successful Family Science event requires much more than providing good activities. It requires figuring out how much of everything you need for 50, 200, even 400 families. It requires shopping for or gathering these materials, preparing them for use, and setting them up before your event. *Science Night Family Fun from A to Z* makes all these tasks as easy as possible with a variety of planning tools and templates for copying. But first, to get you started, this "Planning Your Event" section contains general tips and suggestions for your event.

Selecting a Location

In choosing a location, consider whether you would prefer to have your event in one large space such as a cafeteria or gymnasium, in several smaller spaces such as classrooms, or spread out over the whole school. Your choice of room for the event may affect what kind of tables you will use and how many you will need. For a single large room, you may be able to use cafeteria-type tables and have many families working at each table. If activities are set up in individual classrooms, you can use smaller tables or push several flat-topped desks together.

If your event is small enough, holding it in one large room presents significant advantages: families do not have to walk around a building to find the different activities, volunteers can move from one area to another as needed, and you can keep an eye on the progress of the event and quickly answer any questions or solve any problems. Possible disadvantages include noise, general commotion that may be distracting to families working at the stations, and the possibility of people getting in each other's way as they move about. Of course, the larger your event becomes, the more likely it is that you will need to spread out into hallways or multiple rooms.

Activities that involve water will require a little extra planning to determine where the water will come from, how it can be disposed of, and how to clean up spills. Access to a sink makes those activities easier to set up. If sinks are not readily available, you may want to have one or more volunteers occasionally empty buckets at those stations. Sponges and mops are useful for spills, and we've noted the need for these in activities that use water, so you shouldn't be caught off guard.

Volunteers

No Family Science event can happen without volunteers, and we suggest that you recruit them early in the planning process. Volunteers might include high school students, fellow teachers, parents, or community volunteers. Volunteers can help shop for and gather materials for the event, set up activity stations, replenish supplies, staff tables to engage family teams in conversation about the science topics, and clean up after the event. The planning materials provided for each activity in this book make it easy to involve volunteers in these areas.

If you have volunteers staff the tables, which we highly recommend, it's a good idea to give them a copy of the activities before the event and let them try out the activities so they know what to expect. Practice will enable volunteers to help participants, answer questions, and keep the setups well stocked with consumable materials.

Inviting Families

To have a successful event, you need a convenient way to advertise and also to obtain at least an estimate of the number of families that plan to attend. This can be done by sending home a letter with students that includes a RSVP response slip. Getting papers into the hands of parents (and out of desks and backpacks) can be challenging, so use upbeat, inviting language, eye-catching graphics, and colorful paper to get the message across. Included on the next page is a sample flyer that you may use or adapt for your event.

Give a deadline for parents to return the RSVP slip. If time and budget allow, you may want to plan on two rounds of letters home. The first letter would announce the event and provide the RSVP slip; the second letter would say "there's still time to sign up" and provide another RSVP slip. Despite these opportunities, people may show up who did not RSVP, so we recommend you plan to have a few extra materials on hand just in case. If budget or space restrictions are an issue, you may wish to put a cap on the number of families that can attend. If so, include this idea in your advertising and tell families that space is available on a "first come, first served" basis.

Selecting Activities

This book contains 26 activities—one for each letter of the alphabet. We don't imagine that you will do all 26 activities in any one event! Rather, you will probably pick and choose the activities to fit your budget or a theme. For example, a Family Science event held in Hawaii used the letters of the Hawaiian alphabet. Another event used letters that spelled out "Science is fun," and a third spelled out the name of the hosting school. Also, consider choosing activities that will appeal to a wide cross-section of your audience.

Another issue in selecting activities is the number of families you expect and the amount of time allotted to the event. We recommend that you plan for all families to do all of the activities you set up rather than having so many different ones available that some go undone. Depending on the number of families you expect, you may want to have more than one station (location) for each activity. For example, say you expect 100 families and your event is 2 hours long. If you estimate that each activity takes about 15 minutes, each family could do eight different activities over the two-hour period. So, at any one time, about 12 families will be doing the same activity. You would then plan the available space to accommodate these numbers.

You're invited to a fabulous

Come for the fun of it!

Do lots of cool activities, and take home the stuff you make.

Date: ....

Time: ....

Location: ....

- -

We wouldn't miss it!

Family name: ....

Number of adults: ....

Number of children: ....

Please return this slip by ....

Preparing and Transporting Materials

Once you know the number of people attending and the activities you plan to use, you are ready to begin collecting and preparing materials. This can seem like a daunting task, but we have made it as easy as possible with simple formulas to help you calculate the quantities of every item, shopping lists, and setup checklists. As you will see later in the book, these items will organize your planning process and enable you to easily use volunteers to help you.

Once the materials are ready, we suggest that you pack up each activity in its own labeled box or boxes, with the setup checklist included. That way, when the materials arrive at the location for your event, volunteers can easily find the boxes they need and begin to set up the activities.

Structuring the Event

You will need to consider how much structure you want for your Family Science event. You may prefer to include a registration/check-in procedure and/or include an orientation session. Signing-in procedures could include
- checking off names on an RSVP list,
- receiving name tags (you may copy the sample design below), and
- receiving "start cards" or other instructions on where to start and how to proceed through the stations.

Hi! My name is

....

Another option is not to have a registration or check-in at all and simply let families move around the facility, stopping at any stations that are available. In this case, you might send home confirmation letters before the event providing basic instructions and telling families that they may proceed on their own from activity to activity. You may also need to post signs and/or maps indicating where all of the stations are.

For every activity, families will need **an activity handout and a pen or pencil** to write with. Depending on the size of your event and the way teams will proceed through it, you could distribute handouts and writing materials in different ways. For the handouts, you could distribute all of them in a packet at registration, or you could leave handouts for each activity at the individual stations for family teams to pick up when they do the activity. If extra families show up and you run out of handouts, you may wish to have people sign up to have a set sent home.

As for writing implements, you could tell families to bring their own, or you could provide them. (Science is Fun color-change pencils are available from Terrific Science Books, Kits, and More. For ordering information, call 513/727-3269.) If you choose the latter, consider including pencils with the registration packets, attaching pencils to clipboards and distributing the clipboards at registration, or providing pencils at each station.

Encouraging Family Teams to Complete Their Activity Handouts

The activity handouts that families use during the science event are designed to encourage thoughtful observation and discussion. While these handouts won't be graded, you want to encourage teams to do all of the activities carefully and answer the questions as a family. To do this, consider providing an incentive for family teams to complete all of the activities. Incentives could consist of a small prize for each team that shows a complete set of handouts at a checkout location. To coordinate with your science theme, consider distributing inexpensive science-related toys or items such as Terrific Science Press' Instant Science Kits. Each Instant Science kit features fun, reusable science toys; complete instructions and science explanations, and ideas for doing even more science using simple household items. Each kit is briefly described below. For complete ordering information see www.terrificscience.org or call 513/727-3269.

Puff and Hover (ISF 2011)

Explore the power of air and the mysterious Bernoulli's Principle. Contains puffer toy, balls, and a bendable straw.

Talk and Squawk (ISF 2912)

Explore sound with a string that talks and a cup that squawks. Contains special talking plastic, string, yarn, fabric, and a small container.

Twirl and Whirl (ISF 2813)

Investigate the color mixing of light with psychedelic tops. Contains two plastic tops, a cardboard circle, and patterns.

Hop and Pop (ISF 2714)

Jump into action and experiment with stored and kinetic energy. Contains a plastic jumping frog and two popping disks.

Push, Pull...and More (ISF 2615)

Feeling pressure? Make a vacuum using a plastic syringe and explore its effect on lots of things. Contains a safe plastic syringe (no needle) and balloons.

Gaze and Amaze (ISF 2516)

Experiment with hologram glasses that reveal a message...and be amazed! Contains glasses, two point-source lights, and a battery holder.

Media Coverage

Make sure that the community knows about your wonderful Family Science event! As soon as you know the date of your event, contact local newspapers and television news shows and invite them to send a reporter or photographer. The example below is a newspaper article about a Family Science event that was part of the testing process for this book.

Adding Other Fun Ideas

Make your event even more special by adding one or both of these ideas:
- Invite a local bookstore to display and sell science books during the Family Science event.
- Hire a photographer to set up a science-themed photography booth. Families can then pay to have a photo taken using fun science backgrounds, props, and costumes.

Extending Learning and Family Involvement

A successful Family Science event can be a springboard for continued science learning in the classroom. The teacher companion to this book, *Classroom Science from A to Z*, contains ideas for extending the benefits of family science learning into your classroom science curriculum. Each family science activity in this book coordinates with a complementary classroom science lesson in *Classroom Science from A to Z*. Family involvement can continue as students share their classroom experiences with parents, and parents can feel a connection to the classroom learning based on their experience with similar concepts during the Family Science event.

Getting the Most From This Book

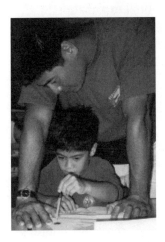

The family science challenges in this book are organized by chapter in alphabetical order. Each chapter begins with an introductory page that provides the following information:
- brief description of the activity,
- table of contents for the chapter,
- key science topics addressed in the activity,
- average time required for the activity, and
- the chapter's links to the corresponding lesson in the companion book, *Classroom Science from A to Z*.

The following terms have a specific meaning in this book; take a moment to become familiar with them before reading the rest of this book.

- **Station**—a location where family teams work on a specific family science challenge. You may choose to have only one station per challenge or several stations per challenge. Your decision will depend on the number of family teams you anticipate and the space available to you.

- **Setup**—a collection of materials that can be used by one family team at a time to do an activity. A station may contain multiple setups to allow more than one team to work at the station simultaneously. A good rule of thumb is to have at least as many total setups (for all activities) as you have family teams. This way, everyone can always be busy and you won't have lots of people standing around.

The rest of "Getting the Most From This Book" describes the items in each activity chapter that will help you get your Family Science event ready in record time!

Table Tents

Table tents help organize your Family Science event by identifying each station. The second page of each chapter contains a photocopy master for a free-standing sign, or "table tent," that can be set at each station. Each table tent contains the activity letter; the title of the activity; and lists of items that need to stay at the station, items that can be taken away when the activity is completed, and items that should be discarded.

To turn the photocopy masters into table tents, photocopy the master three times (permission is granted to photocopy the table tent masters for use in non-profit Family Science events), preferably onto brightly colored cardstock. (Regular office paper will work, but the tents will not be as sturdy.) Then tape the long edges of the three copies together to form a free-standing triangular sign with the text on all three sides facing outward, as shown at left. Place one of these table tents at each station.

Family Science Challenge Handout

Family teams will need written instructions for completing each activity as well as questions to stimulate observations and discussion and a brief explanation to introduce the science concept. The third and fourth page of each chapter is a photocopy master for a two-page family instruction handout. It is designed to be photocopied front to back. You may copy and distribute these handouts for a non-profit Family Science event.

Planning Notes

We provide detailed planning notes to help you every step of the way. "Planning Notes" contains several sections, as described here:

The **Calculating Quantities** section of each lesson contains guidelines for calculating how much of each material you will need for your event. By writing in the number of families you expect and following the simple calculations, you can easily figure out the quantity of each item, as shown in the examples below:

- 1-inch x 8½-inch strips of goldenrod paper
  (2 strips per family) x _____ families = _____ **strips** ✓
  This allows each family one extra beyond what is required for the activity.
  _____ strips ÷ (11 strips per sheet) = _____ **sheets of goldenrod paper** 🛒

- baking soda solution
  How many liters of solution do I need?
  (½ fluid ounce per family) x _____ families = _____ fluid ounces
  _____ fluid ounces x (0.03 liters per fluid ounce) = _____ **liters of solution** ✓

Please note that the "Calculating Quantities" guidelines assume that you will have one station for each activity. If you will have more than one station for any of the activities, you will need to adjust accordingly.

The calculations for liquids are usually based on using 1- and 2-L bottles for storage and dispensing. We recommend using these bottles because they are easy to carry, seal, and pour from, and because they are readily available. Of course, other types of containers may also work, so use what you have available.

In the "Calculating Quantities" section, materials are divided into three categories:

- **Nonconsumable Items Per Station**—lists materials that are needed at every station and that will not be used up, such as trash cans and buckets. The quantities of these materials don't depend on how many setups you are using per station or on the number of people attending the event.

- **Nonconsumable Items Per Setup**—lists materials that are needed for each setup and that will not be used up, such as containers and already-assembled sample toys. The quantities of these materials depend on how many setups you are using per station. For example, if you decide to use four setups for the "Aquatic Action" activity, multiply the quantities of Nonconsumable Items Per Setup by four.

- **Consumable Materials**—lists materials that will be used up or taken away by family teams, such as cotton-tipped swabs, paper towels, handouts, and solutions. The quantities of these materials depend on how many families will attend the event.

  For most activities, you will need to restock setups with consumable materials, such as straws, liquids, and cotton-tipped swabs. For convenience, you can store these items at the stations and have volunteers restock the setups as needed. Restocking water (for activities that use it) is simpler when a sink is available near the station.

  Even though storage bottles are not themselves consumable, when specific kinds of containers such as 1- or 2-L bottles are recommended for making and storing materials such as solutions, the containers are also listed with Consumable Materials.

  Final quantities, if appropriate, are calculated in units typically listed on the products, such as fluid ounces, liters, or grams. Final quantities that need to be transferred to other lists appear in bold type and are denoted with one or both of the following icons:

  🛒 for the Shopping/Gathering List

  ✓ for the Setup Checklist

Getting Ready for the Family Science Challenge explains how to prepare materials for use (for example, making solutions or assembling toys) and how to set up an activity. It contains the following subsections:

- **Tools or General Supplies Needed for Preparation Only**—lists tools that are not intended to be used in the activity but rather only to prepare for it.

- **Preparing Materials for Use**—explains how to prepare materials for use (for example, making solutions, cutting paper, or assembling sample toys). It also provides instructions for labeling materials using the provided label templates or your own labels.

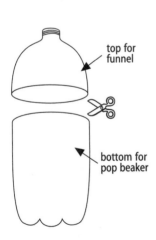

top for funnel

bottom for pop beaker

- **Setting Up the Station**—explains how to set up the station(s), including how to assemble apparatuses, distribute solutions among activity setups, and arrange consumable materials in storage containers. It's a good idea to include some sort of container for all materials set out on the tables. Containers can be labeled with their contents and will keep the items from spilling, becoming strewn around the table, or being soaked if a liquid is spilled on the table. For some products, the container can be the one the products come in, but for others you should include some other sort of container. For example, you could put the small strips of goldenrod paper in the "Radical Writing" activity in a shoe box. You could put items such as pens and markers in an empty soup can. Another useful type of container is a "pop beaker"—a 2-L soft-drink bottle with the top half cut off. Pop beakers make excellent, inexpensive containers for liquids and solids. If you need to store liquids, including water or solutions, make sure to store them in some kind of container that people can carry easily and pour from, such as clean 2-L soft-drink bottles.

Tips contains helpful hints for setting up or performing the activity. These tips are optional but may be helpful.

Disposal describes special procedures, if any, to follow in disposing of materials used or produced in the activity.

Answers and Observations provides plausible answers to questions posed on the family science handout. (When the question calls for a prediction or for observations that may vary greatly, sometimes answers are not provided.)

Answers for Child/Adult Discussion provides plausible answers to questions posed in the Child/Adult Discussion section of the family science handout.

Shopping/Gathering Checklist

This page lists the items needed for the activity and provides spaces for writing quantities needed for your particular event. You will calculate these quantities in the "Calculating Quantities" section of "Planning Notes" and then write these quantities on a photocopy of the shopping/gathering checklist in the book. The totals that need to be transferred to the Shopping/Gathering List are indicated with bold text and the following icon 🛒. Once the quantities are filled in, anyone (including people who have never read the activity) will be able to shop for and gather materials for you. This makes it easier to use the help of volunteers.

Setup Checklist

The Setup Checklist tells you exactly what belongs at the station, down to waste cans for trash and buckets for waste water. That way, during the hustle and bustle of setting up your event, volunteers will be able to effectively help set up the stations. Each Setup Checklist already lists the materials to be placed at the station and provides spaces for writing quantities needed (calculated previously in the Calculating Quantities section). The totals that need to be transferred to the Setup Checklist are indicated with bold text and the following icon: ✓.

Copy Masters for Labels

Many of the stations will require items to be labeled. For your convenience, each chapter contains a photocopy master for a set of labels that can be applied to bottles, containers, or other non-consumable materials. The labels contain the letter of the activity, a description of the contents, and, if appropriate, a brief description of what to do with the item. Using labels helps keep stations organized and gives participants helpful reminders of what to do with materials.

If you wish to use these labels, photocopy the masters provided onto a sheet of 1-inch 2¾-inch copier labels (such as Avery code 5351 or the equivalent size of another brand). If you would rather not use self-adhesive labels, you could photocopy the labels onto regular white paper, cut them out, and tape them on their respective items or write your own labels.

Aquatic Action

Family teams use a simple system to investigate how siphons work.

. . . . **Key Science Topics**

- siphons
- water

. . . . **Average Time Required**

Performance   10–15 minutes

Links to *Classroom Science from A to Z*

You can extend this activity into your science curriculum with the following ideas, included in the book *Classroom Science from A to Z*:

- Links to National Science Standards

- Science Activity 1
  Further the understanding of siphons by manipulating a tube full of water.

- Science Activity 2
  Make, explore, and compare an overflow device and a Tantalus cup.

- Lesson A Teacher Notes

- Lesson A Assessment

- Lesson A Science Explanation

- Lesson A Cross-Curricular Integration

Aquatic
Action

When you are done...

Throw away	Leave at the table	Take with you
paper towels	cups	completed handout
	food color	
	plastic tubing	
	bucket	
	sponge	
	pencil (if provided at station)	

Aquatic Action
Family Science Challenge

Go with the flow to wet and wild fun.

Materials

plastic wash tub or tray • 2 tall, clear plastic cups • water • 2 different food colors • piece of flexible plastic tubing • bucket of water • bucket for waste water • sponge • paper towels

Procedure

Figure 1

❶ Working over the plastic wash tub or tray provided, pour water into two clear plastic cups to about the halfway point. Add two drops of one food color to the water in one cup and add two drops of a different food color to the other cup of water. Set the cups of water on the table.

? *Record the two food colors you used:* _____

❷ Fill the piece of tubing with water by submerging it in a bucket that is about half full of water. While the tubing is submerged, move it around to remove any trapped air. Put your finger tightly over one end of the tubing and have your adult partner put his or her finger over the other end. (See Figure 1.) Lift the tubing out of the bucket, but keep your fingers on the two ends.

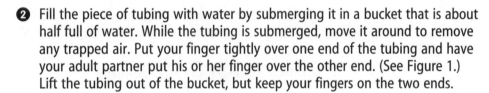
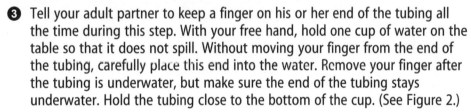

Figure 2

❸ Tell your adult partner to keep a finger on his or her end of the tubing all the time during this step. With your free hand, hold one cup of water on the table so that it does not spill. Without moving your finger from the end of the tubing, carefully place this end into the water. Remove your finger after the tubing is underwater, but make sure the end of the tubing stays underwater. Hold the tubing close to the bottom of the cup. (See Figure 2.)

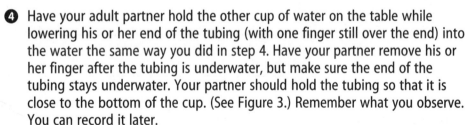

Figure 3

❹ Have your adult partner hold the other cup of water on the table while lowering his or her end of the tubing (with one finger still over the end) into the water the same way you did in step 4. Have your partner remove his or her finger after the tubing is underwater, but make sure the end of the tubing stays underwater. Your partner should hold the tubing so that it is close to the bottom of the cup. (See Figure 3.) Remember what you observe. You can record it later.

? *What did you observe? (Record this after you finish step 7.)*

_____

_____

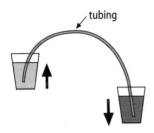

tubing

Figure 4

5 During this step, be sure to hold both ends of the tubing underwater in the cups, close to the bottom. Try raising one cup while lowering the other cup as shown in Figure 4. Then reverse which cup is up and which one is down. Don't let the water overflow a cup or totally empty one either. If this starts to happen, move the cups to the same level.

? *Remember the color of the water, and record it later.* _____

6 Look at both the color and the level of the water in each cup. What do you think will happen if you lift one end of the tubing out of the water? Try it and see.

Prediction: _____

Observation: _____

_____

7 Go back and record your observations from steps 4 and 5, then repeat the activity again if you like. See how empty you can get one of the cups before water stops flowing to the other cup.

8 Clean up the area by pouring water from the cups into the waste bucket. Clean up any spills and leave the materials for the next team.

Child/Adult Discussion

? *Suppose you owned a very large freshwater aquarium with several fish in it. To keep the fish healthy you must clean the water every month or so. Typically this involves removing about a quarter of the water from the tank and replacing it with clean water. Can you suggest a way to do this without having to lift or pour water from the tank?*

_____

_____

_____

Explanation

In this Family Science Challenge you made a siphon that allowed you to move the colored water back and forth from one cup to another. The siphon was made by filling the tubing with water and then placing both ends under the surface of the water in the cups. The water did not move while the two ends of the tubing were at the same level, but when the ends were moved to different heights, things started to happen. Raising one of the cups caused the tubing end in that cup to be higher than the tubing end in the other cup. This difference caused the water to flow out of the higher cup into the lower cup. Switching the position of the cups reversed the flow.

Aquatic Action Planning Notes

This section will help you prepare for and carry out your Family Science event.

Calculating Quantities

"Calculating Quantities" contains information to help you calculate how much of each material you will need for your event. Copy values marked with a 🛒 onto the Shopping/Gathering List and those marked with a ✓ onto the Setup Checklist. If any of the calculations result in fractions, round up to the next whole number.

Nonconsumable Items Per Station

Amounts listed are for one station. If you will have more than one station for this Family Science Challenge, adjust amounts accordingly.

- trash can

Nonconsumable Items Per Setup

You may choose to provide more than one setup at each station to allow a number of family teams to work concurrently.

- 2 tall, clear plastic cups
  (2 clear plastic cups per setup) x _____ *setups =* _____ ***tall, clear plastic cups*** 🛒 ✓

- piece of clear plastic tubing approximately 18 inches long with an inside diameter of ¼–½ inch
  (1 piece of tubing per setup) x _____ *setups =* _____ ***pieces of tubing*** ✓
  (18 inches per piece of tubing) x _____ *pieces of tubing =* _____ ***inches of tubing*** 🛒

- plastic wash tub or tray
  (1 wash tub or tray per setup) x _____ *setups =* _____ ***wash tubs or trays*** 🛒 ✓

- sponge (to clean up spills)
  (1 sponge per setup) x _____ *setups =* _____ ***sponges*** 🛒 ✓

- waste water bucket
  (1 bucket per setup) x _____ *setups =* _____ ***waste water buckets*** 🛒 ✓

Consumable Materials

- food color (2 different colors required)
  (1 bottle of each color per setup) x _____ *setups =* _____ ***bottles of each color of food color*** 🛒 ✓

- water bucket half-filled with water (for filling tubing)
  (1 bucket per setup) x _____ *setups =* _____ ***buckets*** 🛒 ✓

- water in 1- or 2-L plastic soft-drink bottles (if a source of running water will not be readily available near the station)

  (0.5 L per family) x _____ families = **_____** ***liters of water in 1- or 2-L bottles*** ⛟ ✓

- paper towels ⛟ ✓

  estimate (4 paper towels per family) x _____ families = **_____** ***paper towels*** ⛟ ✓

Getting Ready for the Family Science Challenge

Tools or General Supplies Needed for Preparation Only

- 3 sheets of brightly colored cardstock for Table Tent **A**
- adhesive copier labels (template provided) or other materials to make labels
- sharp knife or heavy-duty scissors (if necessary)

Preparing Materials for Use

- Photocopy the Family Science Challenge handout master to make the number of copies needed.

- Photocopy the Table Tent **A** master onto three sheets of brightly colored cardstock and assemble the table tent.

- Photocopy the label template onto a blank sheet of copier labels to print the labels, or make your own labels.

- Label the plastic cups, food color, plastic wash tubs, water bucket, and waste water bucket.

- If the tubing is not already cut, use a sharp knife or heavy-duty scissors to cut it to length.

- If the station will not be located near a source of running water (such as a sink or drinking fountain), fill several 1- or 2-L bottles with water to refill the containers of water as needed. Label the bottles appropriately.

- Half-fill the water buckets for the setups with water.

Setting Up the Station

- Place Table Tent **A** at the station in a prominent location.

- Set out the plastic cups, food color, plastic tubing, plastic wash tub, buckets, sponge, and paper towels.

Answers and Observations

❹ *What did you observe? (Record this after you finish step 7.)*

Nothing happens as long as both cups are on the table and contain the same amount of water.

❻ *Observation:*

Lifting the tubing out of the water stops the siphoning process.

Answers for Child/Adult Discussion

? *Suppose you owned a very large freshwater aquarium with several fish in it. To keep the fish healthy you have to clean the water every month or so. Typically this involves removing about a quarter of the water from the tank and replacing it with clean water. Can you suggest a way to do this without having to pour water from the tank?*

Set up a siphon. Be careful not to siphon any fish!

Aquatic Action Shopping/Gathering List

Use this checklist as a guide to collecting the materials for this Family Science Challenge. Fill in the quantities needed below after doing the calculations called for in the "Calculating Quantities" section.

Total Quantities (from "Planning Notes")

_____ tall, clear plastic cups*

_____ inches of clear plastic tubing with an inside diameter of ¼–½ inch**

_____ plastic wash tub(s) or tray(s)

_____ bottles of each of 2 different food colors

_____ liter(s) water in 1- or 2-L plastic soft-drink bottles

_____ buckets***

_____ paper towels

_____ sponge(s) to clean up spills

_____ trash can(s)

Tools for Getting Ready

☐ 3 sheets of brightly colored cardstock for Table Tent **A**

☐ adhesive copier labels (template provided) or other materials to make labels†

☐ sharp knife or heavy-duty scissors

*   The size and shape of the cups must permit participants to place the ends of the tubing underwater without removing their fingers.

** Clear, flexible plastic tubing is available from pet stores in the aquarium section or from hardware stores or science supply houses.

*** The buckets should be large enough to submerge the tubing completely and allow two participants—one adult and one child—to reach inside and grab the ends of the tubing at the same time.

†   We have provided a label template that can be photocopied directly onto a blank sheet of copier labels to print all of the labels you need for the activity. Use 1-inch x 2¾-inch copier labels, such as Avery Copier Labels (code 5351). If copier labels are not available, copy the label template onto paper, cut out the labels, and use tape to affix the paper labels. Alternatively, make hand-written labels using permanent marker and masking tape or other similar materials.

Aquatic Action Setup Checklist

The following is a list of items you will need to set up the Family Science Challenge. "Planning Notes" gives step-by-step instructions for setting up the Family Science Challenge.

Items Per Station

The following materials should be left on or near the table for all family teams to use. (A station is a location where family teams work on an activity.)

Material	Total Needed	Notes
☐ trash can	_____	_____
☐ Table Tent **A**	_____	Copy master provided

Items Per Setup

The following nonconsumable items will be needed for each setup. You may choose to provide more than one setup at each station to allow a number of family teams to work concurrently.

Material	Total Needed	Notes
☐ bucket for waste water	_____	_____
☐ sponge	_____	For cleanup
☐ 2 tall, clear plastic cups		_____
☐ piece of clear plastic tubing	_____	_____
☐ plastic wash tub or tray	_____	_____
☐ pencil for recording observations*	_____	_____

Consumable Materials

The following materials will be used up or taken away by family teams.

Material	Total Needed	Notes
☐ 2 different food colors	_____	This amount is needed for each color used.
☐ buckets of water	_____	_____
☐ paper towels	_____	For cleanup
☐ Family Science Challenge handouts**	_____	Copy master provided

*   You may wish to pass out pencils at registration or have families bring their own pencils.

** You may wish to pass out Family Science Challenge handouts as a set at registration rather than at each station.

Aquatic Action
Label Template

 **Clear Plastic Cup**
Please leave at the station.

 **Clear Plastic Cup**
Please leave at the station.

 **Clear Plastic Cup**
Please leave at the station.

 **Water**

 **Water**

 **Water Bucket**
Submerge tubing to fill with water.

 **Water Bucket**
Submerge tubing to fill with water.

 **Waste Water Bucket**
Discard used water here.

 **Waste Water Bucket**
Discard used water here.

 **Food Color**
Please leave at the station.

 **Food Color**
Please leave at the station.

 **Food Color**
Please leave at the station.

 **Food Color**
Please leave at the station.

 **Water**

 **Clear Plastic Cup**
Please leave at the station.

 **Water**

Balancing Butterflies

Family teams balance butterfly models and learn about the importance of the center of gravity.

Key Science Topics

- balance
- center of gravity

Average Time Required

Performance   10–15 minutes

Links to *Classroom Science from A to Z*

You can extend this activity into your science curriculum with the following ideas, included in the book *Classroom Science from A to Z:*

- Links to National Science Standards

- Science Activity
  Investigate balance further by trying to balance geometric shapes.

- Lesson B Teacher Notes

- Lesson B Assessment

- Lesson B Science Explanation

- Lesson B Cross-Curricular Integration

Balancing Butterflies

When you are done...

Throw away	Leave at the table	Take with you
card scraps	paper clips	butterfly
	golf tee	completed handout
	ball of clay	
	scissors	
	pencil (if provided at station)	

Balancing Butterflies
Family Science Challenge

Tee up! Take a shot at balancing the butterfly!

Materials

butterfly made of heavy cardstock • scissors • paper clips • golf tee • clay • pencil

Figure 1

Procedure

❶ Select a cardstock butterfly and carefully cut it out. Balance the butterfly on the tip of your index finger. (See Figure 1.)

❷ Once you get the butterfly balanced, place the index finger of your other hand on the top of the butterfly directly over your balance finger. This will ensure your butterfly will not fall.

Figure 2

❸ Have your adult partner draw a circle around the spot where your index finger meets the top of the butterfly. (See Figure 2.) This circle will be called the balance point.

❹ Try to move the balance spot closer to the tip of the head of the butterfly. Slide a paper clip onto the front tip of each of the wings. (See Figure 3.) Does that help? Move the paper clips around as needed until you can balance the butterfly at its head.

Figure 3

❺ Can you get the butterfly to balance at the very tip of its head? Move the paper clips around until the butterfly balances at the very tip of its head. Trace the locations of the paper clips.

❻ Make a stand for the golf tee by rolling a small bit of clay into a ball and setting it on the table. Press the flat end of a golf tee into the clay ball. The point of the golf tee should stand as straight as possible. Mold the clay around the tee to secure the tee in place. (See Figure 4.)

Figure 4

❼ See whether you can balance your butterfly on the point of the golf tee without any paper clips. Now try adding just two paper clips. Then try adding two to four additional paper clips and moving them around.

? *Use the figure below to mark the location of the paper clips that gave you the best results. Use Xs to represent the paper clips.*

? *What do you think would happen if you gently blew on the butterfly balanced on the golf tee? Try it with and without the paper clips and find out. Discuss your observations.*

_____

_____

8 Discard the cardstock scraps in the trash or recycling bin. Put the other materials (including the paper clips and pencils) back where you found them. You may keep your butterfly.

Child/Adult Discussion

? *How does the location of the paper clips affect the balance spots or points?*

_____

_____

Explanation

This investigation allows you to determine the balance point of the paper butterfly. For flat, uniform objects like this butterfly, the balance point occurs at the geometric center of the object. Did you know that if you wanted to find the geometric center of the butterfly using mathematics, you'd need to use calculus? But using physics, you simply find the spot where the butterfly balances on your finger. Isn't science wonderful?

Another interesting thing about this activity is that the paper butterfly balances at its center of gravity, which is the point on the butterfly where the mass seems to be concentrated. (That's why the center of gravity is sometimes called the center of mass.) When you add the paper clips to the butterfly, you add mass, which changes the center of mass (center of gravity), lowering it directly below the balance point. This happens because you no longer have a totally flat, uniform object. Also, each time you change the location of the paper clips, you shift the center of gravity and change the balance point.

When you switch from balancing the butterfly on your finger to balancing it on the golf tee, you provide a smaller support surface. As you have found out, this makes it more challenging to get the butterfly to balance, but it also provides more information on the exact location of the balance point. You probably also noticed that you could blow the butterfly off the golf tee if you blew too strongly. However, by adding paper clips you probably found the butterfly less likely to fall in a gentle puff. This is because the clips lower the center of mass below the support point and help to make the object more stable.

Stuff to Try at Home

Try making balance toys using items such as building toys, craft sticks, wire, corks, small apples or potatoes, forks, and toothpicks. Remember that to balance easily, your toy needs to have some parts that hang below the support point.

Balancing Butterflies Planning Notes

This section will help you prepare for and carry out your Family Science event.

Calculating Quantities

"Calculating Quantities" contains information to help you calculate how much of each material you will need for your event. Copy values marked with a 🛒 onto the Shopping/Gathering List and those marked with a ✓ onto the Setup Checklist. If any of the calculations result in fractions, round up to the next whole number.

Nonconsumable Items Per Station

Amounts listed are for one station. If you will have more than one station for this Family Science Challenge, adjust amounts accordingly.

- shoe box or other small box to hold butterfly patterns 🛒 ✓
- 3 small boxes or other containers for paper clips, golf tees, and balls of clay 🛒 ✓
- trash can or recycling bin 🛒 ✓

Nonconsumable Items Per Setup

You may choose to provide more than one setup at each station to allow a number of family teams to work concurrently.

- paper clips (small, standard size)
  (10 paper clips per setup) x _____ setups + 50 extras = _____ ***paper clips*** 🛒 ✓

- golf tee
  (1 golf tee per setup) x _____ setups + 10 extras = _____ ***golf tees*** 🛒 ✓

- ½-inch-diameter ball of clay
  (1 ball of clay per setup) x _____ setups + 10 extras = _____ ***balls of clay*** ✓
  The average 5-inch stick of clay will yield about 20, ½-inch clay balls, so you will probably need only one stick.

- scissors
  (1 pair of scissors per setup) x _____ setups = _____ ***pairs of scissors*** 🛒 ✓

Consumable Materials

- heavy cardstock for butterfly patterns
  (1 butterfly per family) x _____ families = _____ ***butterflies*** ✓
  _____ butterflies ÷ (2 butterflies per sheet) = _____ ***sheets of cardstock*** 🛒

Getting Ready for the Family Science Challenge

Tools or General Supplies Needed for Preparation Only

- 3 sheets of brightly colored cardstock for Table Tent **B**
- adhesive copier labels (template provided) or other materials to make labels
- scissors or paper cutter

Preparing Materials for Use

- Photocopy the Family Science Challenge handout master to make the number of copies needed.

- Photocopy the Table Tent **B** master onto three sheets of brightly colored cardstock and assemble the table tent.

- Photocopy the label template onto a blank sheet of copier labels to print the labels, or make your own labels.

- Photocopy the butterfly pattern masters (provided) onto cardstock or other stiff paper. Cut the masters to separate the butterfly patterns. (You don't need to cut out the butterflies themselves.)

- Label the containers for the butterfly patterns and extra paper clips, golf tees, and balls of clay.

Setting Up the Station

- Place Table Tent **B** at the station in a prominent location.

- Set out the paper clips, golf tees, balls of clay, and butterfly patterns in their labeled containers.

- Place 10 paper clips, a golf tee, and a ball of clay at each setup.

Answers and Observations

❼ *What do you think would happen if you gently blew on the butterfly balanced on the golf tee? Try it with and without the paper clips and find out. Discuss your observations.*

Gentle blowing on the balanced butterfly with added paper clips should cause it to move slightly but remain balanced.

Answers for Child/Adult Discussion

? *How does the location of the paper clips affect the balance spots or points?*

The balance point moves to a new center of gravity, closer to the added paper clips than the original balance point.

Balancing Butterflies Shopping/Gathering List

Use this checklist as a guide to collecting the materials for this Family Science Challenge. Fill in the quantities needed below after doing the calculations called for in the "Calculating Quantities" section.

Total Quantities (from "Planning Notes")

_____ paper clips (small, standard size)

_____ golf tees

_____ ½-inch-diameter balls of clay

_____ scissors

_____ small boxes or other containers

_____ shoe boxes or other small boxes

_____ sheets of heavy cardstock*

_____ trash can(s) or recycling bin(s)

Tools for Getting Ready

☐ 3 sheets of brightly colored cardstock for Table Tent **B**

☐ adhesive copier labels (template provided) or other materials to make labels**

☐ scissors or paper cutter

* Regular office paper, such as computer paper or copy machine paper, is not stiff enough for this activity, so the butterflies must be copied onto heavy cardstock or other stiff paper.

** We have provided a label template that can be photocopied directly onto a blank sheet of copier labels to print all of the labels you need for the activity. Use 1-inch x 2¾-inch copier labels, such as Avery Copier Labels (code 5351). If copier labels are not available, copy the label template onto paper, cut out the labels, and use tape to affix the paper labels. Alternatively, make hand-written labels using permanent marker and masking tape or other similar materials.

Balancing Butterflies Setup Checklist

The following is a list of items you will need to set up the Family Science Challenge. "Planning Notes" gives step-by-step instructions for setting up the Family Science Challenge.

Items Per Station

The following materials should be left on or near the table for all family teams to use. (A station is a location where family teams work on an activity.)

Material	Total Needed	Notes
☐ Table Tent **B**	_____	Copy master provided
☐ labeled shoe box or other small box	_____	For the butterfly patterns
☐ small labeled boxes	_____	For extra paper clips, golf tees, and balls of clay
☐ trash can	_____	

Items Per Setup

The following nonconsumable items will be needed for each setup. You may choose to provide more than one setup at each station to allow a number of family teams to work concurrently at the station.

Material	Total Needed	Notes
☐ paper clips	_____	_____
☐ golf tee	_____	_____
☐ ½-inch-diameter ball of clay	_____	_____
☐ scissors	_____	_____
☐ pencil for writing on butterflies and recording observations*	_____	_____

Consumable Materials

The following materials will be used up or taken away by family teams.

Material	Total Needed	Notes
☐ cardstock butterflies	_____	_____
☐ Family Science Challenge handouts**	_____	Copy master provided

* You may wish to pass out pencils at registration or have families bring their own pencils.

** You may wish to pass out Family Science Challenge handouts as a set at registration rather than at each station.

Balancing Butterflies
Butterfly Pattern Masters

Balancing Butterflies Label Template

B **Paper clips**
Please leave at the station.

B **Paper clips**
Please leave at the station.

B **Golf Tees**
Please leave at the station.

B **Golf Tees**
Please leave at the station.

B **Balls of Clay**
Please leave at the station.

B **Balls of Clay**
Please leave at the station.

B **Cardstock Butterflies**
1 per family; you may take it with you.

B **Cardstock Butterflies**
1 per family; you may take it with you.

B **Paper clips**
Please leave at the station.

B **Paper clips**
Please leave at the station.

B **Golf Tees**
Please leave at the station.

B **Golf Tees**
Please leave at the station.

B **Balls of Clay**
Please leave at the station.

B **Balls of Clay**
Please leave at the station.

B **Cardstock Butterflies**
1 per family; you may take it with you.

B **Cardstock Butterflies**
1 per family; you may take it with you.

Cool 'Copters

Family teams explore how to help their paper helicopters spin better.

Key Science Topics

- air resistance
- gravity

Average Time Required

Performance 10–15 minutes

Links to *Classroom Science from A to Z*

You can extend this activity into your science curriculum with the following ideas, included in the book *Classroom Science from A to Z*:

- Links to National Science Standards

- Science Activity
  Investigate how shape and mass change the falling behavior of a paper whirligig.

- Lesson C Teacher Notes

- Lesson C Assessment

- Lesson C Science Explanation

- Lesson C Cross-Curricular Integration

Cool 'Copters

When you are done...

Throw away	Leave at the table	Take with you
paper scraps	paper clips markers or crayons scissors pencil (if provided at station)	flying character helicopter helicopter you colored completed handout

Cool 'Copters
Family Science Challenge

Can you help the helicopter spin better?

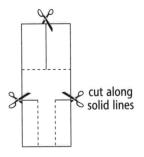

cut along
solid lines

Figure 1

Materials

flying character paper strip • blank helicopter paper strip • paper clips
• markers or crayons • scissors

Procedure

❶ Select a flying character paper strip from the station supplies. Hold the paper strip above your head and drop it with the bottom pointing down.

? *What happens?*

_____

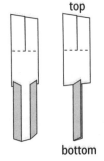

top

bottom

Figure 2

❷ Turn your paper strip into a helicopter toy by carefully cutting along the solid lines as shown in Figure 1. <u>Do not cut along the dotted lines.</u> Fold the bottom side flaps in as shown in Figure 2. Make sure the top flaps are both still unfolded. Hold the helicopter toy above your head and drop it with the bottom pointing down.

? *What happens?*

_____

❸ Fold the top flaps down along the dotted line to opposite sides of the helicopter center. (See Figure 3.) Hold the helicopter toy above your head and drop it as before.

? *What happens?*

_____

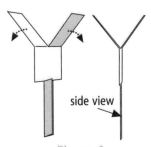

side view

Figure 3

❹ Place a paper clip on the helicopter toy at the bottom with the side flaps folded in. (See Figure 4.) Drop the helicopter now and see what happens. Try adding a few more paper clips and try again.

? *What happens?*

_____

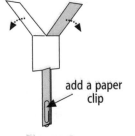

add a paper
clip

Figure 4

❺ Now you get to make a helicopter of your own. Select one of the blank helicopter strips from the station supplies and color it however you like. Then carefully cut along the solid lines. <u>Do not cut along the dotted lines.</u>

❻ Test your helicopter as in steps 1–4.

? *What happens?*

_____

❼ You may keep both of your helicopters. Discard any paper scraps in the trash or recycling bin and leave the remaining materials for the next group.

Child/Adult Discussion

? *How does folding the side flaps on the helicopter affect its travel? How does folding the top flaps on the helicopter affect its travel? What effect did adding paper clips have?*

_____

_____

_____

_____

Explanation

When you let go of the helicopter, two forces begin acting on it: gravity and air resistance. Gravity is the downward pull toward the surface of the Earth. Air resistance is an upward force that acts on the portion of an object's surface area that is parallel to the ground.

When you drop a sheet of paper, it does not stay in any particular position. Air resistance acts over the whole surface of paper, and it flutters to the ground. When you drop the unfolded helicopter, it behaves just like an ordinary piece of paper.

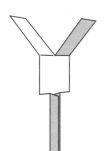

When you fold in the helicopter's side flaps (leaving the top flaps straight up), the extra thickness of paper concentrates the mass at the center part of the bottom. Now, when you drop the helicopter (bottom pointing down), it often falls straight. Air resistance does not affect the helicopter's fall much, since little of the paper's surface is parallel to the ground as it falls.

When you fold open the top flaps (keeping the side flaps folded in) you create angled blades which the molecules in the air hit and bounce off at an angle. This causes two different things to happen to the helicopter: 1) it falls more slowly, and 2) it spins. Adding a paper clip to the bottom of the helicopter adds mass, and this helps to stabilize the helicopter in flight.

Did you notice that the characters on the pre-made helicopter toys are all characters made famous, in part, by flying or falling?

Stuff to Try at Home

Try making helicopters out of other materials you may have around the house. If you have a maple tree, collect some of its seed pods in the spring and see if you can get them to spin as they fall.

Cool 'Copters Planning Notes

This section will help you prepare for and carry out your Family Science event.

Calculating Quantities

"Calculating Quantities" contains information to help you calculate how much of each material you will need for your event. Copy values marked with a 🛒 onto the Shopping/Gathering List and those marked with a ✓ onto the Setup Checklist. If any of the calculations result in fractions, round up to the next whole number.

Nonconsumable Items Per Station

Amounts listed are for one station. If you will have more than one station for this Family Science Challenge, adjust amounts accordingly.

- box for flying character strips 🛒 ✓
- box for blank helicopter strips 🛒 ✓
- trash can or recycling bin 🛒 ✓
- (optional) stapler 🛒 ✓

Nonconsumable Items Per Setup

You may choose to provide more than one setup at each station to allow a number of family teams to work concurrently.

- box of paper clips
  (1 box of paper clips per setup) x _____ *setups =* _____ **boxes of paper clips** 🛒 ✓

- set of crayons or markers
  (1 set per setup) x _____ *setups =* _____ **sets of crayons or markers** 🛒 ✓

- scissors
  (1 pair of scissors per setup) x _____ *setups =* _____ **pairs of scissors** 🛒 ✓

Consumable Materials
- flying character strip
  (1 strip per family) x _____ *families =* _____ **strips** ✓
  _____ *strips ÷ (4 per sheet) =* _____ **sheets of paper** 🛒

- blank helicopter strip
  (1 strip per family) x _____ *families =* _____ **strips** ✓
  _____ *strips ÷ (4 per sheet) =* _____ **sheets of paper** 🛒

Getting Ready for the Family Science Challenge

Tools or General Supplies Needed for Preparation Only
- 3 sheets of brightly colored cardstock for Table Tent **C**
- adhesive copier labels (template provided) or other materials to make labels
- paper cutter

Preparing Materials for Use
- Photocopy the Family Science Challenge handout master to make the number of copies needed.

- Photocopy the Table Tent **C** master onto three sheets of brightly colored cardstock and assemble the table tent.

- Photocopy the label template onto a blank sheet of copier labels to print the labels, or make your own labels.

- Prepare the flying character strips by photocopying the template (provided) onto regular white paper. Use a paper cutter to cut out the strips along the heavy solid lines.

- Prepare the blank helicopter strips by photocopying the template (provided) onto regular white paper. Use a paper cutter to cut out the strips along the heavy solid lines.

- Label the boxes for the flying character strips and the blank helicopter strips.

Setting Up the Station
- Place Table Tent **C** at the station in a prominent location.

- Set out the flying character strips and the blank helicopter strips in their labeled boxes.

- At each setup, place a pair of scissors, a box of paper clips, and a set of markers or crayons.

Tips
- You may wish to put a stapler at the station so families can staple their helicopters to their Family Science Challenge handouts.

Answers and Observations

❶ *What happens?*

The helicopter flutters to the ground, just as any piece of paper would.

❷ *What happens?*

The helicopter falls to the ground. If it was dropped with the bottom pointing down, it will probably fall straight down at least part of the way.

❸ *What happens?*

The helicopter rotates as it falls to the ground. It may tumble out of control at some point in the fall.

❹ *What happens?*

The helicopter rotates as it falls to the ground. It will usually fall straight down.

❻ *What happens?*

The helicopter behaves much like the first one.

Answers for Child/Adult Discussion

? *How does folding the side flaps on the helicopter affect its travel? How does folding the top flaps on the helicopter affect its travel? What effect did adding paper clips have?*

Folding the side flaps makes the helicopter more likely to fall straight to the ground. Folding the top flaps out makes the helicopter rotate (at least initially). With a paper clip attached, the flight is more stable, with the rotation continuing until the helicopter hits the ground.

Cool 'Copters Shopping/Gathering List

Use this checklist as a guide to collecting the materials for this Family Science Challenge. Fill in the quantities needed below after doing the calculations called for in the "Calculating Quantities" section.

Total Quantities (from "Planning Notes")

_____ sheets of paper (sum of lines below)

_____ sheets of paper for flying character strips

_____ sheets of paper for blank helicopter strips

_____ boxes for flying character strips and blank helicopter strips

_____ box(es) of paper clips*

_____ sets of crayons or markers

_____ scissors

_____ trash can(s) or recycling bin(s)

_____ (optional) stapler(s)

Tools for Getting Ready

☐ 3 sheets of brightly colored cardstock for Table Tent **C**

☐ adhesive copier labels (template provided) or other materials to make labels**

☐ paper cutter

* Although any size of paper clips will work, it is best to use smaller ones for the Family Science Challenge. Larger ones will make the helicopter drop too fast.

** We have provided a label template that can be photocopied directly onto a blank sheet of copier labels to print all of the labels you need for the activity. Use 1-inch x 2¾-inch copier labels, such as Avery Copier Labels (code 5351). If copier labels are not available, copy the label template onto paper, cut out the labels, and use tape to affix the paper labels. Alternatively, make hand-written labels using permanent marker and masking tape or other similar materials.

Cool 'Copters
Setup Checklist

The following is a list of items you will need to set up the Family Science Challenge. "Planning Notes" gives step-by-step instructions for setting up the Family Science Challenge.

Items Per Station

The following materials should be left on or near the table for all family teams to use. (A station is a location where family teams work on an activity.)

Material	Total Needed	Notes
☐ Table Tent **C**	_____	Copy master provided
☐ labeled boxes	_____	For flying character strips and blank helicopter strips
☐ trash can or recycling bin	_____	_____
☐ (optional) stapler	_____	_____

Items Per Setup

The following nonconsumable items should be placed at each setup. You may choose to provide more than one setup at each station to allow a number of family teams to work concurrently at the station.

Material	Total Needed	Notes
☐ box of paper clips	_____	_____
☐ set of crayons or markers	_____	_____
☐ scissors	_____	_____
☐ pencil for recording observations*	_____	_____

Consumable Materials

The following materials will be used up or taken away by family teams.

Material	Total Needed	Notes
☐ Family Science Challenge handouts**	_____	Copy master provided
☐ flying character strips	_____	_____
☐ blank helicopter strips	_____	_____

*   You may wish to pass out pencils at registration or have families bring their own pencils.

** You may wish to pass out Family Science Challenge handouts as a set at registration rather than at each station.

Cool 'Copters
Helicopter Templates

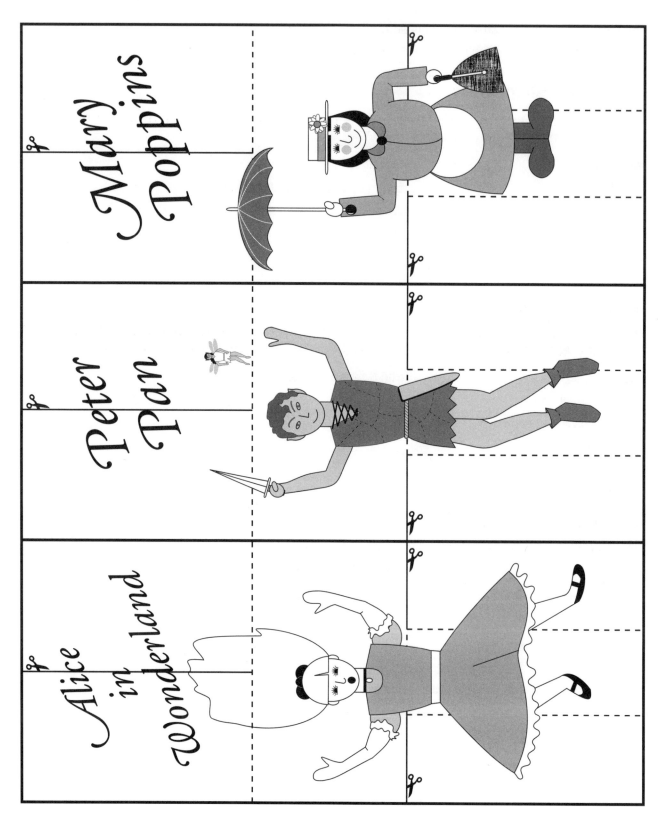

Mary Poppins

Peter Pan

Alice in Wonderland

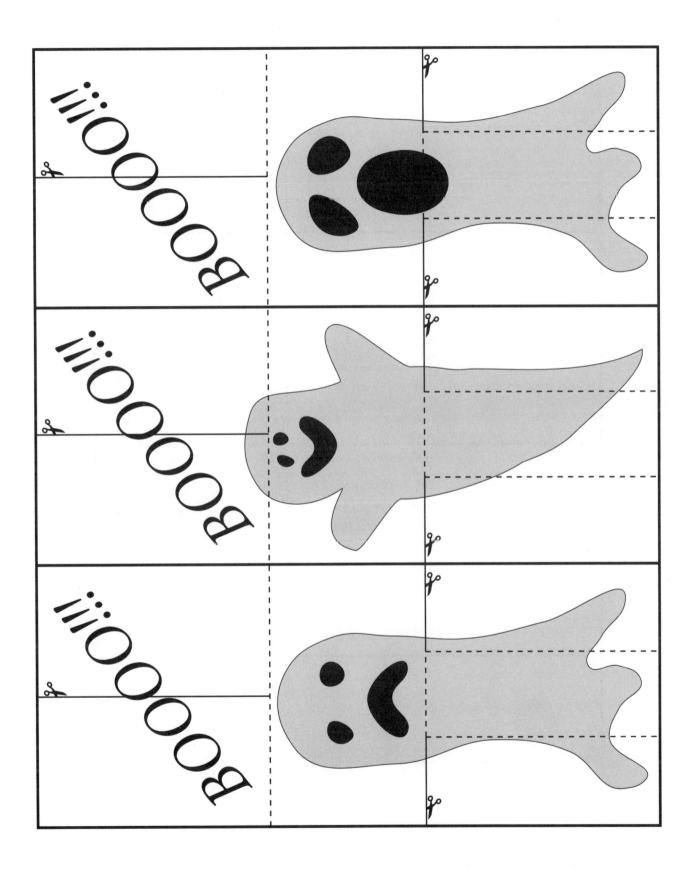

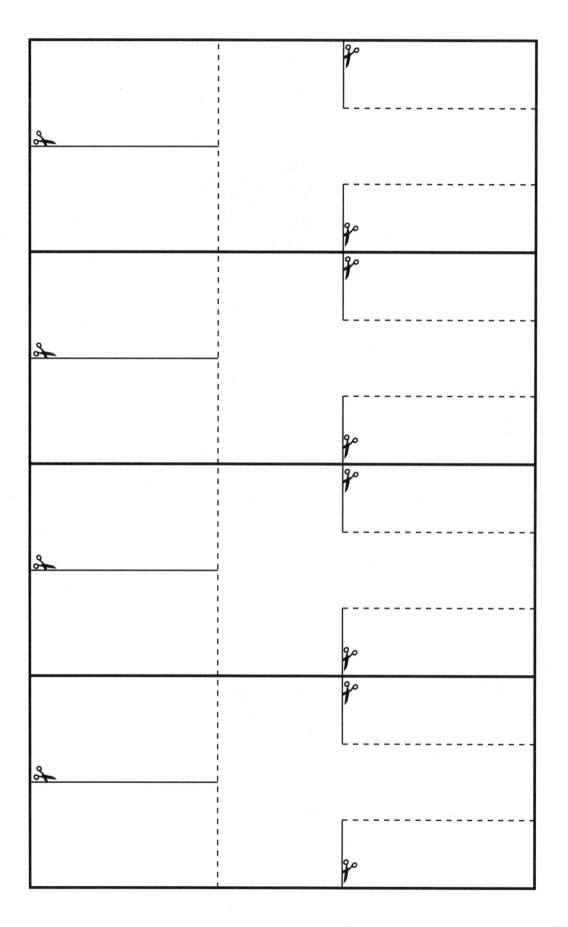

Cool 'Copters
Label Template

C Flying Character Strips
1 per family

C Blank Helicopter Strips
1 per family

C Flying Character Strips
1 per family

C Blank Helicopter Strips
1 per family

C Flying Character Strips
1 per family

C Blank Helicopter Strips
1 per family

C Flying Character Strips
1 per family

C Blank Helicopter Strips
1 per family

C Flying Character Strips
1 per family

C Blank Helicopter Strips
1 per family

C Flying Character Strips
1 per family

C Blank Helicopter Strips
1 per family

C Flying Character Strips
1 per family

C Blank Helicopter Strips
1 per family

C Flying Character Strips
1 per family

C Blank Helicopter Strips
1 per family

Disco Raisins

Under the right circumstances, raisins—even if they aren't from California—will "dance"! Family teams investigate this behavior in raisins and other objects under these same conditions.

.... ## Key Science Topics

- buoyancy
- floating and sinking
- gases
- relative densities

.... ## Average Time Required

Performance   10 minutes

Links to *Classroom Science from A to Z*

You can extend this activity into your science curriculum with the following ideas, included in the book *Classroom Science from A to Z:*

- Links to National Science Standards

- Science Activity
  Students investigate the effects on the buoyancy of raisins when different amounts of vinegar and baking soda are mixed in water.

- Lesson D Teacher Notes

- Lesson D Assessment

- Lesson D Science Explanation

- Lesson D Cross-Curricular Integration

Disco Raisins

When you are done...

Throw away	Leave at the table	Take with you
used popcorn kernels	cups	completed handout
used raisins	cork	
paper towels	other test items	
soft drink (in waste bucket)	spoon	
	pencil (if provided at station)	

Disco Raisins
Family Science Challenge

Discover what happens when raisins take the plunge.

Materials

scissors • raisins • unpopped popcorn kernels • pieces of cork • other solid items to test (as provided) • "water" cup • water • "soft-drink" cup • carbonated soft drink • spoon • paper towels • bucket for waste liquids

Procedure

⚠ *Do not drink or eat any of the materials used in this activity.*

❶ Carefully use the scissors to cut two raisins in half. Cut one of the raisin halves in half again. Collect two kernels of popcorn, two small pieces of cork, and two of any other items provided for you as test items.

? *What do you think will happen if you place one of each of the different solid items you have into the water? Will the solids sink or float? Record your predictions in the Observation Table. What do you think the solids will do in the soft drink? Will they sink or float? Record your predictions.*

Observation Table				
	Will it sink or float in water?		Will it sink or float in the soft drink?	
Solid	Predictions (step 1)	Observations (step 2)	Predictions (step 1)	Observations (step 3)
raisin half				
raisin quarter				
popcorn kernel				
cork piece				
other test object:				

❷ Half-fill the clear plastic cup labeled "Water" with water. Test your predictions using only one piece of each type of solid. Record your observations in the table.

❸ Half-fill the clear plastic cup labeled "Soft Drink" with carbonated soft drink. Tightly cap the remaining soft drink. Test your soft-drink predictions and observe for several minutes. Record your observations in the table.

❹ Clean up the station as follows:

1. Use the spoon to fish the solids out of the liquids. Discard used raisins and popcorn in the trash. Pat the cork and other test items dry with a paper towel and return them to the appropriate containers.

2. Pour the used soft drink and water into the waste bucket. Return both the cups and the spoon to the station for others to use.

Child/Adult Discussion

? *Discuss the similarities and differences in the behavior of the solids in the water and in the soft drink. What do you think caused the differences you observed?*

_____

_____

_____

_____

Explanation

In this activity, you observed the floating and sinking behavior of different solids in water and carbonated soft drink. The ability of a solid to sink or float is based on its density compared to the density of the liquid. Solids that are less dense than the liquid will float, and solids that are more dense will sink. The raisin and unpopped popcorn sank in the water because they were more dense than water. The cork, on the other hand, floated in the water because cork is less dense than water.

In the case of the soft drink, another factor is introduced: carbonation. The carbon dioxide gas that is in the soft drink causes the bubbles you see in soft drinks. These bubbles of carbon dioxide gas attach themselves to solids that you put in the soft drink.

In the case of the raisin piece and popcorn kernel, the bubbles that form on their surfaces actually lift these solids to the surface. The bubbles act like water wings or "floaties" on the solids. The new bubble-raisin or bubble-popcorn "systems" that result are more buoyant, and therefore they are less dense than the soft drink. At the surface, the bubbles pop and the carbon dioxide gas escapes into the air. This causes the raisin or popcorn to sink once again, and the process repeats itself. More bubbles form on the raisin or popcorn, and the solids again ascend to the surface. This process repeats as long as sufficient carbon dioxide gas is available.

While bubbles form on the surface of the cork, it does not bob up and down, since it is already less dense than the soft drink. Other solids, such as paper clips or pebbles, are so dense that the bubbles that form on them from the soft drink are not sufficient to make them rise.

Stuff to Try at Home

Try the activity at home using different brands of carbonated soft drinks. Do the raisins behave differently in different drinks? How about trying a "flat" soft drink versus one that's not? Any differences?

Disco Raisins Planning Notes

This section will help you prepare for and carry out your Family Science event.

Calculating Quantities

"Calculating Quantities" contains information to help you calculate how much of each material you will need for your event. Copy values marked with a 🛒 onto the Shopping/Gathering List and those marked with a ✓ onto the Setup Checklist. If any of the calculations result in fractions, round up to the next whole number.

Nonconsumable Items Per Station

Amounts listed are for one station. If you will have more than one station for this Family Science Challenge, adjust amounts accordingly.

- 2 boxes or other containers for raisins and popcorn kernels (You may wish to leave them in their original containers.) 🛒 ✓
- bucket for waste liquids 🛒 ✓
- sponge 🛒 ✓
- trash can 🛒 ✓

Nonconsumable Items Per Setup

You may choose to provide more than one setup at each station to allow a number of family teams to work concurrently.

- scissors
  (1 pair of scissors per setup) x _____ *setups =* _____ **pairs of scissors** 🛒 ✓

- pieces of cork
  (2 pieces per setup) x _____ *setups =* _____ **pieces of cork** 🛒 ✓

- other test materials, such as paper clips, buttons, or Styrofoam® pieces
  (2 pieces of one material per setup) x _____ *setups =* _____ **pieces** 🛒 ✓

- clear 8-ounce plastic cups
  (2 cups per setup) x _____ *setups =* _____ **cups** 🛒 ✓

- spoons
  (1 spoon per setup) x _____ *setups =* _____ **spoons** 🛒 ✓

- boxes or other containers to hold raisins, popcorn, cork, and other test materials
  (1 box per test material per setup) x _____ *test materials =* _____ *boxes per setup*
  _____ *boxes per setup x* _____ *setups =* _____ **total boxes or other containers** 🛒 ✓

Consumable Materials

- raisins
  (2 raisins per family) x _____ *families =* _____ **raisins** 🛒 ✓

- unpopped popcorn
  (2 kernels per family) x _____ *families =* _____ **kernels** 🛒 ✓

- water in 1- or 2-liter plastic soft-drink bottles (if a source of running water will not be readily available near the station)
  estimate (4 ounces per family) x _____ *families =* _____ *ounces*
  _____ *ounces ÷ (34 ounces per liter) =* _____ **liters of water** ✓
  _____ *liters of water =* _____ **1-L bottles** 🛒 ✓ *; OR*
  _____ *1-L bottles ÷ 2 =* _____ **2-L bottles** 🛒 ✓

- colorless or lightly colored carbonated soft drink
  (4 ounces per family) x _____ *families = ounces*
  _____ *ounces ÷ (34 ounces per liter) =* _____ **liters of soft drink** 🛒 ✓

- paper towels 🛒 ✓
  estimate (2 towels per family) x _____ *families =* _____ **paper towels** 🛒 ✓

Getting Ready for the Family Science Challenge

Tools or General Supplies Needed for Preparation Only

- 3 sheets of brightly colored cardstock for Table Tent **D**
- adhesive copier labels (template provided) or other materials to make labels
- small, sharp knife

Preparing Materials for Use

- Photocopy the Family Science Challenge handout master to make the number of copies needed.

- Photocopy the Table Tent **D** master onto three sheets of brightly colored cardstock and assemble the table tent.

- Photocopy the label template onto a blank sheet of copier labels to print the labels, or make your own labels.

- Check the raisins before use. If they are too dried out, they may not be usable because the loss of water will increase their density. To solve this problem, soak dried-out raisins in water for about 1 hour, drain, and pat dry. Treated raisins of this type typically retain ample water for a couple of days.

- Carefully cut the cork into pieces about the size of the popcorn kernels, if possible.

- Prepare the other test material pieces as needed.

- For each setup, label one 8-ounce cup "Water" and another cup "Soft Drink."

- If the station will not be located near a source of running water (such as a sink or drinking fountain), fill several 1- or 2-L bottles with water to refill the containers of water as needed. Label the bottles appropriately.

- Label the boxes or other containers that will hold the test pieces. Label the waste bucket.

Setting Up the Station

- Place Table Tent **D** at the station in a prominent location.

- Set the labeled containers of raisins and popcorn kernels at the station so they are accessible to all setups.

- Put the cork and other test materials in their labeled boxes and put one set at each setup.

- Place a cup labeled "Water," a cup labeled "Soft Drink," a spoon, and a pair of scissors at each setup.

- Place the bottles of soft drink and water at the station so they are accessible to all setups.

- Place the waste bucket and a sponge at the station so that they are easily accessible for all setups but are out of the way.

Disposal

After the event, dispose of waste liquid from the bucket by pouring it down the drain. If some solids still remain in the waste liquid, dispose of the liquid in a toilet. Throw away used popcorn kernels and raisin halves; the other materials can be used again. Do not allow unused raisins or popcorn kernels to be eaten or to be put where they might be eaten later.

Answers and Observations

Observation Table				
	Will it sink or float in water?		Will it sink or float in the soft drink?	
Solid	Predictions (step 1)	Observations (step 2)	Predictions (step 1)	Observations (step 3)
raisin half		sink		will sometimes sink and rise
raisin quarter		sink		sink and rise
popcorn kernel		sink		sink and rise
cork piece		float		float
other test object:		will vary with object used		will vary with object used

Answers for Child/Adult Discussion

? *Discuss the similarities and differences in the behavior of the solids in the water and in the soft drink. What do you think caused the differences you observed?*

The differences are caused by the bubbles that adhere to the raisins and popcorn kernels, lowering their densities and causing them to float to the surface, where the bubbles pop. The densities then return to their original values, and the solids sink.

Disco Raisins
Shopping/Gathering List

Use this checklist as a guide to collecting the materials for this Family Science Challenge. Fill in the quantities needed below after doing the calculations called for in the "Calculating Quantities" section.

Total Quantities (from Planning Notes)

_____ scissors

_____ raisins

_____ unpopped popcorn kernels

_____ pieces of cork

_____ other solid items to test*

_____ clear 8-ounce plastic cups

_____ liters of water

_____ 1- or 2-liter bottles

_____ liters of colorless or lightly colored carbonated soft drink

_____ spoons

_____ paper towels

_____ boxes or containers

_____ sponge(s)

_____ waste bucket(s)

_____ trash can(s)

Tools for Getting Ready

☐ 3 sheets of brightly colored cardstock for Table Tent **D**

☐ adhesive copier labels (template provided) or other materials to make labels**

☐ small, sharp knife

* Recommended test items include paper clips, buttons, and pieces of Styrofoam®.

** We have provided a label template that can be photocopied directly onto a blank sheet of copier labels to print all of the labels you need for the activity. Use 1-inch x 2¾-inch copier labels, such as Avery Copier Labels (code 5351). If copier labels are not available, copy the label template onto paper, cut out the labels, and use tape to affix the paper labels. Alternatively, make hand-written labels using permanent marker and masking tape or other similar materials.

Disco Raisins
Setup Checklist

The following is a list of items you will need to set up the Family Science Challenge. "Planning Notes" gives step-by-step instructions for setting up the Family Science Challenge.

Items Per Station

The following materials should be left on or near the table for all family teams to use. (A station is a location where family teams work on an activity.)

Material	Total Needed	Notes
☐ Table Tent **D**	_____	Copy master provided
☐ bucket for waste liquids	_____	_____
☐ sponge	_____	_____
☐ trash can	_____	_____

Items Per Setup

The following nonconsumable items should be placed at each setup. You may choose to provide more than one setup at each station to allow a number of family teams to work concurrently at the station.

	Total Needed	Notes
☐ scissors	_____	_____
☐ labeled boxes of test items	_____	One each of cork and other items
☐ clear plastic cup labeled "Water"	_____	_____
☐ clear plastic cup labeled "Soft Drink"	_____	_____
☐ spoon	_____	_____
☐ pencil for recording observations*	_____	_____

Consumable Materials

The following materials will be used up or taken away by family teams.

Material	Total Needed	Notes
☐ labeled bottle(s) of water	_____	_____
☐ labeled bottle(s) of colorless or lightly colored soft drink	_____	_____
☐ raisins	_____	_____
☐ unpopped popcorn kernels	_____	_____
☐ paper towels	_____	_____
☐ Family Science Challenge handouts**	_____	Copy master provided

* You may wish to pass out pencils at registration or have families bring their own pencils.

** You may wish to pass out Family Science Challenge handouts as a set at registration rather than at each station.

Reproduced from *Science Night Family Fun from* Ⓐ *to* Ⓩ

Disco Raisins
Label Template

D Water
Do not drink this water.

D Cork
Use 2; return to container.

D Water
Do not drink this water.

D Cork
Use 2; return to container.

D Water
Do not drink this water.

D Popcorn Kernels
Use 2; discard after use.
Do not eat.

D Soft Drink
Do not drink this soft drink.

D Popcorn Kernels
Use 2; discard after use.
Do not eat.

D Soft Drink
Do not drink this soft drink.

D Other Test Items
Use 2; return to container.

D Soft Drink
Do not drink this soft drink.

D Other Test Items
Use 2; return to container.

D Raisins
Use 2; discard after use.
Do not eat.

D Waste Bucket
Discard used liquids here.

D Raisins
Use 2; discard after use.
Do not eat.

D Waste Bucket
Discard used liquids here.

 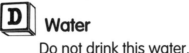

Enlighten Yourself

Family teams observe what happens when the pressure changes as trapped gases are heated or cooled.

Key Science Topics

- air pressure
- behavior of gases
- combustion
- temperature

Average Time Required

Performance   10–15 minutes

Links to *Classroom Science from A to Z*

You can extend this activity into your science curriculum with the following ideas, included in the book *Classroom Science from A to Z*:

- Links to National Science Standards

- Science Activity
  Students use water of different temperatures to crush a plastic bottle.

- Lesson E Teacher Notes

- Lesson E Assessment

- Lesson E Science Explanation

- Lesson E Cross-Curricular Integration

Enlighten Yourself

When you are done…

Throw away	Leave at the table	Take with you
paper towels	birthday candles	completed handout
	pan	
	jar	
	pencil (if provided at station)	

Enlighten Yourself Family Science Challenge

Rise to the challenge and explore the unexpected.

Materials

pie pan-birthday candle apparatus with colored water • matches • narrow-mouthed glass jar or bottle • paper towels • pitcher of water

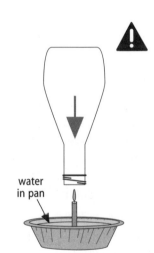

Figure 1

Procedure

❶ Select a pie pan-candle apparatus. (See Figure 1.) The candle should be standing upright in a piece of clay in the middle of the pie pan. (If the candle is too short to light, replace it with a new candle from the station.) The pie pan should be about half-filled with colored water.

❷ Have your adult partner use a match to light the candle.

Work carefully around the open flame.

❸ Observe closely as your adult partner carefully lowers the open mouth of the jar over the candle and into the water (see Figure 2) without resting the jar on the bottom of the pan. (See Figure 3.)

? *What happens to the water? What happens to the flame?*

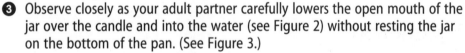

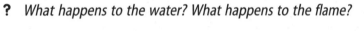

water in pan

Figure 2

❹ Once things stop happening, lift the jar from over the candle. Dry the candle wick thoroughly with a paper towel. (The candle wick will not relight if wet.) Fill the jar with water from the pitcher, then empty the water back into the pitcher. (This cleans out the jar and allows the jar to fill with fresh air.) Wipe the water from inside the neck of the jar using a rolled-up paper towel.

❺ Now consider the following questions and then repeat the experiment to check your responses. Remember the candle wick and the neck of the jar need to be dry in order for the activity to work.

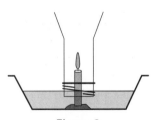

Figure 3

? *Did you see any bubbles coming from under the mouth of the jar before the water movement began?*

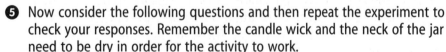

? *Did the water move before the flame went out?*

_____

? *Did the water move after the flame went out?*

_____

6 Please clean up the station by wiping up any spills. Leave the pie pan-candle apparatus as you found it.

Child/Adult Discussion

? *Why do you think the water moved into the jar?*

_____

_____

_____

Explanation

In this activity, a jar is placed over a lit candle sitting in a pan of water. As the jar is lowered over the candle, the air in the jar is heated. Heating a gas causes its volume to increase. Because the jar is open at the mouth, much of the gas originally in the jar is pushed out. This escaping air can at times be seen as bubbles at the point when the mouth of the jar is pushed beneath the water's surface, but these bubbles do not last long. The water level then begins to rise up into the neck of the jar, the candle goes out, and the water rises even more. To understand what caused these observations, it is useful to consider what happens when the candle burns.

In the reaction, candle wax reacts with oxygen to produce carbon dioxide gas and water vapor. The flame went out as the amount of oxygen fell below that needed to sustain combustion. (While oxygen is consumed in the combustion of candle wax, oxygen still remains in the bottle even after the flame goes out.)

The water movement up the neck of the jar results not from the consumption of oxygen, but rather from the lowering of the pressure inside the container, which is caused by two factors. The first and most important factor is that the water produced in the combustion reaction is initially in the gaseous state, but it quickly cools below 100° C and as a result much of it condenses to the liquid state. Because liquid water occupies much, much less space than gaseous water, the gaseous volume inside the jar decreases rather dramatically. A secondary (and less influential) factor is that the pressure inside the container decreases as the gases cool after the flame goes out. Because the atmospheric pressure outside the jar is greater than the air pressure inside the jar, water is pushed into the jar. The water movement ceases when the atmospheric pressure equals the sum of the gas pressure inside and the pressure exerted by the column of water inside the jar.

Stuff to Try at Home

With your adult partner's help, investigate what effect the size and shape of the bottle has on how long the candle will burn and how high the water will rise. Remember, do not play with matches or work unsupervised around flames.

Enlighten Yourself Planning Notes

This section will help you prepare for and carry out your Family Science event.

Calculating Quantities

"Calculating Quantities" contains information to help you calculate how much of each material you will need for your event. Copy values marked with a 🛒 onto the Shopping/Gathering List and those marked with a ✓ onto the Setup Checklist. If any of the calculations result in fractions, round up to the next whole number.

Nonconsumable Items Per Station

Amounts listed are for one station. If you will have more than one station for this Family Science Challenge, adjust amounts accordingly.

- 2 containers, one for candles and the other for matches 🛒 ✓
- trash can 🛒 ✓
- (optional) sponge 🛒 ✓

Nonconsumable Items Per Setup

You may choose to provide more than one setup at each station to allow a number of family teams to work concurrently.

- aluminum pie pan
  *(1 pie pan per setup) x _____ setups = _____ **aluminum pie pans*** 🛒 ✓

- water to half-fill pie pans and fill pitchers

- ½-inch-diameter ball of clay
  *(1 ball of clay per setup) x _____ setups = _____ **balls of clay*** 🛒 ✓
  The average 5-inch stick of clay will yield about 20, ½-inch clay balls, so you will probably need only one stick.

- narrow-mouthed glass jar or bottle
  *(1 jar per setup) x _____ setups = _____ **jars*** 🛒 ✓

- pitcher
  *(1 pitcher per setup) x _____ setups = _____ **pitchers*** 🛒 ✓

Consumable Materials

- paper towels
  *estimate (3 paper towels per family) x _____ families = _____ **paper towels*** 🛒 ✓

- birthday candle
  *estimate (1 candle per family) x _____ families + several extras = _____ **birthday candles*** 🛒 ✓
  Do not use trick re-lighting birthday candles.

- matches

  estimate (4 matches per family) x _____ families = _____ matches 🛒 ✓

Getting Ready for the Family Science Challenge

Tools or General Supplies Needed for Preparation Only

- 3 sheets of brightly colored cardstock for Table Tent **E**
- adhesive copier labels (template provided) or other materials to make labels
- food color

Preparing Materials for Use

- Photocopy the Family Science Challenge handout master to make the number of copies needed.

- Photocopy the Table Tent **E** master onto three sheets of brightly colored cardstock and assemble the table tent.

- Photocopy the label template onto a blank sheet of copier labels to print the labels, or make your own labels.

- Roll the clay into balls about ½ inch in diameter. (If your clay comes in sticks, cut the sticks into ¼-inch lengths and roll the pieces into balls.) Stick a clay ball in the center of each pie pan and push a birthday candle into each clay ball so the candle stands upright. Half-fill the pie pan with colored water.

- Label and fill a pitcher of water per setup.

Setting Up the Station

- Place Table Tent **E** at the station in a prominent location.

- Put a pie pan-birthday candle apparatus and matches at each setup. You may want to include a sponge to wipe up spills.

- Place a pitcher of water at each setup so that it is easily accessible but not in the way.

Answers and Observations

❸ *What happens to the water? What happens to the flame?*

The level of the water in the jar rises and the flame goes out.

❓ *Did the water move before the flame went out?*

The water may begin moving before or after the flame goes out.

cut ¼-inch slices

? *Did the water move after the flame went out?*

Yes, the water usually continues or begins to move and moves more quickly after the flame goes out.

Answers for Child/Adult Discussion

? *Why do you think the water moved into the jar?*

See the Explanation on the Family Science Challenge handout.

Enlighten Yourself Shopping/Gathering List

Use this checklist as a guide to collecting the materials for this Family Science Challenge. Fill in the quantities needed below after doing the calculations called for in the "Calculating Quantities" section.

Total Quantities (from "Planning Notes")

_____ aluminum pie pans

_____ birthday candles*

_____ box(es) or container(s) for pie pans and candles

_____ narrow-mouthed glass jars or bottles**

_____ 1-inch-diameter balls of clay

_____ liter(s) of water

_____ matches

_____ rolls of paper towels

_____ pitcher(s)

_____ trash can(s)

_____ (optional) sponge(s)

Tools for Getting Ready

☐ 3 sheets of brightly colored cardstock for Table Tent **E**

☐ adhesive copier labels (template provided) or other materials to make labels***

☐ food color

*   Do not use trick re-lighting birthday candles.

**   The jars should be at least 3 inches taller than the birthday candles. A 12-ounce juice bottle or a glass salad dressing bottle works well with this activity.

*** We have provided a label template that can be photocopied directly onto a blank sheet of copier labels to print all of the labels you need for the activity. Use 1-inch x 2¾-inch copier labels, such as Avery Copier Labels (code 5351). If copier labels are not available, copy the label template onto paper, cut out the labels, and use tape to affix the paper labels. Alternatively, make hand-written labels using permanent marker and masking tape or other similar materials.

Enlighten Yourself Setup Checklist

The following is a list of items you will need to set up the Family Science Challenge. "Planning Notes" gives step-by-step instructions for setting up the Family Science Challenge.

Items Per Station

The following materials should be left on or near the table for all family teams to use. (A station is a location where family teams work on an activity.)

Material	Total Needed	Notes
☐ Table Tent **E**	_____	Copy master provided
☐ 2 labeled containers	_____	For matches and candles
☐ trash can(s)	_____	
☐ (optional) sponge(s)	_____	

Items Per Setup

The following nonconsumable items should be placed at each setup. You may choose to provide more than one setup at each station to allow a number of family teams to work concurrently at the station.

Material	Total Needed	Notes
☐ aluminum pie pan	_____	
☐ clay ball	_____	
☐ narrow-mouthed glass jar or bottle	_____	
☐ pitcher of water	_____	
☐ pencil for recording observations*	_____	

Consumable Materials

The following materials will be used up or taken away by family teams.

Material	Total Needed	Notes
☐ birthday candles	_____	
☐ matches	_____	
☐ paper towels	_____	
☐ Family Science Challenge handouts**	_____	Copy master provided

*   You may wish to pass out pencils at registration or have families bring their own pencils.

** You may wish to pass out Family Science Challenge handouts as a set at registration rather than at each station.

Enlighten Yourself
Label Template

[E] Water

[E] Water

[E] Water

[E] Water

[E] Water

[E] Water

[E] Water

[E] Water

[E] Water

[E] Water

[E] Water

[E] Water

[E] Water

[E] Water

[E] Water

[E] Water

Frisky Fish

What makes a frisky fish wiggle in your hand? Family teams investigate the reasons these fish curl up.

.... **Key Science Topics**

- absorption
- capillary action
- evaporation

.... **Average Time Required**

Performance   5–10 minutes

Links to *Classroom Science from A to Z*

You can extend this activity into your science curriculum with the following ideas, included in the book *Classroom Science from A to Z:*

- Links to National Science Standards

- Science Activity
  Students use capillary action to make a paper "worm" grow.

- Lesson F Teacher Notes

- Lesson F Assessment

- Lesson F Science Explanation

- Lesson F Cross-Curricular Integration

Frisky Fish

When you are done...

Throw away	Leave at the table	Take with you
paper towels	pencil (if provided at station)	completed handout

*Ask the Station Monitor whether you should keep or leave the fish.

Reproduced from *Science Night Family Fun from* A *to* Z

Frisky Fish
Family Science Challenge

Don't sweat the small stuff—you'll discover the secret of the frisky fish.

Materials

cellophane fish in its plastic wrapper • container of water • paper towels

Procedure

❶ Remove a cellophane fish from its wrapper and lay the cellophane fish in the palm of your hand.

? *What happens?*

_____

_____

❷ Put the wrapper in the palm of your adult partner's hand. Then put the fish on top of the wrapper.

? *What happens?*

_____

_____

❸ Brainstorm with your adult partner about what might be causing the movement of the fish.

? *Record your ideas.*

_____

_____

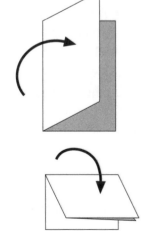

❹ Fold a paper towel in half and then in half again. (See Figure 1.)

❺ Slightly dampen the folded paper towel by dipping it in water and squeezing out as much of the excess water as you can. (Caution: Too much water could cause the fish to become waterlogged.) Lay the damp, folded paper towel on the table.

Figure 1

6 Have your adult partner lay the cellophane fish on the moist paper towel.

? *What happens?*

_____

_____

7 Wipe up any water and discard wet paper towels. Ask the station monitor what you should do with the fish.

Child/Adult Discussion

? *Was the fish's movement when placed directly on your hand more like the fish's action on the plastic wrapper or on the moist paper towel?*

_____

_____

? *Based on your answer, which factor do you think had the greater effect on the fish's motion: heat from your hand or moisture (sweat) from your hand?*

_____

Explanation

The cellophane fish curls and twists primarily because it absorbs moisture from the sweat glands in your hand and subsequently loses water due to evaporation. The frisky fish is made from a special cellophane that is "hygroscopic," a term that comes from the Greek words "hygro," meaning "wet," and "scopic," meaning "to view or find."

As water is absorbed into the cellophane fish, the water moves through small pores, or holes, in the cellophane by a process called capillary action. The heat of your hand then causes the water to evaporate. The lightness of the cellophane makes the fish very susceptible to air currents, which adds to the "dancing" effect. Because every person is different, the absorption/evaporation process happens at a different rate for each person depending upon the warmth of the hand and the amount of moisture on the palm.

When the curled fish is placed on a warm, dry surface, it flattens out because the warmth evaporates the moisture and no additional moisture is available to be absorbed. However, placing the fish on the wet paper towel causes the fish to curl as it did in your hand because it once again absorbs water. The fish didn't move when you placed it on the wrapper because the wrapper prevented the fish from absorbing any water from the palm of your hand.

Stuff to Try at Home

If you're able to take your fish home, try seeing how it behaves after it has been in your freezer for a while. How about putting it on an ice cube? Remember not to let the fish get soggy.

Frisky Fish Planning Notes

This section will help you prepare for and carry out your Family Science event.

Calculating Quantities

"Calculating Quantities" contains information to help you calculate how much of each material you will need for your event. Copy values marked with a 🛒 onto the Shopping/Gathering List and those marked with a ✓ onto the Setup Checklist. If any of the calculations result in fractions, round up to the next whole number.

Nonconsumable Items Per Station

Amounts listed are for one station. If you will have more than one station for this Family Science Challenge, adjust amounts accordingly.

- box or other container for the fish 🛒 ✓
- trash can 🛒 ✓

Nonconsumable Items Per Setup

You may choose to provide more than one setup at each station to allow a number of family teams to work concurrently.

- large, open, waterproof container, such as a pop beaker
  *(1 container per setup) x _____ setups = _____ **containers** 🛒 ✓*

Consumable Materials

- cellophane fish
  The first calculation below assumes each family will keep the fish they use. If you do not wish to allow families to keep the fish, plan on providing three fish per setup (in case a fish gets too waterlogged) and perform the second calculation to determine the number of fish needed.

  *(1 fish per family) x _____ families = _____ **cellophane fish** 🛒 ✓ ; OR*
  *(3 fish per setup) x _____ setups = _____ **cellophane fish** 🛒 ✓*

- paper towels
  *(estimate 2 towels per family) x _____ families = _____ **paper towels** 🛒 ✓*

- water in 1- or 2-L plastic soft-drink bottles (if a source of running water will not be readily available near the station)
  *(0.015 L water per family) x _____ families = _____ **liters of water** 🛒 ✓*
  *_____ liters of water = _____ **1-L bottles** 🛒 ✓ ; OR*
  *_____ 1-L bottles ÷ 2 = _____ **2-L bottles** 🛒 ✓*

Getting Ready for the Family Science Challenge

Tools or General Supplies Needed for Preparation Only

- 3 sheets of brightly colored cardstock for Table Tent **F**
- adhesive copier labels (template provided) or other materials to make labels

Preparing Materials for Use

- Photocopy the Family Science Challenge handout master to make the number of copies needed.

- Photocopy the Table Tent **F** master onto three sheets of brightly colored cardstock and assemble the table tent.

- Photocopy the label template onto a blank sheet of copier labels to print the labels, or make your own labels.

- No preparation is required for the cellophane fish. Leave them in their original wrappers. Label the fish container with the appropriate label (master provided) to indicate whether family teams may keep the fish or not.

- Label the open containers for water.

- If the station will not be located near a source of running water (such as a sink or drinking fountain), fill several 1- or 2-L bottles with water to refill the containers of water as needed. Label the bottles appropriately.

Setting Up the Station

- Place Table Tent **F** at the station in a prominent location.

- Place the paper towels and trash can at the station. Either place the labeled box of fish at the station or place three fish at each setup.

- Place a labeled, open container at each setup. Fill each container about half full with water. If you are providing refill bottles of water, place them where they are easily accessible but are not in the way.

Tips

- To help ensure that the cellophane fish do not get too wet and that no more than one fish per family is used, we recommend you assign a station monitor to hand out the fish.

- If you wish to allow families to keep their cellophane fish, you may want to indicate this on the table tent. Let the station monitor know if the used fish should be collected and kept for future use. Choose the appropriate label (master provided) to indicate whether family teams may keep the fish or not.

Answers and Observations

❶ *What happens?*

The fish curls up.

❷ *What happens?*

The fish stops moving (except possibly to uncurl).

❻ *What happens?*

The fish curls up.

Answers for Child/Adult Discussion

? *Was the fish's movement when placed directly on your hand more like the fish's action on the plastic wrapper or on the moist towel?*

The fish's movement on the hand was more like its movement on the moist towel.

? *Based on your answer, which factor do you think had the larger effect on the fish's motion: heat from your hand or moisture (sweat) from your hand?*

The moisture from the hand had a bigger effect on making the fish move.

Reference

Sarquis, M.; Sarquis, J.; Williams, J. "Fortune-Telling Fish," *Teaching Chemistry with TOYS;* McGraw-Hill: New York, 1995; pp 83–85.

Frisky Fish Shopping/Gathering List

Use this checklist as a guide to collecting the materials for this Family Science Challenge. Fill in the quantities needed below after doing the calculations called for in the "Calculating Quantities" section.

Total Quantities (from Planning Notes)

_____ cellophane fish*

_____ paper towels

_____ liters of water

_____ large, open, waterproof containers**

_____ 1- or 2-L plastic soft-drink bottles (if necessary)

_____ box(es) or other container(s)

_____ trash can(s)

Tools for Getting Ready

☐ 3 sheets of brightly colored cardstock for Table Tent **F**

☐ adhesive copier labels (template provided) or other materials to make labels***

* Cellophane fish are available in quantities of 30 (item #PR9906S) and 144 (item #PR9906L) from Terrific Science Books, Kits, & More, 513/727-3269.

** A pop beaker made by cutting off the top of a 2-L plastic soft-drink bottle works well.

*** We have provided a label template that can be photocopied directly onto a blank sheet of copier labels to print all of the labels you need for the activity. Use 1-inch x 2¾-inch copier labels, such as Avery Copier Labels (code 5351). If copier labels are not available, copy the label template onto paper, cut out the labels, and use tape to affix the paper labels. Alternatively, make hand-written labels using permanent marker and masking tape or other similar materials.

Frisky Fish
Setup Checklist

The following is a list of items you will need to set up the Family Science Challenge. "Planning Notes" gives step-by-step instructions for setting up the Family Science Challenge.

Items Per Station

The following materials should be left on or near the table for all family teams to use. (A station is a location where family teams work on an activity.)

Material	Total Needed	Notes
☐ Table Tent **F**	_____	Copy master provided
☐ trash can	_____	_____
☐ labeled box or other container	_____	For fish

Items Per Setup

The following nonconsumable items should be placed at each setup. You may choose to provide more than one setup at each station to allow a number of family teams to work concurrently at the station.

Material	Total Needed	Notes
☐ labeled, open container of water	_____	_____
☐ pencil for recording observations*	_____	_____

Consumable Materials

The following materials will be used up or taken away by family teams.

Material	Total Needed	Notes
☐ cellophane fish in wrappers	_____	_____
☐ paper towels	_____	_____
☐ Family Science Challenge handouts**	_____	Copy master provided
☐ labeled bottles of water	_____	Needed if a sink or drinking fountain is not close by

* You may wish to pass out pencils at registration or have families bring their own pencils.

** You may wish to pass out Family Science Challenge handouts as a set at registration rather than at each station.

 # Frisky Fish
Label Template

F Water

F Water

F Water

F Water

F Water

F Water

F Water

F Water

F Cellophane Fish
Use 1 per family. You may keep your fish when finished.

F Cellophane Fish
Use 1 per family. You may keep your fish when finished.

F Cellophane Fish
Use 1 per family. You may keep your fish when finished.

F Cellophane Fish
Use 1 per family. You may keep your fish when finished.

F Cellophane Fish
Use 1 per family. Please return to the station monitor when finished.

F Cellophane Fish
Use 1 per family. Please return to the station monitor when finished.

F Cellophane Fish
Use 1 per family. Please return to the station monitor when finished.

F Cellophane Fish
Use 1 per family. Please return to the station monitor when finished.

Gobs of Fun

Family teams make Gluep, a fun polymer putty material, and investigate its physical properties.

.... **Key Science Topics**

- cross-linking
- physical properties
- polymers
- viscosity

.... **Average Time Required**

Performance   10–15 minutes

Links to *Classroom Science from A to Z*

You can extend this activity into your science curriculum with the following ideas, included in the book *Classroom Science from A to Z*:

- Links to National Science Standards

- Science Activity
  Students make three different recipes of Gluep and compare their properties.

- Lesson G Teacher Notes

- Lesson G Assessment

- Lesson G Science Explanation

- Lesson G Cross-Curricular Integration

Gobs of Fun

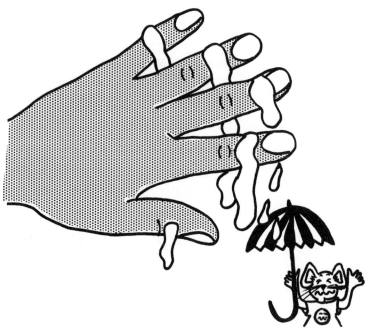

When you are done...

Throw away	Leave at the table	Take with you
paper towels	glue-water mixture borax solution measuring cups pencil (if provided at station)	Gluep completed handout

Gobs of Fun
Family Science Challenge

Follow the recipe for gooey, gloopy fun.

Materials

glue-water mixture • borax solution (provided by the station monitor) • measuring cup • zipper-type plastic bags • paper towels

Procedure

❶ Cap the bottle of glue-water mixture and shake it well. Pour glue-water mixture into a measuring cup to the 2-tablespoon mark. Have your adult partner hold a zipper-type plastic bag open while you pour the measured glue-water mixture into the bag.

? *What does the glue-water mixture look like?*

_____

_____

❷ Take your bag containing the glue-water mixture to the station monitor, who will pour 2 teaspoons borax solution into your bag. Zip the bag closed and squeeze the bag gently to mix the contents. Continue mixing until a gel-like mass forms. This is Gluep.

There is little danger in handling the Gluep unless you have very sensitive skin. If your skin is very sensitive, do not remove the Gluep from the bag. If you do handle the Gluep, be sure to wash your hands after use. Do not give Gluep to very young children, who may try to eat it. It could cause choking.

❸ Open the bag and examine the properties of the Gluep by kneading it, rolling it into a ball or rope, bouncing it, stretching it, snapping it, and tearing it.

? *Describe what you find.*

_____

_____

_____

_____

❹ Put your Gluep back in the plastic bag to take home if you desire. Otherwise, dispose of it in a trash can. Wipe off the area you were working in.

Do not keep your Gluep for more than a few days, because it typically becomes moldy with handling. Dispose of Gluep in a trash can. Gluep does not readily stick to clothes, walls, or desks, but it does stick to paper. However, do not put Gluep on natural wood furniture; it will leave a water mark. If Gluep falls on the carpet, de-gel it by adding vinegar to it and washing the area with soap and water.

Child/Adult Discussion

? *The Gluep has some properties of a solid and some properties of a liquid. List these properties.*

solid:_____

_____

liquid: _____

_____

Explanation

In this activity, you examined some properties of polymers ("poly" means "many;" "mers" means "units.") Polymers are made by combining many individual units called monomers ("mono" means "one") into a single polymer unit. Polymers are an interesting group of chemicals found in many forms around us, including plastics and the biochemical molecules that make up our bodies.

What makes Gluep so different from the glue, borax, and water from which it is made? Most brands of white glue contain millions of individual chains of a polymer called polyvinyl acetate, which have been dissolved in water. Before you add the borax, these chains are able to slip and slide freely over one another like strands of freshly cooked spaghetti. Although they can slip around, the polyvinyl acetate chains are so long that they do interfere with one another, causing the glue to be rather thick and to pour more slowly than water. (In other words, the glue is more viscous than water.)

When you add the borax (sodium tetraborate) solution to the glue, you caused the polyvinyl acetate chains to be linked together—just as rungs link the two sides of a ladder. The borax forms bridges with the polymer chains, binding them together (cross-linking them) and producing a gel-like material that is more viscous than the glue solution. Figure 1 shows a model of this process, with students representing the monomers of polyvinyl acetate and the cross-linkers. Gluep has a variety of interesting properties. These properties vary with the amount of cross-linking, and the amount of cross-linking varies with the proportions of the ingredients: polyvinyl acetate, water, and borax.

Figure 1

Gobs of Fun
Planning Notes

This section will help you prepare for and carry out your Family Science event.

Calculating Quantities

"Calculating Quantities" contains information to help you calculate how much of each material you will need for your event. Copy values marked with a 🛒 onto the Shopping/Gathering List and those marked with a ✓ onto the Setup Checklist. If any of the calculations result in fractions, round up to the next whole number.

Nonconsumable Items Per Station

Amounts listed are for one station. If you will have more than one station for this Family Science Challenge, adjust amounts accordingly.

- box or other container to hold plastic bags 🛒 ✓
- sponge or mop and pail 🛒 ✓
- trash can 🛒 ✓
- 20- to 30-ounce squeeze bottles with pop-up lid to dispense borax solution
- goggles

Nonconsumable Items Per Setup

You may choose to provide more than one setup at each station to allow a number of family teams to work concurrently.

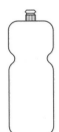

- 20- to 30-ounce squeeze bottle with pop-up lid to dispense glue-water mixture 🛒 ✓
- 2 small cups for tablespoon and teaspoon measures 🛒 ✓

Consumable Materials

- zipper-type plastic bags
  *(1 plastic bag per family) x _____ families = _____ **zipper-type plastic bags*** 🛒 ✓

- glue-water mixture
  How many liters of mixture do I need?
  *(0.03 L per family) x _____ families = _____ **liters of glue-water mixture** ✓*
  How much white glue do I need to make the mixture?
  *_____ liters of mixture x (2 cups of glue per liter of mixture) = _____ **cups of glue** 🛒*

- borax solution
  How many liters of solution do I need?
  *(0.01 L per family) x _____ families = _____ **liters of borax solution** ✓*
  How much borax (powder) do I need to make the solution?
  *_____ liters of solution x (¼ cup borax per liter of solution) = _____ **cups of borax (powder)** 🛒 OR*
  *_____ cups x (10 grams per tablespoon) = _____ **grams of borax (powder)** 🛒*

- 1- or 2-L plastic bottles to make and store glue-water mixture and borax solution

    _____ *liters glue-water mixture +* _____ *liters borax solution =* **_____ 1-L bottles**
    🛒 ✓ *OR*

    _____ *1-L bottles ÷ 2 =* **_____ 2-L bottles** 🛒 ✓

- paper towels

    estimate (2 towels per family) x _____ *families =* **_____ paper towels** 🛒 ✓

Getting Ready for the Family Science Challenge

Tools or General Supplies Needed for Preparation Only

- 3 sheets of brightly colored cardstock for Table Tent **G**
- adhesive copier labels (template provided) or other materials to make labels
- measuring cups and spoons
- permanent marker
- funnel or paper cone
- goggles

Preparing Materials for Use

- Photocopy the Family Science Challenge handout master to make the number of copies needed.

- Photocopy the Table Tent **G** master onto three sheets of brightly colored cardstock and assemble.

- Photocopy the label template onto a blank sheet of copier labels to print the labels, or make your own labels.

    Some people may have an allergic reaction to dry, powdered borax. Avoid inhaling or ingesting the borax solution. Use adequate ventilation in preparing the solution and wash your hands after contact with the solid.

- While wearing goggles, prepare the borax solution in the required number of empty 1- or 2-L plastic bottles by almost filling each bottle with water and using a funnel to add ¼ cup borax for each liter of water used. Cap the bottle(s) and shake well to dissolve. Label the bottle(s). Do not worry if some borax does not dissolve.

- Prepare the glue-water mixture in the required number of empty 1- or 2-L plastic bottles by half-filling a bottle with glue and then adding water until the bottle is almost full. Shake well to mix. Label the bottle(s).

- Prepare a 2-tablespoon measuring cup for each setup as follows: Determine the 2 tablespoon level by measuring two tablespoons of water into a cup with a measuring spoon. Mark the level of the water with a permanent marker and write "2 tablespoons " near the line. If using pre-marked medicine cups, you may wish to make the 2 tablespoon mark stand out more using a permanent marker.

- Prepare a 2-teaspoon measuring cup for the station monitor to use. Do this by using the same method used in previous step.

- Label the squeeze bottles with pop-up lids for the glue-water mixture and the borax solution. Label the box for storing the plastic bags.

Setting Up the Station

- Place Table Tent **G** at the station in a prominent location.

- Have a sponge or mop and pail handy to clean up spills.

- Put the plastic bags in their labeled box and place at the station.

- Pour the glue-water mixture into the appropriately labeled bottles with pop-up lids and place them at each setup. Place the storage bottles of glue-water mixture at the station out of the way to refill the squeeze bottles as needed.

- Place a 2-tablespoon measuring cup at each setup.

- Pour borax solution into the appropriately labeled bottle with a pop-up lid. Place the storage bottles of borax solution at the station out of the way to refill the squeeze bottles as needed. Provide the station monitor with a pair of safety goggles to use, the 2-teaspoon measuring cup, and the borax solution.

Safety

To avoid any complications with the handling or use of the borax solution, have the station monitor measure and pour the borax solution into the family team bags. The station monitor should wear safety goggles during this process.

Some people have developed an allergic reaction to dry, powdered borax. As a result, care should be taken when handling it. Avoid inhalation and ingestion. Use adequate ventilation in preparing the borax solution and wash your hands after contact with the solid.

There is typically no danger in handling the Gluep, but you should wash your hands after use. Persons with especially sensitive skin or persons who know they are allergic to borax or detergent products should determine their sensitivity to the Gluep by touching a small amount. Should redness or itching occur, wash the area with a mild soap and avoid further contact.

If Gluep spills on the carpet, apply vinegar to the spot and follow with a soap-and-water rinse. Do not let the Gluep harden on the carpet. Do not place gluep on natural wood furniture; it will leave a water mark.

Disposal

The borax and glue solutions can be stored in closed containers for several months. Shake well before use if stored for long periods of time and check for signs of mold. Discard the solutions if they are moldy.

Answers and Observations

❶ *What does the glue-water mixture look like?*

The glue-water mixture is an opaque, white liquid.

❸ *Describe what you find.*

The mixture has changed and has many properties of a solid. It can be rolled into a ball, bounced, and stretched when pulled slowly. The Gluep will not maintain its shape and tends to spread out or flow.

Answers for Child/Adult Discussion

? *The Gluep has some properties of a solid and some properties of a liquid. List these properties.*

Solid: It stretches when pulled slowly but breaks when pulled quickly. It bounces.

Liquid: When placed on a table, it spreads out, and it does not retain its original shape.

References

Casassa, E.Z., Sarquis, M., and Van Dyke, C.H. "The Gelation of Polyvinyl Alcohol with Borax," *Journal of Chemical Education, 63*, 1986, pp 57–60.

"Gluep," *Fun with Chemistry: A Guidebook of K–12 Activities;* Sarquis, M., Sarquis, J., Eds.; Institute for Chemical Education: Madison, WI, 1993; Vol. 2, pp 81–88.

"Glue Polymer," *Chain Gang—The Chemistry of Polymers;* Sarquis, M., Ed.; Terrific Science: Middletown, OH, 1995; pp 103–109.

Sarquis, M. "A Dramatization of Polymeric Bonding Using Slime," *Journal of Chemical Education, 63*, 1986, pp 60–61.

Gobs of Fun Shopping/Gathering List

Use this checklist as a guide to collecting the materials for this Family Science Challenge. Fill in the quantities needed below after doing the calculations called for in the "Calculating Quantities" section.

Total Quantities (from "Planning Notes")

_____ zipper-type plastic bags

_____ box(es) or other container(s)

_____ cups of Elmer's (or equivalent) white glue*

_____ cups OR _____ grams of borax (powder)**

_____ small cups***

_____ 20- to 30-ounce squeeze bottles with pop-up lids†

_____ 1- or 2-L plastic soft-drink bottles

_____ goggles

_____ paper towels

_____ sponge(s) or mop and pail

_____ trash can(s)

Tools for Getting Ready

☐ 3 sheets of brightly colored cardstock for Table Tent **G**

☐ adhesive copier labels (template provided) or other materials to make labels††

☐ measuring cup and spoons

☐ water to make borax solution and glue-water mixture

☐ permanent marker

☐ funnel or paper cone

☐ goggles

* Neither washable "school glue" nor Elmer's colored glues work well for this activity.

** Borax can be found in grocery stores in the laundry section.

*** Cups 3 ounces or smaller are needed so that the 2-teaspoon mark is high enough from the bottom of the cup to be visible. Transparent pill bottles work well. Solo makes 3-ounce disposable bathroom cups, which are available in many grocery stores. Medicine cups (they hold 1 ounce) with teaspoon and tablespoon measure marks are available as a special-order item from some pharmacies and from Frey Scientific, 800/225-3739.

† Bottles with pop-up squeeze lids will make pouring liquids easier. These lids are on the bottles of many brands of bottled water, sports drinks, liquid detergent, soap, hand lotion, and shampoo. The 20- to 30-ounce size makes the bottles very manageable for young children.

†† We have provided a label template that can be photocopied directly onto a blank sheet of copier labels to print all of the labels you need for the activity. Use 1-inch x 2¾-inch copier labels, such as Avery Copier Labels (code 5351). If copier labels are not available, copy the label template onto paper, cut out the labels, and use tape to affix the paper labels. Alternatively, make hand-written labels using permanent marker and masking tape or other similar materials.

Gobs of Fun
Setup Checklist

The following is a list of items you will need to set up the Family Science Challenge. "Planning Notes" gives step-by-step instructions for setting up the Family Science Challenge.

Items Per Station

The following materials should be left on or near the table for all family teams to use. (A station is a location where family teams work on an activity.)

Material	Total Needed	Notes
☐ Table Tent **G**	_____	Copy master provided
☐ labeled container	_____	For plastic bags
☐ sponge or mop and pail	_____	_____
☐ trash can	_____	_____
☐ squeeze bottles with pop-up lids	_____	For borax solution

Items Per Setup

The following nonconsumable items should be placed at each setup. You may choose to provide more than one setup at each station to allow a number of family teams to work concurrently at the station.

Material	Total Needed	Notes
☐ small cups	_____	For teaspoon and tablespoon measures
☐ squeeze bottle with pop-up lid	_____	For glue-water mixture
☐ pencil for recording observations*	_____	_____

Consumable Materials

The following materials will be used up or taken away by family teams.

Material	Total Needed	Notes
☐ zipper-type plastic bags	_____	_____
☐ refill bottle(s) of glue-water mixture	_____	_____
☐ refill bottle(s) of borax solution	_____	_____
☐ paper towels	_____	_____
☐ Family Science Challenge handouts**	_____	Copy master provided

*   You may wish to pass out pencils at registration or have families bring their own pencils.

**   You may wish to pass out Family Science Challenge handouts as a set at registration rather than at each station.

Reproduced from *Science Night Family Fun from* [A] *to* [Z]

Gobs of Fun
Label Template

Glue-Water Mixture

Cap and SHAKE WELL—
Use 2 tablespoons.

Glue-Water Mixture

Cap and SHAKE WELL—
Refill squeeze bottle as necessary.

Borax Solution

Use 2 teaspoons.

Borax Solution

Refill squeeze bottle as necessary.

Plastic Bags

1 per family

Glue-Water Mixture

Cap and SHAKE WELL—
Use 2 tablespoons.

Glue-Water Mixture

Cap and SHAKE WELL—
Refill squeeze bottle as necessary.

Borax Solution

Use 2 teaspoons.

Borax Solution

Refill squeeze bottle as necessary.

Plastic Bags

1 per family

Glue-Water Mixture

Cap and SHAKE WELL—
Use 2 tablespoons.

Glue-Water Mixture

Cap and SHAKE WELL—
Refill squeeze bottle as necessary.

Borax Solution

Use 2 teaspoons

Borax Solution

Refill squeeze bottle as necessary.

Plastic Bags

1 per family

Glue-Water Mixture

Cap and SHAKE WELL—
Use 2 tablespoons.

Hovering Paper Clip

Family teams use a mysteriously hovering paper clip to explore the properties of magnetism.

·············· Key Science Topic

- magnetism

·············· Average Time Required

Performance   15 minutes

Links to *Classroom Science from A to Z*

You can extend this activity into your science curriculum with the following ideas, included in the book *Classroom Science from A to Z:*

- Links to National Science Standards

- Science Activity
  Maneuver a paper clip through a homemade maze and free it from a trap using a magnet.

- Lesson H Teacher Notes

- Lesson H Assessment

- Lesson H Science Explanation

- Lesson H Cross-Curricular Integration

Hovering Paper Clip

When you are done...

Leave at the table	Take with you
magnet	completed handout
aluminum foil	
spatula	
test objects	
Hovering Paper Clip toy	
pencil (if provided at station)	

Hovering Paper Clip
Family Science Challenge

Break through the mystery of the hovering clip.

Materials

Hovering Paper Clip toy • magnet • piece of cardboard • piece of aluminum foil • metal spatula • assorted objects that are and are not attracted to a magnet

Procedure

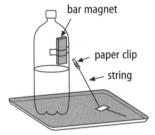

Figure 1

1 Examine the Hovering Paper Clip toy. Is the paper clip hovering? If it isn't, lift the paper clip up toward the magnet and release it when you think it is in the proper position to hover. Keep trying until the paper clip hovers.

2 Gently tug on the string so that the paper clip falls.

? *How easy was this?*

_____

_____

3 Make the paper clip hover again.

4 Select the magnet from the container of objects provided at the station. Without touching the hovering paper clip, use this magnet to see whether you can make the paper clip hover toward it and away from the toy. Try using your magnet to guide the paper clip back to the bottle without letting the paper clip fall and without touching it. Return the magnet to the container.

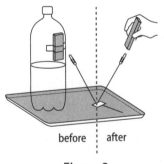

before ⋮ after

Figure 2

5 Select the piece of cardboard and the piece of aluminum foil from the container. Try passing each of these objects between the hovering paper clip and the magnet on the bottle without touching the magnet or paper clip.

? *What happens?*

_____

_____

6 Try passing a metal spatula between the magnet and the paper clip without allowing the spatula to touch the magnet or the paper clip.

? *What happens?*

_____

_____

7 Some of the objects in the container are attracted to magnets. Try to hang some of them from the magnet in the hover toy. Can you still get the paper clip to hover?

? *What happens?*

_____

_____

8 When you are done with the activity, make sure the paper clip is left hovering. Return the objects to the container.

Child/Adult Discussion

? *How do you think the Hovering Paper Clip toy works?*

_____

_____

_____

Explanation

Since the sixth century B.C., people have observed that magnets are attracted only to certain metals. Iron is the most commonly recognized metal that is attracted to magnets. A few other metals, including nickel and cobalt, can also be attracted to magnets if the magnets are strong enough. Many other metals, including aluminum, copper, and zinc, are not attracted to magnets.

Magnets are thought to establish a magnetic field around themselves that extends outside the magnet itself. Objects made of the proper metal experience a force when placed in this field. This force causes the paper clip to be attracted to the magnet and hover. When you pass a thin object that isn't attracted by the magnetic field through the space between the magnet and the paper clip, the magnetic field is not significantly affected, and the paper clip continues to hover. Depending on the strength of the magnet in the toy, it could probably attract several other objects to it while still causing the paper clip to hover.

Stuff to Try At Home

Do you use magnets at home? Look around your house and see what you can find. Try checking cabinet and refrigerator doors, handbags, and screwdrivers. Did you know that TVs and VCRs use magnets? You can't see them because they are part of the inner workings of these machines.

Hovering Paper Clip Planning Notes

This section will help you prepare for and carry out your Family Science event.

Calculating Quantities

"Calculating Quantities" contains information to help you calculate how much of each material you will need for your event. Copy values marked with a 🛒 onto the Shopping/Gathering List and those marked with a ✓ onto the Setup Checklist. If any of the calculations result in fractions, round up to the next whole number.

Nonconsumable Items Per Setup

You may choose to provide more than one setup at each station to allow a number of family teams to work concurrently.

- magnet
  (1 magnet per setup) x _____ setups = _____ **magnets** 🛒 ✓

- wide-mouthed container, such as a butter tub or cardboard box
  (1 container per setup) x _____ setups = _____ **wide-mouthed containers** 🛒 ✓

- piece of cardboard approximately 1 inch x 3 inches
  (1 piece of cardboard per setup) x _____ setups = _____ **pieces of cardboard** 🛒 ✓

- piece of aluminum foil approximately 1 inch x 3 inches
  (1 piece of aluminum foil per setup) x _____ setups = _____ **pieces of aluminum foil** 🛒 ✓

- metal spatula
  (1 metal spatula per setup) x _____ setups = _____ **metal spatulas** 🛒 ✓

- a variety of objects that are *and* objects that are not attracted to magnets, such as the following:
  - coin
  - marble
  - rubber band
  - cotton ball
  - birthday candle
  - shoelace
  - pieces of plastic
  - copper wire
  - plastic paper clip
  - cork
  - iron nail
  - nail that is not attracted to magnets
  - stainless steel table knife
  - wooden ruler or craft stick

  (1 set of objects per setup) x _____ setups = _____ **sets of objects** 🛒 ✓

- 2-L plastic soft-drink bottle
  (1 bottle per setup) x _____ setups = _____ **2-L plastic soft-drink bottles** 🛒

- 1 of the following magnets for the Hovering Paper Clip toy:
  - strong bar magnet
  - horseshoe magnet
  - disk magnet

  (1 magnet per setup) x _____ setups = _____ **magnets** 🛒

- cafeteria tray or shallow box

  (1 tray or box per setup) x _____ setups = _____ **trays or boxes** 🛒

- paper clip

  (1 paper clip per setup) x _____ setups = _____ **paper clips** 🛒

- 12-inch length of lightweight string or thread

  (12 inches of string per setup) x _____ setups = _____ **inches of string** 🛒

Getting Ready for the Family Science Challenge

Tools or General Supplies Needed for Preparation Only

- 3 sheets of brightly colored cardstock for Table Tent **H**
- adhesive copier labels (template provided) or other materials to make labels
- scissors or utility knife
- water, pebbles, or sand
- marker or pen
- tape
- (optional) sheet of paper

Preparing Materials for Use

- Photocopy the Family Science Challenge handout master to make the number of copies needed.

- Photocopy the Table Tent **H** master onto three sheets of brightly colored cardstock and assemble the table tent.

- Photocopy the label template onto a blank sheet of copier labels to print the labels, or make your own labels.

- Build the Hovering Paper Clip toy as follows:

  - Fill the 2-L soft-drink bottle about half full with water or about one-quarter full with sand or pebbles to help stabilize it. Cap the bottle.

  - Tape the magnet to the bottle just below the neck, as shown in Figure 1.

  - Place the bottle with the attached magnet on a tray or in a shallow box, such as the lid from a box containing reams of paper. Alternatively, remove the top and cut down the sides of a large box to a height of 1–2 inches. Trace the position of the bottle on the tray or box and label the resulting circle "Place Bottle Here." (If necessary, you can tape paper to the tray first to avoid permanently marking the tray.)

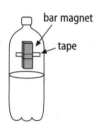

bar magnet

tape

Figure 1

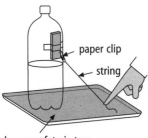

Figure 2

(a)

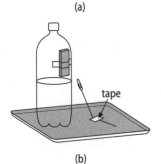

(b)

Figure 3

○ Cut the string into 12-inch lengths. Tie the string to the paper clip and place the paper clip on the magnet. Starting with the end of the string resting on the bottom of the tray or box, slide the string along the bottom of the box and away from the bottle until there is no more slack and the string, bottle, and tray bottom form a triangle. (See Figure 2.)

○ Now slowly move your finger along the string, keeping your finger on the bottom of the tray. (See Figure 3a.) This will shorten the amount of string rising above the tray. When the paper clip falls, move your finger back just a little to give the paper clip a bit more string. Keeping your finger on the string, lift the paper clip as high as the string will allow and carefully let go. If the paper clip hovers in mid-air, tape the string to the tray or box where your finger is. (See Figure 3b.) If the paper clip doesn't hover, give the paper clip a bit more string and test it again.

○ At least ½–1 inch of space should be left between the hovering paper clip and the magnet to allow for objects to easily pass between them. If the magnet is not strong enough to create a magnetic field that allows at least this required space, try to find a stronger magnet, or be sure to include very thin objects that are attracted (such as a steel table knife) and not attracted (such as a wooden ruler) to magnets for participants to choose from.

• Cut the cardboard and aluminum foil into strips about 1 inch x 3 inches.

• Place a magnet, a piece of cardboard, a piece of aluminum foil, a metal spatula, and a set of the objects attracted to and not attracted to magnets in each wide-mouthed container.

• Label the Hovering Paper Clip toys and the containers of assorted objects to test.

Setting Up the Station

• Place Table Tent **H** at the station in a prominent location.

• Place one labeled container of assorted objects to test at each setup.

• Carefully set a tray or box containing a completed Hovering Paper Clip toy at each setup. Put the paper clip in its hovering position.

Answers and Observations

❷ *How easy was this?*

The amount of force needed to make the paper clip fall depends on the strength of the magnet. The stronger the magnet, the greater the force needed. The weaker the magnet, the smaller the force needed.

❺ *What happens?*

Since neither cardboard nor aluminum foil is attracted to magnets, the magnetic field is not disrupted, and the paper clip remains suspended.

❻ *What happens?*

The paper clip falls because metal that is attracted to the magnet disrupts the magnetic field.

❼ *What happens?*

Answers will vary depending on the strength of the magnet.

Answers for Child/Adult Discussion

? *How do you think the Hovering Paper Clip toy works?*

The magnetic field created by the magnet attracts the paper clip, which is made mostly of iron. The strength of this field is sufficient to hold the paper clip in the air and defy gravity.

Hovering Paper Clip Shopping/Gathering List

Use this checklist as a guide to collecting the materials for this Family Science Challenge. Fill in the quantities needed below after doing the calculations called for in the "Calculating Quantities" section.

Total Quantities (from "Planning Notes")

_____ magnets

_____ wide-mouthed containers

_____ pieces of cardboard approximately 1 inch x 3 inches

_____ pieces of aluminum foil approximately 1 inch x 3 inches

_____ metal spatulas

_____ sets of objects that are and objects that are not attracted to magnets*

_____ 2-L plastic soft-drink bottles

1 of the following magnets for each Hovering Paper Clip toy**:

_____ strong bar magnets

_____ horseshoe magnets

_____ disk magnets

_____ cafeteria trays or shallow boxes***

_____ paper clips

_____ inches of lightweight string or thread

Tools for Getting Ready

☐ 3 sheets of brightly colored cardstock for Table Tent **H**

☐ adhesive copier labels (template provided) or other materials to make labels†

☐ scissors or utility knife

☐ water, pebbles, or sand

☐ marker or pen

☐ tape

☐ (optional) piece of paper

* When choosing objects to test for magnetic attraction, be sure to include metallic objects that aren't attracted to magnets, such as aluminum foil, pennies, or copper wire to demonstrate that not all metals are attracted to magnets.

** The magnet for the Hovering Paper Clip toy can be a bar, disk, or horseshoe magnet.

*** The lid from a box containing reams of paper works well. Or you could remove the top and cut down the sides of a larger box until they are 1–2 inches tall.

† We have provided a label template that can be photocopied directly onto a blank sheet of copier labels to print all of the labels you need for the activity. Use 1-inch x 2¾-inch copier labels, such as Avery Copier Labels (code 5351). If copier labels are not available, copy the label template onto paper, cut out the labels, and use tape to affix the paper labels. Alternatively, make hand-written labels using permanent marker and masking tape or other similar materials.

Hovering Paper Clip Setup Checklist

The following is a list of items you will need to set up the Family Science Challenge. "Planning Notes" gives step-by-step instructions for setting up the Family Science Challenge.

Items Per Station

The following materials should be left on or near the table for all family teams to use. (A station is a location where family teams work on an activity.)

Material	Total Needed	Notes
☐ Table Tent **H**	_____	Copy master provided

Items Per Setup

The following nonconsumable items will be needed for each setup. You may choose to provide more than one setup at each station to allow a number of family teams to work concurrently at the station.

☐ magnet	_____	_____
☐ container of assorted objects to test	_____	_____
☐ Hovering Paper Clip toy	_____	Includes prepared tray, paper clip, bottle, and magnet
☐ pencil for recording observations*	_____	_____

Consumable Materials

The following materials will be used up or taken away by family teams.

Material	Total Needed	Notes
☐ Family Science Challenge handouts**	_____	Copy master provided

*   You may wish to pass out pencils at registration or have families bring their own pencils.

** You may wish to pass out Family Science Challenge handouts as a set at registration rather than at each station.

Hovering Paper Clip Label Template

H Hovering Paper Clip Toy

H Hovering Paper Clip Toy

H Assorted objects to test
Please return to the container.

H Assorted objects to test
Please return to the container.

H Hovering Paper Clip Toy

H Hovering Paper Clip Toy

H Assorted objects to test
Please return to the container.

H Assorted objects to test
Please return to the container.

H Hovering Paper Clip Toy

H Hovering Paper Clip Toy

H Assorted objects to test
Please return to the container.

H Assorted objects to test
Please return to the container.

H Hovering Paper Clip Toy

H Hovering Paper Clip Toy

H Assorted objects to test
Please return to the container.

H Assorted objects to test
Please return to the container.

Inky Elevators

Family teams learn how to use chromatography to separate colored pigments in marker ink.

. . . . ## Key Science Topics

- capillary action
- chromatography

. . . . ## Time Required

Performance   10–15 minutes

Links to *Classroom Science from A to Z*

You can extend this activity into your science curriculum with the following ideas, included in the book *Classroom Science from A to Z:*

- Links to National Science Standards

- Science Activity
  Students use chromatography to separate inks on different types of paper and on chalk.

- Lesson I Teacher Notes

- Lesson I Assessment

- Lesson I Science Explanation

- Lesson I Cross-Curricular Integration

Inky Elevators

When you are done...

Throw away	Leave at the table	Take with you
paper towels	markers	your paper towel strips
	cups	completed handout
	sharpened pencil for activity	
	pencil for recording (if provided at station)	

Inky Elevators
Family Science Challenge

Going up? Take your ink to new heights.

Materials

3 white paper towel strips • sharpened pencil • water-soluble markers of several different colors • clear plastic cup • water • paper towels • waste water bucket

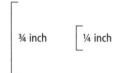

¾ inch   ¼ inch

Figure 1

Procedure

❶ Use a pencil to draw a horizontal line about ¾ inch (see Figure 1) above the bottom edge of one paper towel strip. Use a black, water-soluble marker to trace along the pencil line.

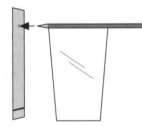

Figure 2

❷ Hold the strip next to the clear plastic cup so that the bottom edge of the strip almost reaches the bottom of the cup. Push the point of a pencil through the top of the strip exactly even with the rim of the cup. (See Figures 2 and 3.)

❸ Lift the pencil from the cup and push the paper to the middle of the pencil. Continue to hold the pencil while your partner pours about ¼ inch (Figure 1) of water into the cup.

❹ Set the pencil across the rim of the cup so that the bottom of the paper is in the water. The marker line should be above the water. (See Figure 4.) If the marker line accidentally dips below the water level, discard the paper, rinse out the cup, and start over.

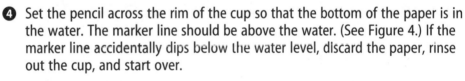

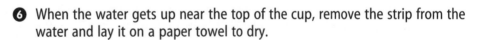
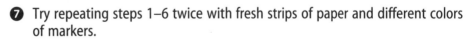

Figure 3

❺ Observe the water and the black line.

❻ When the water gets up near the top of the cup, remove the strip from the water and lay it on a paper towel to dry.

❼ Try repeating steps 1–6 twice with fresh strips of paper and different colors of markers.

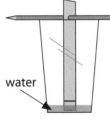

water

Figure 4

❽ Clean up the station by emptying the water from the cup into the waste water bucket and wiping up any spills. You may take your strips with you. Leave the markers and sharpened pencil at the station for the next group.

Child/Adult Discussion

? *Where do you think the colors that you observed come from? Did different markers give different color patterns?*

_____

_____

_____

_____

Explanation

While the inks in the colored markers you used in this exploration appear to be a single color, they actually contain mixtures of several different-colored pigments. The procedure you followed allowed you to separate these pigments. Scientists call this technique chromatography (kro-mah-TOG-ra-fee). Depending on what scientists are trying to separate, they use different materials for the chromatography process. In this activity, you use water and paper to separate the pigments in water-soluble markers.

The paper is porous, which means it has many tiny openings throughout it. Water moves up these openings, which scientists call "capillaries." The upward movement of water is called "capillary action." The marker ink is water-soluble—that is, it dissolves in water. When the water reaches the marker line, it dissolves the ink and continues to travel up the paper, carrying the ink with it.

As the water-ink mixture moves through the capillaries, the pigments in the ink begin to separate. The separation results because the different pigments have different amounts of attraction for the paper and the water. The ones with the strongest attraction for paper and the weakest attraction for water move the least amount. What properties would the farthest-moving pigments have?

Stuff to Try at Home

Investigate to find out whether food colors are made of single colors or mixtures of colors. To do this, follow the same procedure you did here, except instead of tracing the pencil line in step 1 with a marker, squeeze a couple of drops of food color onto the pencil line. You can also try blending several colors together yourself and seeing whether you can get the mixture to separate on the strip of paper towel.

Inky Elevators Planning Notes

This section will help you prepare for and carry out your Family Science event.

Calculating Quantities

"Calculating Quantities" contains information to help you calculate how much of each material you will need for your event. Copy values marked with a 🛒 onto the Shopping/Gathering List and those marked with a ✓ onto the Setup Checklist. If any of the calculations result in fractions, round up to the next whole number.

Nonconsumable Items Per Station

Amounts listed are for one station. If you will have more than one station for this Family Science Challenge, adjust amounts accordingly.

- box or other container for paper towel strips 🛒 ✓
- waste water bucket 🛒 ✓
- sponge 🛒 ✓
- trash can 🛒 ✓
- (optional) stapler 🛒 ✓

Nonconsumable Items Per Setup

You may choose to provide more than one setup at each station to allow a number of family teams to work concurrently.

- water-soluble markers of several different colors
  (3 different-colored markers per setup) x _____ *setups =* _____ ***markers*** 🛒 ✓
  Do not use washable markers.

- 8-ounce clear plastic cups
  (1 cup per setup) x _____ *setups =* _____ ***cups*** 🛒 ✓

- sharpened pencils
  (1 pencil per setup) x _____ *setups =* _____ ***pencils*** 🛒 ✓

Consumable Materials

- white paper towel strips
  estimate (4 strips per family) x _____ *families =* _____ ***strips*** ✓
  _____ *strips ÷ (22 strips per sheet) =* _____ ***sheets of paper towels*** 🛒

- water in 1- or 2-L plastic soft-drink bottles (if a source of running water will not be readily available near the station)
  estimate (0.02 liter per family) x _____ *families =* _____ ***liters*** 🛒 ✓
  _____ *liters of water x (1 L per 1-L bottle) =* _____ ***1-L bottles*** 🛒 ✓; OR
  _____ *1-L bottles ÷ 2 =* _____ ***2-L bottles*** 🛒 ✓

• paper towels for cleanup and strip drying

estimate (3 towels per family) x _____ families = _____ ***paper towels*** 🛒 ✓

Getting Ready for the Family Science Challenge

Tools or General Supplies Needed for Preparation Only

• 3 sheets of brightly colored cardstock for Table Tent **I**
• adhesive copier labels (template provided) or other materials to make labels
• scissors or paper cutter

Preparing Materials for Use

• Photocopy the Family Science Challenge handout master to make the number of copies needed.

• Photocopy the Table Tent **I** master onto three sheets of brightly colored cardstock and assemble the table tent.

• Photocopy the label template onto a blank sheet of copier labels to print the labels, or make your own labels.

• Cut the white paper towels into strips about 1 inch wide and about 1 inch longer than the height of the cups you will be using. We estimate that an 11-inch x 13.8-inch paper towel will yield about 22 strips. Put the strips in a box and label the box.

Setting Up the Station

• Place Table Tent **I** at the station in a prominent location.

• Place the labeled box of paper towel strips and a bucket for collecting waste water at each station, out of the way of the setups. Keep additional whole paper towels and a sponge handy for cleanups.

• Place a plastic cup, a sharpened pencil, and several water-based markers of various colors at each setup.

• If the station will not be located near a source of running water (such as a sink or drinking fountain), fill several 1- or 2-L bottles with water to refill the containers of water as needed.

• You may wish to put a stapler at the station so families can staple their colored paper strips to their Family Science Challenge handouts.

Tips

• Test the markers yourself to be sure the ones you have selected give a colorful separation when used in the activity.

Answers for Child/Adult Discussion

? *Where do you think the colors that you observed come from? Did different markers give different color patterns?*

The ink in the marker was a mixture of the colors observed. The hues and patterns of the colors are different for different markers.

Inky Elevators Shopping/Gathering List

Use the checklist as a guide to collecting the materials for this Family Science Challenge. Fill in the quantities needed below after doing the calculations called for in the "Calculating Quantities" section.

Total Quantities (from "Planning Notes")

_____ white paper towels

_____ box(es) or other container(s)

_____ water-soluble markers of several different colors*

_____ 8-ounce clear plastic cups

_____ sharpened pencils

_____ water

_____ 1- or 2-L plastic soft-drink bottles

_____ paper towels for strip drying and cleanup

_____ sponge(s)

_____ bucket(s) for collecting waste water

_____ trash can(s)

_____ (optional) stapler(s)

Tools for Getting Ready

☐ 3 sheets of brightly colored cardstock for Table Tent I

☐ adhesive copier labels (template provided) or other materials to make labels**

☐ scissors or paper cutter

* Water-soluble pens made for overhead projectors, such as the Vis-a-Vis® brand, or watercolor markers, such as the Mr. Sketch® markers, work well with this activity. DO NOT USE WASHABLE MARKERS. Black, brown, or purple markers usually provide the best range of colors during the chromatography. Red, blue, and yellow markers usually will not separate at all and should not be used.

** We have provided a label template that can be photocopied directly onto a blank sheet of copier labels to print all of the labels you need for the activity. Use 1-inch x 2¾-inch copier labels, such as Avery Copier Labels (code 5351). If copier labels are not available, copy the label template onto paper, cut out the labels, and use tape to affix the paper labels. Alternatively, make hand-written labels using permanent marker and masking tape or other similar materials.

Reproduced from *Science Night Family Fun from* 🅐 *to* 🆉

Inky Elevators Setup Checklist

The following is a list of items you will need to set up the Family Science Challenge. "Planning Notes" gives step-by-step instructions for setting up the Family Science Challenge.

Items Per Station

The following materials should be left on or near the table for all family teams to use. (A station is a location where family teams work on an activity.)

Material	Total Needed	Notes
☐ Table Tent **I**	_____	Copy master provided
☐ labeled box for paper towel strips	_____	_____
☐ sponge	_____	_____
☐ waste water bucket	_____	_____
☐ trash can	_____	_____
☐ (optional) stapler	_____	_____

Items Per Setup

The following nonconsumable items should be placed at each setup. You may choose to provide more than one setup at each station to allow a number of family teams to work concurrently.

Material	Total Needed	Notes
☐ 8-ounce plastic cup	_____	
☐ sharpened pencil	_____	
☐ different-colored markers	_____	At least three colors per setup
☐ pencils for recording observations*	_____	

Consumable Materials

The following materials will be used up or taken away by family teams.

Material	Total Needed	Notes
☐ strips of white paper towels	_____	
☐ labeled bottles of water`	_____	If station is not close to a source of water
☐ paper towels		For placing strips on to dry and for cleaning up
☐ Family Science Challenge handouts**	_____	Copy master provided

*   You may wish to pass out pencils at registration or have families bring their own pencils.

** You may wish to pass out Family Science Challenge handouts as a set at registration rather than at each station.

Inky Elevators Label Template

 **Paper towel strips**
3 strips per family

 **Paper towel strips**
3 strips per family

I **Water**
Pour about 1/4 inch water into a cup.

 **Water**
Pour about 1/4 inch water into a cup.

I **Water**
Pour about 1/4 inch water into a cup.

 **Water**
Pour about 1/4 inch water into a cup.

I **Paper towel strips**
3 strips per family

 **Paper towel strips**
3 strips per family

I **Water**
Pour about 1/4 inch water into a cup.

 **Water**
Pour about 1/4 inch water into a cup.

I **Water**
Pour about 1/4 inch water into a cup.

 **Water**
Pour about 1/4 inch water into a cup.

I **Water**
Pour about 1/4 inch water into a cup.

 **Water**
Pour about 1/4 inch water into a cup.

I **Water**
Pour about 1/4 inch water into a cup.

 **Water**
Pour about 1/4 inch water into a cup.

Jive Jabberwackies

Family teams build their own talking cups and use them to explore the relationship between the size of the cup and the pitch of the sound produced.

Key Science Topics

- frequency
- sound
- waves
- wavelength

Average Time Required

Performance   5–15 minutes

Links to *Classroom Science from A to Z*

You can extend this activity into your science curriculum with the following ideas, included in the book *Classroom Science from A to Z:*

- Links to National Science Standards

- Science Activity
  Students experiment to determine what factors cause the sound of the Jabberwackies to change.

- Lesson J Teacher Notes

- Lesson J Assessment

- Lesson J Science Explanation

- Lesson J Cross-Curricular Integration

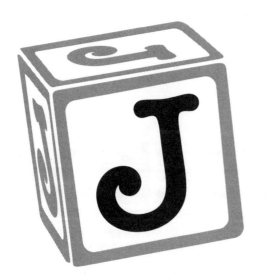

Jive Jabberwackies

When you are done...

Leave at the table	Take with you
premade large Jabberwacky	Jabberwacky you made
premade medium Jabberwacky	completed handout
fabric scraps	
pencil (if provided at station)	

Jive Jabberwackies
Family Science Challenge

Reach new highs (and lows) with a homemade sound toy.

Materials

piece of fabric • container of water • large and medium-sized Jabberwacky toys • 18-inch piece of string • small paper cup • paper clip • plastic yarn needle

Procedure

❶ Select a moistened piece of fabric. Squeeze out any excess water from the fabric.

❷ Have your adult partner hold the medium-sized Jabberwacky toy by the cup while you wrap the piece of fabric around the string just below the cup. (See Figure 1.) Use short, jerking motions to pull the piece of fabric down the string of the Jabberwacky toy. What do you hear?
Don't pull too hard on the string or you may break the Jabberwacky.

❸ Predict whether the sound of the large Jabberwacky toy will be higher, lower, or the same as the sound of the larger toy. Record your prediction below, and then try the experiment and record your observations.

Prediction _____

Observation _____

Figure 1

❹ What do you think will happen if you try the experiment with a piece of string without a cup attached to it? Record your prediction below, then try the experiment and record your observations.

Prediction _____

Observation _____

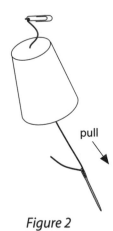

pull

Figure 2

❺ Select one of the small paper cups to make your own Jive Jabberwacky toy as follows:

a. Tie a paper clip to the end of a piece of string.

b. Thread the plastic yarn needle with the piece of string.

c. With the threaded needle, poke a small hole in the center of the outside bottom of the cup and gently push the needle and string through the hole until the paper clip is flat against the outside bottom of the cup. (See Figure 2.)

d. Remove the needle and try your Jabberwacky.

Figure 3

6 Here are some other experiments you can try to see whether you can change the sound produced:

   a. Try holding the bottom of the string at the same time you pull the moist fabric down the string.

   b. Try to produce a "clucking" sound by running just your thumb and forefinger (no fabric) down the string.

   c. Remove the string and thread it through the cup so that the paper clip is on the bottom of the inside of the cup. (See Figure 3.) Try the Jabberwacky.

7 You may take the Jive Jabberwacky toy you made with you, but leave the sample Jabberwacky toys, fabric pieces, and plastic yarn needle at the station.

Child/Adult Discussion

? *Which Jabberwacky had the lowest sound? Which had the highest? What do you think caused the differences you heard in the experiments you tried?*

_____

_____

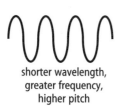

shorter wavelength,
greater frequency,
higher pitch

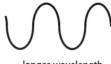

longer wavelength,
lower frequency,
lower pitch

Figure 4

Explanation

Sounds are actually vibrating waves created by moving objects. When you pull the string of the Jabberwacky, you cause it to vibrate. The string causes the air to vibrate, which in turn causes your eardrum to vibrate. The middle ear magnifies the sound and the auditory nerve sends a signal to the brain, which perceives the signal as sound. The sound we hear depends upon the wavelength (the length of the sound wave from crest to crest) and the frequency (the number of wavelengths per second) of the vibrating wave. The shorter the wavelength, the greater the frequency, and therefore the higher the pitch of the sound. (See Figure 4.)

As you observed in the activity, different-sized cups produce different sounds. This is because the different sizes of cups affect different wavelengths of sound. Smaller cups affect sound waves with shorter wavelengths to produce sounds of higher pitch. Large cups affect sound waves with long wavelengths and produce sounds of lower pitch.

Stuff to Try at Home

Try making a Jabberwacky out of a cup made of Styrofoam® or other material and compare the sound it makes with the Jabberwacky you made in this Family Science Challenge. Try different lengths of string to see how string length affects the sound.

Jive Jabberwackies Planning Notes

This section will help you prepare for and carry out your Family Science event.

Calculating Quantities

"Calculating Quantities" contains information to help you calculate how much of each material you will need for your event. Copy values marked with a 🛒 onto the Shopping/Gathering List and those marked with a ✓ onto the Setup Checklist. If any of the calculations result in fractions, round up to the next whole number.

Nonconsumable Items Per Station

Amounts listed are for one station. If you will have more than one station for this Family Science Challenge, adjust amounts accordingly.

- pop beaker made from a cut-off 2-L soft-drink bottle 🛒 ✓
- about ½ liter water 🛒 ✓
- small container such as a plastic cup or bowl 🛒 ✓
- container such as a shoe box 🛒 ✓
- trash can

Nonconsumable Items Per Setup

You may choose to provide more than one setup at each station to allow a number of family teams to work concurrently.

- large paper or soft plastic bucket
  (1 bucket per setup) x _____ setups = _____ **large paper or plastic buckets** 🛒

- 24-ounce paper cup
  (1 cup per setup) x _____ setups = _____ **24-ounce paper cups** 🛒

- lightweight string for sample Jabberwackies
  (2, 18-inch pieces of string per setup) x _____ setups = _____ pieces
  _____ pieces ÷ *(2 pieces per yard)* = _____ **yards of string** 🛒

- paper clips for sample Jabberwackies
  (2 paper clips per setup) x _____ setups = _____ **paper clips** 🛒

- plastic yarn needle
  (1 needle per setup) x _____ setups = _____ **plastic yarn needles** 🛒 ✓

- heavier-weight fabric, such as denim or broadcloth
  (2, 2-inch x 2-inch pieces per setup) x _____ setups = _____ **pieces of fabric** ✓
  _____ pieces ÷ *(324 pieces per square yard)* = _____ **square yards of fabric** 🛒

Consumable Materials

- lightweight string
  (1, 18-inch piece per family) x _____ families = _____ **pieces of string** ✓
  _____ pieces ÷ (2 pieces per yard) = _____ **yards of string** 🛒

- 12-ounce or smaller paper cups
  (1 cup per family) x _____ families = _____ **12-ounce or smaller paper cups** 🛒 ✓

- paper clips
  (1 paper clip per family) x _____ families = _____ **paper clips** 🛒 ✓

Getting Ready for the Family Science Challenge

Tools or General Supplies Needed for Preparation Only

- 3 sheets of brightly colored cardstock for Table Tent **J**
- adhesive copier labels (template provided) or other materials to make labels
- yardstick
- scissors
- plastic yarn needle
- (optional) markers, construction paper or felt, glue, or other materials to decorate the Jabberwackies as poultry.

Preparing Materials for Use

- Photocopy the Family Science Challenge handout master to make the number of copies needed.

- Photocopy the Table Tent **J** master onto three sheets of brightly colored cardstock and assemble.

a "pop beaker"

- Photocopy the label template onto a blank sheet of copier labels to print the labels, or make your own labels.

- For each station, cut off the top half of a 2-L soft-drink bottle to make a "pop beaker." (See figure.)

- Cut the lightweight string into 18-inch pieces. Place the string in a shoe box or other container and label it.

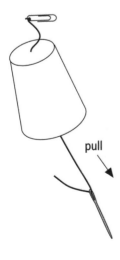

pull

- For each station, make a medium and large Jabberwacky toy following the procedure below using a 24-ounce paper cup and a paper or soft plastic bucket.
  ◦ Tie a paper clip to the end of a piece of string.
  ◦ Thread the plastic yarn needle with the piece of string.
  ◦ With the threaded needle, poke a small hole in the center of the outside bottom of the cup or bucket and gently pull the string through until the paper clip is flat against the outside bottom of the cup or bucket. (See figure.) Remove the needle.
  ◦ (optional) Decorate the Jabberwackies as different types of poultry.

- Cut the fabric into pieces about 2 inches x 2 inches. (The exact dimensions of the fabric pieces are not critical.)

- Place the paper clips in the small container and label it.

- Label the Jabberwackies and the pop beaker.

Setting Up the Station

- Place Table Tent **J** at the station in a prominent location.

- At each station place the labeled containers of string pieces and paper clips, a pop beaker, stacks of 12-ounce or smaller paper cups, and a medium and large Jabberwacky toy.

- Fill the pop beaker about one-quarter full with water.

- Place several fabric pieces to soak in the pop beaker.

Answers and Observations

3 *Observation*

The sound produced has a higher pitch than the sound made by the large Jabberwacky.

4 *Observation*

A sound is produced, but it is not very loud.

Answers for Child/Adult Discussion

? *Which Jabberwacky had the lowest sound? Which had the highest? What do you think causes the differences you heard?*

The lowest sound was produced by the largest Jabberwacky toy, while the highest sound was made by the Jabberwacky made from the smallest cup. Different-sized cups amplify different wavelengths of sound.

Jive Jabberwackies Shopping/Gathering List

Use this checklist as a guide to collecting the materials for the Family Science Challenge. Fill in the quantities needed below after doing the calculations called for in the "Calculating Quantities" section.

Total Quantities (from "Planning Notes")

_____ 2-L plastic soft-drink bottles

_____ liters of water

_____ small container(s) such as a plastic cup or bowl

_____ container(s) such as a shoe box

_____ large paper or soft plastic buckets*

_____ 24-ounce paper cups

_____ yards of lightweight string (sum of lines below)

    _____ yards for sample Jabberwackies

    _____ yards for consumable materials

_____ paper clips (sum of lines below)

    _____ clips for sample Jabberwackies

    _____ clips for consumable materials

_____ plastic yarn needles**

_____ square yards of heavier-weight fabric (such as denim or broadcloth)

_____ 12-ounce or smaller paper or flexible plastic cups

_____ trash can

Tools for Getting Ready

☐ 3 sheets of brightly colored cardstock for Table Tent **J**

☐ adhesive copier labels (template provided) or other materials to make labels***

☐ yardstick

☐ scissors

☐ plastic yarn needle**

☐ materials to decorate the Jabberwackies as poultry

* Examples of large paper buckets you can use are paint buckets, popcorn tubs, or take-out chicken buckets.

** Plastic yarn needles are available at fabric stores and craft stores.

*** We have provided a label template that can be photocopied directly onto a blank sheet of copier labels to print all of the labels you need for the activity. Use 1-inch x 2¾-inch copier labels, such as Avery Copier Labels (code 5351). If copier labels are not available, copy the label template onto paper, cut out the labels, and use tape to affix the paper labels. Alternatively, make hand-written labels using permanent marker and masking tape or other similar materials.

Jive Jabberwackies Setup Checklist

The following is a list of items you will need to set up the Family Science Challenge. "Planning Notes" gives step-by-step instructions for setting up the Family Science Challenge.

Items Per Station

The following materials should be left on or near the table for all family teams to use. (A station is a location where family teams work on an activity.)

Material	Total Needed	Notes
☐ Table Tent **J**	_____	Copy master provided
☐ cut-off 2-L plastic soft-drink bottle of water, labeled	_____	For soaking fabric pieces in water
☐ small container	_____	For paper clips
☐ piece of heavy fabric about 2 inches x 2 inches	_____	_____
☐ trash can	_____	_____

Items Per Setup

The following nonconsumable items should be placed at each setup. You may choose to provide more than one setup at each station to allow a number of family teams to work concurrently at the station.

Material	Total Needed	Notes
☐ large Jabberwacky	_____	_____
☐ medium Jabberwacky	_____	_____
☐ pencil for recording observations*	_____	_____

Consumable Materials

The following materials will be used up or taken away by family teams.

Material	Total Needed	Notes
☐ 12-ounce or smaller paper cups	_____	_____
☐ paper clips	_____	_____
☐ 18-inch lengths of lightweight string	_____	_____
☐ Family Science Challenge handouts**	_____	_____

* You may wish to pass out pencils at registration or have families bring their own pencils.

** You may wish to pass out Family Science Challenge handouts as a set at registration rather than at each station.

Jive Jabberwackies
Label Template

J **Paper clips**
One per family

J **Large Jabberwacky**
Please leave at the station.

J **18-inch lengths of string**
One per family

J **Medium Jabberwacky**
Please leave at the station.

J **Paper clips**
One per family

J **Large Jabberwacky**
Please leave at the station.

J **18-inch lengths of string**
One per family

J **Medium Jabberwacky**
Please leave at the station.

J **Large Jabberwacky**
Please leave at the station.

J **Large Jabberwacky**
Please leave at the station.

J **Medium Jabberwacky**
Please leave at the station.

J **Medium Jabberwacky**
Please leave at the station.

J **Large Jabberwacky**
Please leave at the station.

J **Large Jabberwacky**
Please leave at the station.

J **Medium Jabberwacky**
Please leave at the station.

J **Medium Jabberwacky**
Please leave at the station.

Kooky Pencils

Family teams use science to marble a wooden pencil.

. . . . ## Key Science Topics

- adhesion
- density
- mixtures

. . . . ## Average Time Required

Performance   15 minutes

Links to *Classroom Science from A to Z*

You can extend this activity into your science curriculum with the following ideas, included in the book *Classroom Science from A to Z*:

- Links to National Science Standards

- Science Activity
  Use the suminagashi technique to decorate paper with swirled ink.

- Lesson K Teacher Notes

- Lesson K Assessment

- Lesson K Science Explanation

- Lesson K Cross-Curricular Integration

Kooky Pencils

When you are done...

Throw away	Leave at the table	Take with you
paper towels	marbling container	completed handout
toothpicks	paints	marbled, labeled pencil
	newspaper	(Leave at the station until dry and come back later to pick it up.)
	pencil (if provided at station)	

Names _____ _____

_____ _____

Kooky Pencils
Family Science Challenge

Create a colorful, one-of-a-kind design.

Materials

(optional) paint smocks or aprons • newspaper • marbling container • water
• toothpicks • 2 colors of Testor brand enamel model paints • label or tape
• wooden pencil • drying rack or spring-type clothespin • paper towels

Procedure

Work over the newspaper at all times.

1 If paint smocks or aprons are available, put one on over your clothes. Locate a marbling container full of water. (See Figure 1.) It might have a small residue of paint on the surface of the water; don't worry about this.

2 Dip a clean toothpick partway into one color of paint. Hold the toothpick over the water and allow 4–5 drops of paint to fall at different places on the surface of the water.

? *What do you observe?*

_____

_____

Figure 1

3 Repeat step 2 with a clean toothpick and a second color of paint. Don't add too much paint—you want the drops to float on the water. Use the toothpick to slowly swirl the paints into a marbled pattern.

? *What do you observe?*

_____

_____

4 Dip one end of another clean toothpick about halfway into the marbling mixture. Look through the side of the marbling container when you do this. Lift the toothpick straight up out of the marbling mixture. Lay it on the newspaper.

? *What did you see through the side of the container when you dipped the toothpick?*

_____

_____

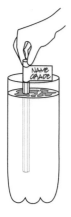

Figure 2

5 Write your name and grade on a label or piece of tape. Attach this label to a pencil right below the eraser. If clothespins are available, clip a clothespin onto the pencil, close to the label.

6 Now marble the pencil. Here's how: Hold the pencil either by the eraser or by the clothespin and carefully dip the pencil, eraser-end up, into the marbling mixture. (See Figure 2.) Lower the pencil as far as you can without getting the label wet. Slowly twirl the pencil as you raise it through the swirls of floating paint. (Twirling is necessary to keep the paint from clumping in one spot.) Hold the pencil over the newspaper.

7 Stand the pencil in the drying rack or rest it on the newspaper, propped up on the clothespin as shown. (See Figure 3.) The paint will take a while to dry. Stop back at the station at the end of the Family Science event to collect your pencil.

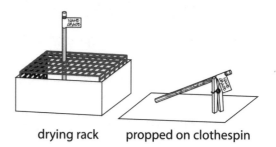

drying rack   propped on clothespin

Figure 3

8 Leave the newspaper on the table. Skim paint from the water's surface using an extra piece of newspaper or a paper towel. Dispose of the used newspaper or paper towel in a trash can. Wipe up any spills. Leave the marbling container and water for the next family to use.

Child/Adult Discussion

? *Why do you think the paint floated on the water?*

_____

_____

? *Would the activity work if the paint sank instead of floating on the water?*

_____

_____

Explanation

The enamel model paint used in this activity is a special type of oil-based paint. When the paint is dropped into the water, it floats on the surface. This behavior is caused by two important factors: 1) oil does not mix with water (in other words, oil and water are immiscible), and 2) oil is less dense than water (thus the oil floats on top of the water). When the toothpick and pencil are pushed through the film of oil paint, the paint adheres to the surface of these objects.

Reproduced from *Science Night Family Fun from* **A** *to* **Z**

Kooky Pencils Planning Notes

This section will help you prepare for and carry out your Family Science event.

Calculating Quantities

"Calculating Quantities" contains information to help you calculate how much of each material you will need for your event. Copy values marked with a 🛒 onto the Shopping/Gathering List and those marked with a ✓ onto the Setup Checklist. If any of the calculations result in fractions, round up to the next whole number.

Nonconsumable Items Per Station

Amounts listed are for one station. If you will have more than one station for this Family Science Challenge, adjust amounts accordingly.

- 2 boxes or other containers to hold pencils and pencil labels 🛒 ✓
- sponge or mop and pail 🛒 ✓
- trash can 🛒 ✓
- 1 of the following sets of materials for drying the pencils:
  Set A: Drying Rack ✓
  - 2 short cardboard boxes about 5 to 6 inches high, such as shoe boxes 🛒
  - 2 pieces of ½-inch mesh hardware cloth, sized for the cardboard box 🛒
    slightly less than the width of the box = _____ *inches wide*
    length of the box plus three times the height = _____ *inches long*

  Set B: Clothespins
  - spring-type clothespins
    estimate (1 per family) x _____ families = _____ *spring-type clothespins* 🛒 ✓
  - box or other container to hold clothespins 🛒 ✓

Nonconsumable Items Per Setup

You may choose to provide more than one setup at each station to allow a number of family teams to work concurrently.

- tall, narrow-diameter marbling container such as a tennis ball container or 1-L soft drink bottle cut off to make a tall pop beaker
  (1 container per setup) x _____ setups = _____ *containers* 🛒 ✓
- water (enough to fill the marbling containers) 🛒 ✓
- (optional) paint smocks or aprons
  (4 smocks or aprons per setup) x _____ setups = _____ *paint smocks or aprons* 🛒 ✓

Consumable Materials

- paper towels 🛒 ✓

  *estimate (1 per family) x _____ families = _____ **paper towels** 🛒 ✓*

- small stack of old newspapers 🛒 ✓
- 2 different colors of Testor brand enamel model paints

  estimate (one ¼-ounce bottle of each color per 25 families)
  *_____ families ÷ 25 = _____ **bottles of each color** 🛒 ✓*

2 bottles of Testor brand
enamel paint

- wooden pencils

  *(1 pencil per family) x _____ families + several extras = _____ **wooden pencils** 🛒 ✓*

- pencil labels (template provided)

  *(1 label per family) x _____ families + several extras = _____ **pencil labels** 🛒 ✓*

- wooden toothpicks

  *(3 toothpicks per family) x _____ families = _____ **toothpicks** 🛒 ✓*

Getting Ready for the Family Science Challenge

Tools or General Supplies Needed for Preparation Only

- 3 sheets of brightly colored cardstock for Table Tent **K**
- adhesive copier labels (template provided) or other materials to make labels
- masking or electrical tape

Preparing Materials for Use

- Photocopy the Family Science Challenge handout master to make the number of copies needed.

- Photocopy the Table Tent **K** master onto three sheets of brightly colored cardstock and assemble the table tent.

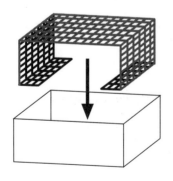

- Photocopy the label template onto a blank sheet of copier labels to print the labels, or make your own labels.

- Make labels (template provided) for the families to use on their pencils or provide tape for families to make their own.

- If using drying racks, make them as follows: Bend one piece of hardware cloth to form a mesh insert for the shoe box, as shown in the figure at left. To protect against sharp edges, tape all the edges of the hardware cloth. If necessary, fold the bottom of the hardware cloth rack in to lower it a bit. Repeat with the other piece of hardware cloth and box. Label the drying racks.

- Label the marbling containers.

- If the station will not be located near a source of running water (such as a sink or drinking fountain), fill several 1- or 2-L bottles with water to refill the containers of water as needed. Label the bottles appropriately.

- If using clothespins for drying, label the container for the clothespins.

- Label the toothpick box and the containers for the pencils and pencil labels.

Setting Up the Station

- Spread newspaper over the working surface and place Table Tent **K** at the station in a prominent location.

- Place the drying rack(s) (or clothespins) at the station.

- Put the pencils and pencil labels in labeled boxes or other containers at the station.

- Place two different colors of enamel model paint at each setup.

- For each setup, fill a marbling container almost full water. (The water level in each marbling container should be high enough to submerge a pencil up to just below its eraser.) Place the filled marbling container on the newspaper.

- Have a sponge or mop and pail close by to clean up spills that may occur.

Tips

- The oil-based paint can stain clothing and furniture. Extra care should be taken to prevent paint stains. Tell participants to wear old clothing, or provide smocks or aprons. You may wish to have turpentine or another appropriate oil-paint solvent available to clean up paint spills after the event.

- Inexpensive disposable aprons can be ordered through your school cafeteria.

- To prevent disappointment, test the activity in advance with the paint and pencils you've selected to be sure they work.

Disposal

Skim paint from the water's surface using a piece of newspaper or a paper towel. Dispose of newspapers or paper towels in the trash. Dispose of the water down the drain.

Answers and Observations

❷ *What do you observe?*

The paint floats and remains clumped together.

❸ *What do you observe?*

The paint still floats, but it forms swirls of color.

❹ *What did you see through the side of the container when your dipped the toothpick?*

Some of the paint sticks to the toothpick as the toothpick is submerged.

Child/Adult Discussion

? *Why do you think the paint floated on the water?*

The paint floated on the water because it's less dense than the water and also because it didn't mix with the water.

? *Would the activity work if the paint sank instead of floating on the water?*

No, because you couldn't pass the pencil through the paint.

Kooky Pencils Shopping/Gathering List

Use this checklist as a guide to collecting the materials for this Family Science Challenge. Fill in the quantities needed below after doing the calculations called for in the "Calculating Quantities" section.

Total Quantities (from "Planning Notes")

_____ wooden pencils*

_____ adhesive copier labels (template provided) or other materials to make pencil labels**

_____ boxes to hold pencils and pencil labels

_____ pieces of ½-inch mesh hardware cloth (____ x ____ inches) and _____ cardboard boxes, **OR** spring-type clothespins and _____ box(es) to hold clothespins***

_____ tall, narrow-diameter marbling containers †

_____ liters of water

_____ 2-L plastic soft-drink bottles for storing water

_____ bottles each of 2 different colors of Testor brand enamel model paints††

_____ wooden toothpicks in original container

_____ small stack(s) of old newspapers†††

_____ paper towels

_____ sponge(s) or mop and pail

_____ trash can(s)

_____ (optional) paint smocks or aprons

Tools for Getting Ready

☐ 3 sheets of brightly colored cardstock for Table Tent **K**

☐ adhesive copier labels (template provided) or other materials to make labels**

☐ masking or electrical tape

*   Unpainted pencils are preferable because they produce a more attractive final product, but regular painted wooden pencils can be used. Sanford manufactures unpainted wooden pencils called "American Naturals" that are available at most office supply stores. Large quantities (6 dozen or more) are available through Gray Enterprises, 800/970-7367, www.kingpen.com. Wooden craft sticks can also be used for this activity and are an economical alternative to pencils.

** We have provided a label template that can be photocopied directly onto a blank sheet of copier labels to print all of the labels you need for the activity. Use 1-inch x 2¾-inch copier labels, such as Avery Copier Labels (code 5351). If copier labels are not available, copy the label template onto paper, cut out the labels, and use tape to affix the paper labels. Alternatively, make hand-written labels using permanent markers and masking tape or other similar materials.

*** Clothespins are handy for drying the pencils, but for large numbers of participants it may be more practical to use drying racks. Hardware cloth must be cut with metal shears; the hardware store will cut it to size.

†   This container must be at least as tall as the pencils used. A 1-L bottle with the top cut off or a clear plastic tennis-ball canister will work.

†† Testor brand epoxy model paints can be purchased in small bottles at hobby or toy stores.

††† Newspaper should be spread on the table to protect it from paint spills.

Kooky Pencils Setup Checklist

The following is a list of items you will need to set up the Family Science Challenge. "Planning Notes" gives step-by-step instructions for setting up the Family Science Challenge.

Items Per Station

The following materials should be left on or near the table for all family teams to use. (A station is a location where family teams work on an activity.)

Material	Total Needed	Notes
☐ Table Tent **K**	_____	Copy master provided
☐ labeled boxes	_____	For wooden pencils and pencil labels
☐ drying racks or box of clothespins	_____	Appropriately labeled
☐ trash can	_____	

Items Per Setup

The following nonconsumable items should be placed at each setup. You may choose to provide more than one setup at each station to allow a number of family teams to work concurrently.

Material	Total Needed	Notes
☐ marbling container	_____	
☐ pencil for recording observations*	_____	
☐ (optional) paint smocks or aprons	_____	

Consumable Materials

The following materials will be used up or taken away by family teams.

Material	Total Needed	Notes
☐ toothpicks	_____	
☐ 2 colors of Testor enamel model paints	_____	
☐ bottle(s) of water	_____	
☐ wooden pencils	_____	
☐ pencil labels	_____	
☐ old newspapers	_____	
☐ paper towels	_____	
☐ Family Science Challenge handouts**	_____	Copy master provided

*   You may wish to pass out pencils at registration or have families bring their own pencils.

** You may wish to pass out Family Science Challenge handouts as a set at registration rather than at each station.

Kooky Pencils
Label Template

K Refill Bottle of Water

K Refill Bottle of Water

K Pencils

1 per family; you may take it with you.

K Pencils

1 per family; you may take it with you.

K Toothpicks

3 per family

K Toothpicks

3 per family

K Drying Rack

Leave pencil upright until dry.

K Drying Rack

Leave pencil upright until dry.

K Drying Rack

Leave pencil upright until dry.

K Drying Rack

Leave pencil upright until dry.

K Marbling Container

Fill almost to the top.

K Marbling Container

Fill almost to the top.

K Pencil Labels

1 per family

K Pencil Labels

1 per family

K Clothespins

1 per family; leave at station after use.

K Clothespins

1 per family; leave at station after use.

Kooky Pencils
Pencil Label Template

K Name_____
    Grade_____

K Name_____
    Grade_____

K Name_____
    Grade_____

K Name_____
    Grade_____

K Name_____
    Grade_____

K Name_____
    Grade_____

K Name_____
    Grade_____

K Name_____
    Grade_____

K Name_____
    Grade_____

K Name_____
    Grade_____

K Name_____
    Grade_____

K Name_____
    Grade_____

K Name_____
    Grade_____

K Name_____
    Grade_____

K Name_____
    Grade_____

K Name_____
    Grade_____

Lincoln Drops

Water has very special properties, including high surface tension. Family teams discover this as they investigate how many water drops will fit on the head of a penny.

. . . . **Key Science Topics**

- cohesion
- surface tension
- water and its properties

. . . . **Average Time Required**

Performance   5–10 minutes

Links to *Classroom Science from A to Z*

You can extend this activity into your science curriculum with the following ideas, included in the book *Classroom Science from A to Z*:

- Links to National Science Standards

- Science Activity
  Students investigate surface tension in plain water and soapy water.

- Lesson L Teacher Notes

- Lesson L Assessment

- Lesson L Science Explanation

- Lesson L Cross-Curricular Integration

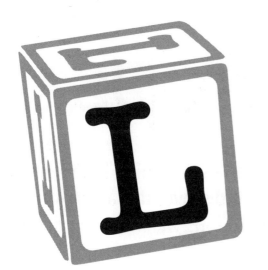

Lincoln Drops

When you are done…

Throw away	Leave at the table	Take with you
paper towels	pennies	completed handout
	droppers	
	cups	
	liquids	
	pencil (if provided at station)	

Names _____   _____

_____   _____

Lincoln Drops
Family Science Challenge

Push the limit… don't spill the water.

Materials

pennies • paper towels • cup of water with dropper • cup of soapy water with dropper

Procedure

? *How many drops of water do you think can be placed on the head of a penny before any of the water spills off?*

Prediction: _____

← edge of penny

Figure 1

❶ Place a clean, dry penny on a paper towel. Fill the "water" dropper with water. Carefully place drops of water on the penny, one at a time, keeping track of the number of drops. After you've placed about 10 drops on the penny, look at the penny from the side. In Figure 1, draw what the water looks like on the penny.

❷ Continue placing drops of water on the penny, refilling the dropper as necessary. Keep track of the number of drops (including the 10 you've already placed) that you could place before the water spilled off the penny. Record this number in the chart at the left beside Trial 1.

❸ Wipe the penny with a paper towel. See if you can beat your record. You have three more tries. Record your results each time, and remember to dry off the penny each time before starting over.

? *If you were able to beat your record for Trial 1, what did you do differently?*

_____

_____

_____

❹ Return the dropper to the cup of water and set aside for others to use.

❺ Dry the penny as before and place it on a paper towel. Select a cup of soapy water with its dropper.

? *How many drops of the soapy water do you think will fit on the penny?*

Prediction: _____

Plain Water	
Trial	Results
1	
2	
3	
4	

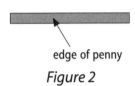

edge of penny

Figure 2

Soap-Water	
Trial	Results
1	
2	
3	
4	

6 Begin adding drops of soapy water to the head of the penny. After you've added 10 drops of the soapy water, stop and look at the penny from the side. In Figure 2, draw what the soapy water looks like on the penny.

7 Continue putting drops of soapy water on the penny, refilling the dropper as necessary. Keep track of the total number of drops you could place before the solution spilled off the penny. (Don't forget the 10 drops you put on in step 6.) Record this number in the chart at the left beside Trial 1.

8 Wipe off the penny with a paper towel. See if you can beat your record. You have three more tries. Record your results and remember to wipe off the penny each time before starting over.

? *If you were able to beat your record for Trial 1, what did you do that was different?*

_____

_____

_____

9 When you are done, drop your penny in the Used Penny Container.

Child/Adult Discussion

? *What was the greatest number of drops you could place on the penny? Which liquid yielded this result?*

_____

_____

? *What factors do you think affected the number of drops that could be placed on the penny?*

_____

_____

Explanation

Water has a high surface tension, which means the surface of the water acts like a thin, invisible "skin." This high surface tension causes the dome you see when you look at the penny from the side after placing about 10 drops of water on it. Surface tension results from the strong attraction that water molecules have for each other. We call this attraction "cohesion." Surface tension affects the number of drops of water that fit on the penny. Other factors influence this number as well, such as the height of the dropper above the penny; the placement of the drops; the angle at which the dropper is held; the size of the drops; whether the penny is clean, scratched, or deformed; and whether soap is present.

The dramatically lower number of drops of soapy water that fit on the penny was caused by soap's ability to reduce the surface tension of water. Soap is one of a group of chemicals called surfactants, or surface-acting agents. Surfactants cause water to spread out rather than to dome like the plain water did.

Lincoln Drops Planning Notes

This section will help you prepare for and carry out your Family Science event.

Calculating Quantities

"Calculating Quantities" contains information to help you calculate how much of each material you will need for your event. Copy values marked with a 🛒 onto the Shopping/Gathering List and those marked with a ✓ onto the Setup Checklist. If any of the calculations result in fractions, round up to the next whole number.

Nonconsumable Items Per Station

Amounts listed are for one station. If you will have more than one station for this Family Science Challenge, adjust amounts accordingly.

- 2 large, open containers, such as "pop beakers," for pennies 🛒 ✓
- sponge 🛒 ✓
- trash can 🛒 ✓
- pennies
  (1 penny per family) x _____ families = _____ pennies 🛒 ✓
  This number could be reduced if a station monitor is available to thoroughly rinse pennies periodically to remove soap solution and avoid contamination.

Nonconsumable Items Per Setup

You may choose to provide more than one setup at each station to allow a number of family teams to work concurrently.

- droppers
  (2 droppers per setup) x _____ setups = _____ droppers 🛒 ✓

- plastic cups
  (2 plastic cups per setup) x _____ setups = _____ plastic cups 🛒 ✓

Consumable Materials

- paper towels
  estimate (4 towels per family) x _____ families = _____ paper towels 🛒 ✓

- water in 1- or 2-L plastic soft-drink bottles (if a source of running water will not be readily available near the station)
  (0.015 L water per family) x _____ families = _____ liters of water in 1- or 2-L soft-drink bottles 🛒 ✓

- soapy water solution in 1- or 2-L soft-drink bottles

    For each 100 families, prepare 1L of soap solution by mixing 1L water with 5 teaspoons of dishwashing liquid. Store in a 1- or 2-L soft-drink bottle.

    I will need _____ **liters of soapy water solution in 1- or 2-L soft-drink bottles** ✓ 🛒

    How much dishwashing liquid do I need to buy?

    (5 teaspoons per liter of solution) x _____ *liters of solution =* _____ **teaspoons of dishwashing liquid** 🛒

Getting Ready for the Family Science Challenge
Tools or General Supplies Needed for Preparation Only

- 3 sheets of brightly colored cardstock for Table Tent **L**
- adhesive copier labels (template provided) or other materials to make labels
- teaspoon measure

Preparing Materials for Use

- Photocopy the Family Science Challenge handout master to make the number of copies needed.

- Photocopy the Table Tent **L** master onto three sheets of brightly colored cardstock and assemble the table tent.

- Photocopy the label template onto a blank sheet of copier labels to print the labels, or make your own labels.

- For each liter of soapy water needed, mix 5 teaspoons dishwashing liquid in 1 L water in a 1- or 2-L bottle. Label the bottle appropriately.

- If the station will not be located near a source of running water (such as a sink or drinking fountain), fill several 1- or 2-L bottles with water to refill the containers of water as needed. Label the bottles appropriately.

- Prepare the Used Penny Container by half-filling a large container, such as a pop beaker made by cutting off the top of a 2-L plastic soft-drink bottle, with water. Label it "Used Penny Container."

- Label the container for the clean pennies.

- For each setup, label one cup and dropper "water" and the other cup and dropper "soapy water."

Setting Up the Station

- Place Table Tent **L** at the station in a prominent location.

- Place a "water" cup and dropper and a "soapy water" cup and dropper at each setup. Half-fill the cups with the appropriate liquids. Cap the bottles of leftover liquids and place them at the station so they are accessible to families but are not in the way.

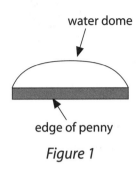

water dome

edge of penny

Figure 1

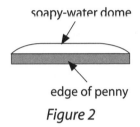

soapy-water dome

edge of penny

Figure 2

• Place the clean pennies in their container and put the container at the station. Put the Used Penny Container at the station.

Answers and Observations

❶ *Draw what the water looks like on the penny.*

The water will form a dome on the penny. See Figure 1.

❻ *Draw what the soapy water looks like on the penny.*

The soapy water does not mound up like the water does. See Figure 2.

Answers for Child/Adult Discussion

? *What was the greatest number of drops you could place on the penny? Which liquid yielded this result?*

More drops of plain water should fit on the penny than drops of the soapy water.

? *What factors do you think affected the number of drops that could be placed on the penny?*

Factors include the height of the dropper above the penny; the placement of the drops; the angle at which the dropper is held; the size of the drops; whether the penny is clean, scratched, or deformed; and whether soap is present.

Reference

Sarquis, J.L.; Sarquis, M.; Williams, J.P. "A Collection of Surface Tension Activities"; *Teaching Chemistry with TOYS;* Terrific Science: Middletown, OH, 1995; pp 169–175.

Lincoln Drops
Shopping/Gathering List

Use this checklist as a guide to collecting the materials for this Family Science Challenge. Fill in the quantities needed below after doing the calculations called for in the "Calculating Quantities" section.

Total Quantities (from Planning Notes)

_____ pennies

_____ large, open containers for pennies*

_____ droppers

_____ plastic cups

_____ liters of water (sum of lines below)

   _____ liters of plain water

   _____ liters for soapy water solution

_____ teaspoons of dishwashing liquid

_____ 1- or 2-L soft-drink bottles

_____ paper towels

_____ sponge(s)

_____ trash can(s)

Tools for Getting Ready

☐ 3 sheets of brightly colored cardstock for Table Tent **L**

☐ adhesive copier labels (template provided) or other materials to make labels**

☐ teaspoon measure

* "Pop beakers" made by cutting off the tops of 2-L plastic soft-drink bottles work well.

** We have provided a label template that can be photocopied directly onto a blank sheet of copier labels to print all of the labels you need for the activity. Use 1-inch x 2¾-inch copier labels, such as Avery Copier Labels (code 5351). If copier labels are not available, copy the label template onto paper, cut out the labels, and use tape to affix the paper labels. Alternatively, make hand-written labels using permanent marker and masking tape or other similar materials.

Lincoln Drops
Setup Checklist

The following is a list of items you will need to set up the Family Science Challenge. "Planning Notes" gives step-by-step instructions for setting up the Family Science Challenge.

Items Per Station

The following materials should be left on or near the table for all family teams to use. (A station is a location where family teams work on an activity.)

Material	Total Needed	Notes
☐ Table Tent **L**	_____	Copy master provided
☐ pennies	_____	_____
☐ large, open, labeled containers	_____	For clean and used pennies
☐ sponge	_____	_____
☐ trash can	_____	_____

Items Per Setup

The following nonconsumable items should be placed at each setup. You may choose to provide more than one setup at each station to allow a number of family teams to work concurrently.

Material	Total Needed	Notes
☐ labeled droppers	_____	2 per setup
☐ labeled plastic cups	_____	2 per setup; for plain water and soapy water
☐ pencil for recording observations*	_____	_____

Consumable Materials

The following materials will be used up or taken away by family teams.

Material	Total Needed	Notes
☐ labeled bottle(s) of soapy water	_____	_____
☐ labeled bottle(s) of water	_____	_____
☐ several rolls of paper towels	_____	_____
☐ Family Science Challenge handouts**	_____	Copy master provided

* You may wish to pass out pencils at registration or have families bring their own pencils.

** You may wish to pass out Family Science Challenge handouts as a set at registration rather than at each station.

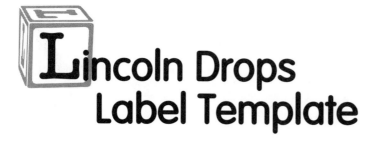

Lincoln Drops
Label Template

L **Used Penny Container**
Do not use the pennies from
this container.

L **Used Penny Container**
Do not use the pennies from
this container.

L **Clean Pennies**
1 per family; after use, put in
the Used Penny Container.

L **Clean Pennies**
1 per family; after use, put in
the Used Penny Container.

L **Water**

L **Water**

L **Water**

L **Water**

L **Water**

L **Water**

L **Soapy Water**

L **Soapy Water**

L **Soapy Water**

L **Soapy Water**

L **Soapy Water**

L **Soapy Water**

Mirror Madness

Family teams investigate how mirrors reflect light and use this property to make a virtual picture.

.... ## Key Science Topics

- light
- light reflection
- mirrors
- symmetry

.... ## Average Time Required

Performance   10–15 minutes

Links to *Classroom Science from A to Z*

You can extend this activity into your science curriculum with the following ideas, included in the book *Classroom Science from A to Z*:

- Links to National Science Standards

- Science Activity
  Students use mirrors to make kaleidoscopes.

- Lesson M Teacher Notes

- Lesson M Assessment

- Lesson M Science Explanation

- Lesson M Cross-Curricular Integration

Mirror Madness

When you are done...

Leave at the table	Take with you
plastic mirror	completed handout
pencil (if provided at station)	

Names _____ _____

_____ _____

Mirror Madness
Family Science Challenge

Reflect a bit and change your image.

Materials

mirror • markers or crayons

Procedure

1 Select a mirror from the station supplies. Put your right hand on the table. Can you use the mirror to make it seem like you've added more fingers to your hand?

? *Look at the reflection of your hand in the mirror. Does the reflected hand have the thumb on the same side as your right hand or as your left hand?*

_____

_____

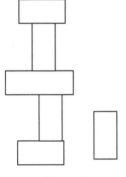

Figure 1

2 Use the pictures at left and below and what you know about mirrors to complete the following tasks.

   a. Move your mirror around to different sides of or places on Figure 1. Can you see 12 rectangles? How about eight? Five rectangles? Three? Two? One?

   b. Make the butterfly in Figure 2 appear whole. Do the two sides have the same markings? The polka dots in the drawn butterfly are on the left side of the butterfly body. Are they in the same orientation in the mirror?

   c. Make two sailboats. (See Figure 3.) Look at the shaded flags on the tops of the sailboats. Do they point in the same direction? Bring the two boats close together, then make them sail away from each other.

   d. Put more fish in the bowl in Figure 4. How many fish were you able to see?

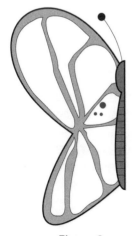

Figure 2

Figure 3

Figure 4

A
B C D
E F G
H I J

❸ The letter A is symmetrical. This means that if you draw an imaginary line down the center of the letter, both halves look the same. Place the mirror along the dotted line to make the letter A appear whole. Use the mirror to determine which other letters of the alphabet are symmetrical. *Hint: Letters can also be horizontally symmetrical.*

_____

_____

❹ On the back of this paper draw your own picture with crayons or markers. Use the mirror to change your picture in different ways.

Child/Adult Discussion

? *In what ways were the mirror images and the original pictures the same? In what ways were they different?*

_____

_____

Explanation

When you look in a mirror, you see yourself because mirrors reflect light in a special way. All surfaces reflect light, but not all surfaces act like mirrors do. The rays of light from the sun or a light bulb travel in parallel paths. If these parallel light rays hit a surface that is rough, they scatter in all different directions. However, if they hit a smooth surface, they stay parallel as they reflect. (See Figure 1.) When these reflected, parallel rays hit your eye, your brain interprets them as if they had been reflected from the object itself.

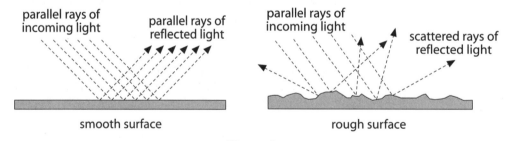

Figure 1

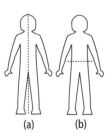

(a)   (b)

Figure 2

A symmetrical half of an object can appear whole if a mirror is held in the correct place next to it. Symmetrical images are those that look the same on one side as they do on the other. For example, in Figure 2a, the left and right halves of the person are symmetrical. However, in Figure 2b, where the line is drawn horizontally, the top and bottom of the figure are not symmetrical with respect to each other.

Mirror Madness Planning Notes

This section will help you prepare for and carry out your Family Science event.

Calculating Quantities

"Calculating Quantities" contains information to help you calculate how much of each material you will need for your event. Copy values marked with a 🛒 onto the Shopping/Gathering List and those marked with a ✓ onto the Setup Checklist. If any of the calculations result in fractions, round up to the next whole number.

Nonconsumable Items Per Setup

You may choose to provide more than one setup at each station to allow a number of family teams to work concurrently.

- mirrors
  (1 mirror per setup) x _____ setups = _____ **mirrors** 🛒 ✓

- markers or crayons
  (1 set of markers or crayons per setup) x _____ setups = _____ **sets of markers or crayons** 🛒 ✓

Getting Ready for the Family Science Challenge
Tools or General Supplies Needed for Preparation Only

- 3 sheets of brightly colored cardstock for Table Tent **M**
- adhesive copier labels (template provided) or other materials to make labels
- (optional) masking tape

Preparing Materials for Use

- Photocopy the Family Science Challenge handout master to make the number of copies needed.

- Photocopy the Table Tent **M** master onto three sheets of brightly colored cardstock and assemble the table tent.

- Photocopy the label template onto a blank sheet of copier labels to print the labels, or make your own labels.

- Plastic, Mylar®, or foil mirrors are safer to use with younger students. If glass mirrors are used, cover the edges of the mirrors with masking tape.

- Place labels on the backs of the mirrors.

Setting Up the Station

• Place Table Tent **M** at the station in a prominent location.

• Place a mirror and a set of markers, pens, or crayons at each setup.

Answers and Observations

❶ *Look at the reflection of your hand in the mirror. Does the reflected hand have the thumb on the same side as your right hand or as your left hand?*

The hand in the mirror has the thumb on the same side as the left hand.

❸ *What other letters of the alphabet are symmetrical?*

Letters A, H, I, M, O, T, U, V, W, X, and Y are vertically symmetrical.
Letters B, C, D, E, H, I, O, and X are horizontally symmetrical.

Answers for Child/Adult Discussion

? *In what ways were the mirror images and the original pictures the same? In what ways were they different?*

The mirror images matched the originals in every way except that what was on the right in the original was on the left in the reflection, and vice versa.

Reference

Sarquis, M. *Community Approach to Science in Elementary Schools (CASES)*. Unpublished work, 1983.

Mirror Madness
Shopping/Gathering List

Use this checklist as a guide to collecting the materials for this Family Science Challenge. Fill in the quantities needed below after doing the calculations called for in the "Calculating Quantities" section.

Total Quantities (from "Planning Notes")

_____ mirrors*

_____ markers or crayons

Tools for Getting Ready

_____ 3 sheets of brightly colored cardstock for Table Tent **M**

_____ adhesive copier labels (template provided) or other materials to make labels**

_____ masking tape (if necessary)

* Small plastic mirrors are less likely than glass ones to have sharp edges and are available in packages of 30 (item #53-130-3280) from Delta Education, P.O. Box 3000, Nashua, NH 03601-9913, 800/442-5444; http://www.delta-ed.com, as well as from other science education suppliers. Double-sided Plexiglas™ mirrors that can be cut with scissors are available in packages of eight (item #F16481) from Frey Scientific, 905 Hickory Lane, P.O. Box 8101, Mansfield, OH 44901-8101, 800/225-FREY; http://www.freyscientific.com.

** We have provided a label template that can be photocopied directly onto a blank sheet of copier labels to print all of the labels you need for the activity. Use 1-inch x 2¾-inch copier labels, such as Avery Copier Labels (code 5351). If copier labels are not available, copy the label template onto paper, cut out the labels, and use tape to affix the paper labels. Alternatively, make hand-written labels using permanent marker and masking tape or other similar materials.

Mirror Madness Setup Checklist

The following is a list of items you will need to set up the Family Science Challenge. "Planning Notes" gives step-by-step instructions for setting up the Family Science Challenge.

Items Per Station

The following materials should be left on or near the table for all family teams to use. (A station is a location where family teams work on an activity.)

Material	Total Needed	Notes
☐ Table Tent **M**	_____	Copy master provided

Items Per Setup

The following nonconsumable items should be placed at each setup. You may choose to provide more than one setup at each station to allow a number of family teams to work concurrently.

Material	Total Needed	Notes
☐ mirror	_____	_____
☐ markers or crayons	_____	_____
☐ pencil for recording observations*	_____	_____

Consumable Materials

The following materials will be used up or taken away by family teams.

Material	Total Needed	Notes
☐ Family Science Challenge handouts**	_____	Copy master provided

*   You may wish to pass out pencils at registration or have families bring their own pencils.

** You may wish to pass out Family Science Challenge handouts as a set at registration rather than at each station.

Mirror Madness Label Template

 Mirror
Please leave at the station.

 Mirror
Please leave at the station.

 Mirror
Please leave at the station.

 Mirror
Please leave at the station.

 Mirror
Please leave at the station.

 Mirror
Please leave at the station.

 Mirror
Please leave at the station.

 Mirror
Please leave at the station.

 Mirror
Please leave at the station.

 Mirror
Please leave at the station.

 Mirror
Please leave at the station.

 Mirror

 Mirror
Please leave at the station.

 Mirror
Please leave at the station.

 Mirror
Please leave at the station.

 Mirror
Please leave at the station.

Nifty Balloon Trick

Family teams use science to perform a seemingly impossible feat—pushing a pointed object through a balloon without popping it.

. . . . **Key Science Topics**

- balloons
- polymers and their properties

. . . . **Average Time Required**

Performance   5–10 minutes

Links to *Classroom Science from A to Z*

You can extend this activity into your science curriculum with the following ideas, included in the book *Classroom Science from A to Z:*

- Links to National Science Standards

- Science Activity
  Investigate ways to poke a hole in a container without spilling its contents.

- Lesson N Teacher Notes

- Lesson N Assessment

- Lesson N Science Explanation

- Lesson N Cross-Curricular Integration

Nifty Balloon Trick

When you are done...

Throw away	Leave at the table	Take with you
used balloons	skewer	completed handout
paper towels	pencil (if provided at station)	

Nifty Balloon Trick
Family Science Challenge

Skewer a balloon.

Materials

2 latex balloons • bamboo skewer • cooking oil in a dropper bottle or cup
• paper towel

Procedure

Figure 1

*Handle skewers with caution. Attention: This activity involves the use of latex
balloons. If anyone in your family is allergic to latex, take the necessary precautions.*

❶ Blow a balloon up to about half its intended size. Be sure the balloon is
several inches shorter than the bamboo skewer. (See Figure 1.) Tie off the
balloon.

❓ *Predict what will happen if you try to push the skewer into the balloon.*

_____

❷ Drop several drops of cooking oil near the tip of the skewer or dip it into the
cup of oil and use a paper towel to spread the oil along the length of the
skewer.

Figure 2

Just in case the balloon pops, do not hold it too close to anyone's face.

❸ Hold the skewer above the end of the balloon opposite the knot. Find the
part that isn't stretched as much as the rest of the balloon. It's often slightly
darker in color. Put the point of the skewer there. Using a screwing, twisting
motion, push the skewer into the balloon. (See Figure 2.) Be careful not to
jerk back or jump when the skewer pierces the balloon.

❹ Push the skewer through the balloon, stopping short of the knot end. Again,
find the part that's not stretched out too much. At this point, use the
screwing, twisting motion as you push the skewer through balloon near the
knot. (See Figure 3.) If it pops, inflate another balloon and try again.

Figure 3

❺ Carefully hold the skewer near the tip and pull the skewer out of the
balloon. Look at the balloon. Place one of your fingers near one of the holes.

❓ *Is air coming out of the balloon?* _____

Figure 4

❻ Blow up and tie off another balloon. Examine the two ends of the balloon
you pushed the skewer through. Compare how thick the latex looks there to
what it looks like on the sides. Find a place where you think the latex looks
the thinnest. What do you think would happen if you tried pushing the oiled
skewer through this spot? (See Figure 4.) Try it.

❓ *What happens?* _____

7 Clean up by throwing the used balloons and paper towels in the trash. Return the skewer to its container.

Child/Adult Discussion

? *Was there a difference between pushing the skewer through the sides of the balloon and pushing it through the top and bottom of the balloon? What might have caused this difference?*

_____

_____

? *What role does the cooking oil play?*

_____

_____

Explanation

Balloons are usually made of a natural material called latex. Latex is made of very, very, very long molecules called polymers. These huge polymer molecules are all twisted and coiled around each other (like a messed-up wad of yarn or string). A balloon can stretch as much as it does because these molecules can uncoil and spread out quite a bit. When you blow up a balloon, the latex at the sides stretches more and becomes thinner than the latex at the top and bottom near the tie end. The more the latex in the balloon stretches, the thinner it becomes. The thinner the latex becomes, the fewer molecules you will find in a given space, and those that are there will be stretched out so much that it is easy for them to tear apart from one another. This can lead to a rip in the side of the balloon. Once a rip forms, the air inside quickly pushes its way out, causing the balloon to pop.

Now consider what happened when you pushed the skewer into the balloon. When a skewer passes through the regions that aren't stretched too greatly, the latex strands can be gently pushed aside without breaking or tearing apart from one another. This is what happened at the top and tie ends (that is, if your balloon didn't pop). The cooking oil was used as a lubricant to help the skewer slide more easily past the latex molecules. It probably wasn't possible to keep the balloon from popping when you pushed the skewer through the thin, stretched-out sides of the balloon. The strands were already stretched out and couldn't slide apart without tearing, and you know what happens once the tear starts…pop!

Stuff to Try At Home

Investigate to find out whether you can use other types of lubricants to help put a skewer through a balloon. You could try bar or liquid soap; hand lotion; lard, butter, or margarine; or different types of oils.

Nifty Balloon Trick Planning Notes

This section will help you prepare for and carry out your Family Science event.

Calculating Quantities

"Calculating Quantities" contains information to help you calculate how much of each material you will need for your event. Copy values marked with a 🛒 onto the Shopping/Gathering List and those marked with a ✓ onto the Setup Checklist. If any of the calculations result in fractions, round up to the next whole number.

Nonconsumable Items Per Station

Amounts listed are for one station. If you will have more than one station for this Family Science Challenge, adjust amounts accordingly.

- large, open container, such as a pop beaker, for bamboo skewers 🛒 ✓
- box or other container for balloons 🛒 ✓
- trash can 🛒 ✓

Nonconsumable Items Per Setup

You may choose to provide more than one setup at each station to allow a number of family teams to work concurrently.

- bamboo skewers
  (1 skewer per setup) x _____ *setups =* _____ ***bamboo skewers*** 🛒 ✓

- dropper bottles or cups
  (1 dropper bottle per setup) x _____ *setups =* _____ ***dropper bottles*** 🛒 ✓ *; OR*
  (1 cup per setup) x _____ *setups =* _____ ***cups*** 🛒 ✓

Consumable Materials

- round latex balloons
  (2 latex balloons per family) x _____ *families =* _____ *balloons*
  To allow for the possibility of balloons popping when they aren't supposed to, plan for extras:
  estimate (_____ *balloons planned above) ÷ 4 =* _____ *extra balloons*
  total number of balloons = _____ ***balloons*** 🛒 ✓

- cooking oil
  (0.01 fluid ounces cooking oil per family) x _____ *families =* _____ ***fluid ounces of cooking oil*** 🛒 ✓

- paper towels
  (1 paper towel per family) x _____ *families =* _____ ***paper towels*** 🛒 ✓

Getting Ready for the Family Science Challenge

Tools or General Supplies Needed for Preparation Only

- 3 sheets of brightly colored cardstock for Table Tent **N**
- adhesive copier labels (template provided) or other materials to make labels

Preparing Materials for Use

- Photocopy the Family Science Challenge handout master to make the number of copies needed.

- Photocopy the Table Tent **N** master onto three sheets of brightly colored cardstock and assemble the table tent.

- Photocopy the label template onto a blank sheet of copier labels to print the labels, or make your own labels.

- Check the skewers for splinters and make sure each skewer has a pointed end.

- Label the containers for the skewers and balloons appropriately. Label the dropper bottle or the cup.

Setting Up the Station

- Place Table Tent **N** at the station in a prominent location.

- Put the skewers and the balloons in their appropriately labeled containers.

- Fill labeled dropper bottles or cups about half full with cooking oil.

Safety

Skewers should be handled with care, and families should hold balloons away from anyone's face, as the balloon may pop. Also, an increasing number of people are allergic to latex. People who are allergic to latex should follow the recommendations of their doctors.

Answers and Observations

❺ *Is air coming out of the balloon?*

Most observers will feel a slight stream of air exiting the balloon.

❻ *What happens?*

The balloon pops more easily when the skewer is pushed through the side of the balloon.

Answers for Child/Adult Discussion

? *Was there a difference between pushing the skewer through the sides of the balloon and pushing it through the top and bottom of the balloon? What might have caused this difference?*

Yes, there was a difference. The latex is thicker at the top and bottom of the balloon, allowing the skewer to push aside the polymer chains that make up the balloon without tearing them. The latex is thin on the sides of the stretched balloon, so the polymer chains cannot slide apart and the balloon tears and pops.

? *What role does the cooking oil play?*

The cooking oil acts as a lubricant and helps the skewer slide more easily through the balloon.

References

"Needle Through a Balloon"; *Chain Gang—The Chemistry of Polymers;* Science in Our World Series; Sarquis, M., Ed.; Terrific Science: Middletown, OH, 1995; pp 45–49.

"Needle Through a Balloon"; *Fun With Chemistry: A Guidebook of K–12 Activities;* Sarquis, M., Sarquis, J., Eds.; Institute for Chemical Education: Madison, WI, 1991; Vol. 1, pp 139–142.

Woodward, L. "Skewering a Balloon," *Polymers All Around You!;* Terrific Science: Middletown, OH, 1992; p 18.

Nifty Balloon Trick
Shopping/Gathering List

Use this checklist as a guide to collecting the materials for this Family Science Challenge. Fill in the quantities needed below after doing the calculations called for in the "Calculating Quantities" section.

Total Quantities (from "Planning Notes")

_____ bamboo skewers*

_____ round latex balloons**

_____ dropper bottles or cups

_____ ounces of cooking oil

_____ paper towels

_____ large open container(s)***

_____ box(es) or other container(s)

_____ trash can(s)

Tools for Getting Ready

☐ 3 sheets of brightly colored cardstock for Table Tent **N**

☐ adhesive copier labels (template provided) or other materials to make labels[†]

* Bamboo skewers can be found in grocery stores, usually near cooking utensils. The skewers should be free of splinters and pointed.

** Latex balloons can be purchased from a department store, magic store, florist's shop, or balloon store. The balloons should not be too old. Avoid balloons with printing on them; they typically pop more easily than plain balloons. Round balloons work better than sausage-shaped balloons because they are less likely to pop. If large quantities are required, balloons may be purchased from National Latex Products, 246 E. 4th St., Ashland, OH 44805, 419/289-3300. A minimum order is required for mail orders.

*** Pop beakers made by cutting off the tops of 2-L plastic soft-drink bottles work well.

[†] We have provided a label template that can be photocopied directly onto a blank sheet of copier labels to print all of the labels you need for the activity. Use 1-inch x 2¾-inch copier labels, such as Avery Copier Labels (code 5351). If copier labels are not available, copy the label template onto paper, cut out the labels, and use tape to affix the paper labels. Alternatively, make hand-written labels using permanent marker and masking tape or other similar materials.

Nifty Balloon Trick
Setup Checklist

The following is a list of items you will need to set up the Family Science Challenge. "Planning Notes" gives step-by-step instructions for setting up the Family Science Challenge.

Items Per Station

The following materials should be left on or near the table for all family teams to use. (A station is a location where family teams work on an activity.)

Material	Total Needed	Notes
☐ Table Tent **N**	_____	Copy master provided
☐ labeled open container	_____	For bamboo skewers
☐ labeled box or other container	_____	For balloons
☐ bamboo skewers	_____	
☐ large trash can	_____	

Items Per Setup

The following nonconsumable items will be needed for each setup. You may choose to provide more than one setup at each station to allow a number of family teams to work concurrently at the station.

Material	Total Needed	Notes
☐ labeled dropper bottle or cup	_____	
☐ pencil for recording observations*	_____	

Consumable Materials

The following materials will be used up or taken away by family teams.

Material	Total Needed	Notes
☐ latex balloons	_____	
☐ cooking oil	_____	
☐ paper towels	_____	
☐ Family Science Challenge handouts**	_____	Copy master provided

*   You may wish to pass out pencils at registration or have families bring their own pencils.

** You may wish to pass out Family Science Challenge handouts as a set at registration rather than at each station.

Nifty Balloon Trick
Label Template

 **Bamboo skewers**
Use 1; please leave at the station.

 **Balloons**
2 per family

 **Cooking Oil**
Please leave at the station.

 **Bamboo skewers**
Use 1; please leave at the station.

 **Balloons**
2 per family

 **Cooking Oil**
Please leave at the station.

 **Bamboo skewers**
Use 1; please leave at the station.

 **Balloons**
2 per family

 **Cooking Oil**
Please leave at the station.

 **Bamboo skewers**
Use 1; please leave at the station.

 **Balloons**
2 per family

 **Cooking Oil**
Please leave at the station.

 **Bamboo skewers**
Use 1; please leave at the station.

 **Balloons**
2 per family

 **Cooking Oil**
Please leave at the station.

Bamboo skewers
Use 1; please leave at the station.

Optical Illusions

Is seeing always believing? Families will make an optical illusion toy and discover that what they see is not always what is there.

Key Science Topics

- persistence of vision
- sight

Average Time Required

Performance   10 minutes

Links to *Classroom Science from A to Z*

You can extend this activity into your science curriculum with the following ideas, included in the book *Classroom Science from A to Z*:

- Links to National Science Standards

- Science Activity 1
  Students use persistence of vision to mix and blend different colors.

- Science Activity 2
  Is what you see what you get? Students investigate more optical illusions.

- Lesson O Teacher Notes

- Lesson O Assessment

- Lesson O Science Explanation

- Lesson O Cross-Curricular Integration

Optical Illusions

When you are done…

Throw away	Leave at the table	Take with you
card scraps	Thaumatrope Toys scissors hole punch crayons or markers pencil (if provided at station)	thaumatrope you made completed handout

Names _____   _____

_____   _____

Optical Illusions
Family Science Challenge

Spin the disk… fool your brain.

Materials

Thaumatrope Toys • thaumatrope pattern • 5-inch x 7-inch index card • scissors • hole punch • rubber bands • crayons or colored markers

Procedure

Figure 1

❶ Select one of the Thaumatrope (THAW muh trope) Toys at the station. Examine it. Grasp its rubber bands between the thumb and forefinger of each hand, about ¼ inch away from the edge of the circle as shown in Figure 1. Roll the rubber bands back and forth quickly so the disk spins over and over. Watch the image on the turning circle.

? *What do you see?*

_____

_____

❷ Select a different Thaumatrope Toy from the station. This time predict what you will see before you spin it. Then spin it and see if your prediction was correct.

❸ Try making your own thaumatrope by doing the following steps:

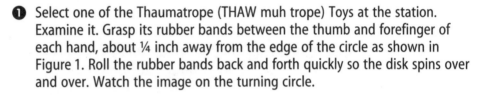

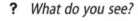

Figure 2

a. Trace the thaumatrope pattern provided onto the index card as shown in Figure 2. Mark the places for the holes, too. Cut the disk out with the scissors. Use a hole punch to punch out the holes.

b. To draw your design, you will need to put half of a picture on one side of the disk and the other half of the picture on the other side. For example, you might use a coffee cup on one side and a doughnut on the other, a dog and a ball, a frog and a lily pad, or a person's head and a hat. Use your imagination! HINT: After drawing the first picture, make sure the picture on the other side will be upside down compared to the first picture.

c. Loop a rubber band through each of the holes in the disk as shown in Figure 3.

Figure 3

4 Try spinning your thaumatrope.

? *What do you see?*

_____

_____

5 Now try spinning your thaumatrope very slowly.

? *Do you see the same thing as when you turned it quickly?*

_____

_____

6 You may keep the thaumatrope you made. Please clean up the station and return the other thaumatrope toys to the appropriate container.

Child/Adult Discussion

? *Why do you think the thaumatrope gave a different result when it was spun quickly and then slowly?*

_____

_____

Explanation

The illusion that the pictures from the two sides of the thaumatrope are a single picture is caused by a phenomenon called persistence of vision. This phenomenon results from a series of complex reactions that occur in your eye and brain. You "see" because light is reflected from the object onto the retina of your eye. The light reacts with chemicals in the retina and causes them to form new compounds that trigger a message to the brain, allowing you to "see" the object. The new compounds made in this process linger briefly— about $1/15$ of a second. As a result, your brain continues to think it sees the object for $1/15$ second after it is removed. Because the image of the object seems to persist, the phenomenon is called persistence of vision. When you spun the disk, it twirled past your eye so quickly that the image on one side persisted into the time the image of the second side appeared. Your brain perceived this motion as a blending of the images. This is the same process that occurs when we watch movies, flip through flip books, or watch television.

Stuff to Try at Home

Try making a flipbook by drawing a series of pictures, each one slightly different from the previous one. Staple the pictures together along one edge and flip through them rapidly.

Optical Illusions Planning Notes

This section will help you prepare for and carry out your Family Science event.

Calculating Quantities

"Calculating Quantities" contains information to help you calculate how much of each material you will need for your event. Copy values marked with a 🛒 onto the Shopping/Gathering List and those marked with a ✓ onto the Setup Checklist. If any of the calculations result in fractions, round up to the next whole number.

Nonconsumable Items Per Station

Amounts listed are for one station. If you will have more than one station for this Family Science Challenge, adjust amounts accordingly.

- 3 containers for dispensing rubber bands, index cards, and premade thaumatrope toys 🛒 ✓
- premade thaumatrope toys ✓

  How many 5-inch x 7-inch index cards do I need?
  (4 index cards per setup) x _____ setups =_____ **index cards** 🛒

  How many rubber bands do I need?
  (8 rubber bands per setup) = _____ **rubber bands** 🛒

Nonconsumable Items Per Setup

You may choose to provide more than one setup at each station to allow a number of family teams to work concurrently.

- thaumatrope patterns ✓
  How many 5-inch x 7-inch index cards do I need?
  (1 index card per setup) x _____ setups = _____ **index cards** 🛒 ✓
- pencils
  (1 pencil per setup) x _____ setups = _____ **pencils** 🛒 ✓
- scissors
  (1 pair of scissors per setup) x _____ setups = _____ **pair(s) of scissors** 🛒 ✓
- hole punch
  (1 hole punch per setup) x _____ setups = _____ **hole punches** 🛒 ✓
- crayons or colored markers
  (1 set of crayons or colored markers per setup) x _____ setups = _____ **sets of crayons or markers** 🛒 ✓

Consumable Materials

- 5-inch x 7-inch unlined index cards
  (1 index card per family) x _____ families = **_____** *index cards* 🛒 ✓
- rubber bands
  (2 rubber bands per family) x _____ families = **_____** *rubber bands* 🛒 ✓

Getting Ready for the Family Science Challenge

Tools or General Supplies Needed for Preparation Only

- 3 sheets of brightly colored cardstock for Table Tent **O**
- adhesive copier labels (template provided) or other materials to make labels
- scissors or paper cutter
- pencil
- glue or tape
- crayons or colored markers
- hole punch
- ruler

Preparing Materials for Use

- Photocopy the Family Science Challenge handout master to make the number of copies needed.

- Photocopy the Table Tent **O** master onto three sheets of brightly colored cardstock and assemble the table tent.

- Photocopy the label template onto a blank sheet of copier labels to print the labels, or make your own labels.

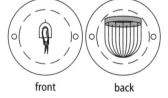
Trace around the pattern.

- To make the Thaumatrope Patterns: Photocopy the Thaumatrope Pattern (provided) onto white paper. Cut apart the circles and glue one onto an index card. Cut out the disk and punch out the two holes with a hole punch. This is your first thaumatrope pattern. Use it as a template to trace around to make more patterns (see figure at left), or make the others in the same way you made the first one. Label each disk "Thaumatrope Pattern."

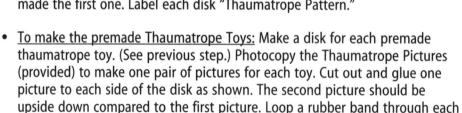
front   back

- To make the premade Thaumatrope Toys: Make a disk for each premade thaumatrope toy. (See previous step.) Photocopy the Thaumatrope Pictures (provided) to make one pair of pictures for each toy. Cut out and glue one picture to each side of the disk as shown. The second picture should be upside down compared to the first picture. Loop a rubber band through each hole as shown at left to complete the toy. Label each thaumatrope "Thaumatrope Toy."

Loop a rubber band through each hole.

- Label the three containers, such as shoe boxes or "pop beakers" (made from cutting off the top of a 2-L bottle), for storing the rubber bands, index cards, and premade thaumatrope toys.

Setting Up the Station

- Place the rubber bands, index cards, and premade thaumatrope toys in their appropriately labeled containers at the station.

- Place scissors, a hole punch, a thaumatrope pattern, and a set of crayons or colored markers at each setup.

Answers and Observations

❺ *Do you see the same thing as when you turned it quickly?*

No, you see the two separate images when you spin the thaumatrope slowly. However, when you spin it quickly, you should see one combined image.

Answers for Child/Adult Discussion

? *Why do you think the thaumatrope gave a different result when it was spun quickly and then slowly?*

The images blurred together more when spun quickly—our eyes didn't have time to see the separate images.

Reference

Sarquis, M.; Woodward, L. "Father's Day Thaumatropes," *Science Projects for Holidays Throughout the Year;* McGraw-Hill: New York, 1999; pp 333–346.

Optical Illusions Shopping/Gathering List

Use this checklist as a guide to collecting the materials for this Family Science Challenge. Fill in the quantities needed below after doing the calculations called for in the "Calculating Quantities" section.

Total Quantities (from "Planning Notes")

_____ 5-inch x 7-inch unlined index cards (sum of lines below)

_____ for the premade thaumatrope toys

_____ for the thaumatrope patterns

_____ for family teams

_____ rubber bands* (sum of lines below)

_____ for the premade thaumatrope toys

_____ for family teams

_____ scissors

_____ hole punch(es)

_____ crayons or colored markers

_____ containers for rubber bands, index cards, and premade thaumatrope toys

_____ trash can(s)

Tools for Getting Ready

☐ 3 sheets of brightly colored cardstock for Table Tent **O**

☐ adhesive copier labels (template provided) or other materials to make labels**

☐ scissors or paper cutter

☐ (optional) pencil for tracing pattern circles

☐ (optional) glue or tape

☐ crayons or colored markers

☐ hole punch

☐ ruler

* Narrow rubber bands such as #18 work best. If you are using another size, test them in advance to ensure they will produce the desired result.

** We have provided a label template that can be photocopied directly onto a blank sheet of copier labels to print all of the labels you need for the activity. Use 1-inch x 2¾-inch copier labels, such as Avery Copier Labels (code 5351). If copier labels are not available, copy the label template onto paper, cut out the labels, and use tape to affix the paper labels. Alternatively, make hand-written labels using permanent marker and masking tape or other similar materials.

Reproduced from *Science Night Family Fun from* Ⓐ *to* Ⓩ

Optical Illusions Setup Checklist

The following is a list of items you will need to set up the Family Science Challenge. "Planning Notes" gives step-by-step instructions for setting up the Family Science Challenge.

Items Per Station

The following materials should be left on or near the table for all family teams to use. (A station is a location where family teams work on an activity.)

Material	Total Needed	Notes
☐ Table Tent **O**	_____	Copy master provided
☐ labeled containers	_____	For rubber bands, index cards, and premade thaumatrope toys
☐ premade thaumatrope toys	_____	_____
☐ trash can	_____	_____

Items Per Setup

The following nonconsumable items should be placed at each setup. You may choose to provide more than one setup at each station to allow a number of family teams to work concurrently at the station.

Material	Total Needed	Notes
☐ thaumatrope pattern	_____	_____
☐ scissors	_____	_____
☐ hole punch	_____	_____
☐ crayons or colored markers	_____	_____
☐ pencil for tracing thaumatropes and recording observations*	_____	_____

Consumable Materials

The following materials will be used up or taken away by family teams.

Material	Total Needed	Notes
☐ index cards	_____	_____
☐ rubber bands	_____	_____
☐ Family Science Challenge handouts**	_____	Copy master provided

* You may wish to pass out pencils at registration or have families bring their own pencils.

** You may wish to pass out Family Science Challenge handouts as a set at registration rather than at each station.

Optical Illusions
Thaumatrope Patterns

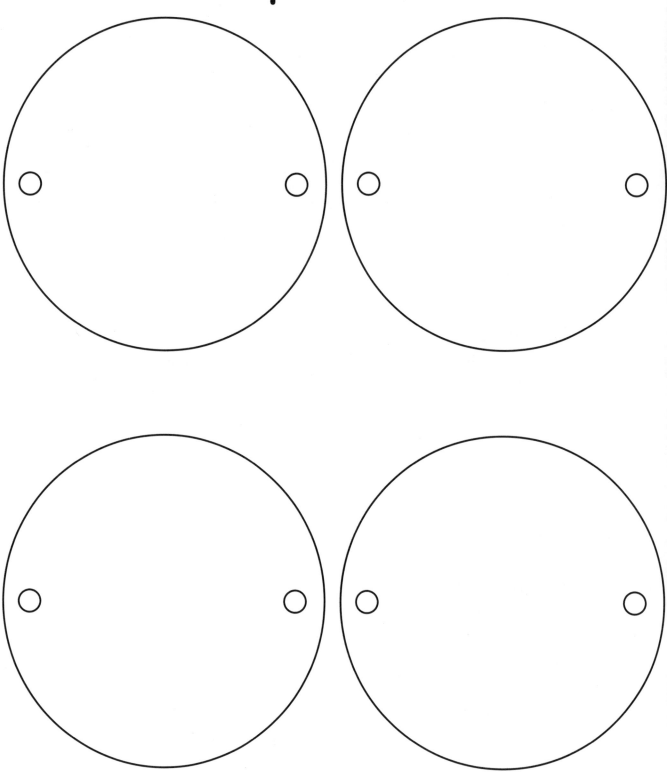

Optical Illusions
Thaumatrope Pictures

Optical Illusions
Label Template

[O] Index Cards
1 per family

[O] Index Cards
1 per family

[O] Rubber Bands
2 per family

[O] Rubber Bands
2 per family

[O] Thaumatrope Toy
Please leave at the station.

[O] Thaumatrope Toy
Please leave at the station.

[O] Thaumatrope Toy
Please leave at the station.

[O] Thaumatrope Toy
Please leave at the station.

[O] Thaumatrope Toy
Please leave at the station.

[O] Thaumatrope Toy
Please leave at the station.

[O] Thaumatrope Toy
Please leave at the station.

[O] Thaumatrope Toy
Please leave at the station.

[O] Thaumatrope Pattern
Please leave at the station.

[O] Thaumatrope Pattern
Please leave at the station.

[O] Thaumatrope Pattern
Please leave at the station.

[O] Thaumatrope Pattern
Please leave at the station.

Popping Patterns

Family teams investigate the relationship between soap bubble colors and when they pop.

Key Science Topics

- color
- light
- reflection
- soap bubbles
- waves

Average Time Required

Performance   10–15 minutes

Links to *Classroom Science from A to Z*

You can extend this activity into your science curriculum with the following ideas, included in the book *Classroom Science from A to Z:*

- Links to National Science Standards

- Science Activity
  Investigate the bubble shapes produced by different bubble blowers.

- Lesson P Teacher Notes

- Lesson P Assessment

- Lesson P Science Explanation

- Lesson P Cross-Curricular Integration

Popping Patterns

When you are done...

Throw away	Leave at the table	Take with you
paper towels	bubble dome apparatus	completed handout
straw	bubble solution	
	pencil (if provided at station)	

Names _____   _____

_____   _____

Popping Patterns
Family Science Challenge

Use the pattern to predict the pop.

Materials

bubble dome apparatus • bubble solution • drinking straws (1 per person)
• paper towels

Procedure

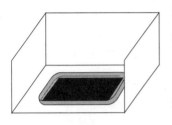

Figure 1

❶ At the station you will find a bubble dome apparatus. It includes a cardboard shield (with white inside) and a bubble tray that has been prepared for your use. Please leave it set up as it is. (See Figure 1.)

❷ Check the black paper in the bottom of the bubble tray. It should be completely saturated with soap solution, and small puddles should be visible. If it looks too dry, add a little more bubble solution, but don't overfill.

❸ Select a clean straw and remove it from the wrapper.

❹ Lower the straw into one of the puddles of soap solution in the bubble tray. Blow gently through the straw to form a large bubble dome. Remove the straw carefully so that the bubble stays on the paper and does not pop.

❺ Observe the swirling of the soap film and the changing colors in the bubble until the bubble pops.

? *Record your observations in the Observation Table below.*

❻ Repeat steps 4–5 several more times, taking turns blowing bubbles. For health reasons, each person should use only his or her own straw.

❼ Discard your straws and wipe up any spilled bubble solution. Leave the other materials for the next family group.

	Observation Table	
Trial #	Colors observed (in order if possible)	Color immediately before popping
1		
2		
3		
4		

Child/Adult Discussion

? *Review your observations. What color do you think indicates that the bubble is ready to pop?*

_____

_____

Explanation

The bubble domes you made in this Family Science Challenge had air in the middle and a thin soap-film wall. The bubble dome remains intact as long as the walls are strong enough to hold the air in. However, over time the wall becomes thinner and thinner. This is because the soap film that makes it up gradually flows away from the top of the bubble due to gravity. Eventually the wall becomes so thin that the bubble pops. Figure 1 provides a diagram of the color sequence that is often seen when a bubble pops. The pattern you see may be slightly different, because air currents may cause the bubble to grow thin too quickly or pop early, disrupting the pattern. The cardboard shield helps protect the bubble from these air currents. Also, the white color of the shield helps reflect light onto the bubble so you can see the colors more clearly.

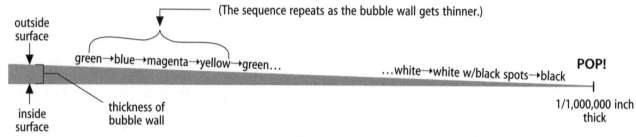

Figure 1

Stuff to Try at Home

Try blowing bubbles at home and see if you can detect the same color changes with bubbles that are floating in the air.

Popping Patterns Planning Notes

This section will help you prepare for and carry out your Family Science event.

Calculating Quantities

"Calculating Quantities" contains information to help you calculate how much of each material you will need for your event. Copy values marked with a 🛒 onto the Shopping/Gathering List and those marked with a ✓ onto the Setup Checklist. If any of the calculations result in fractions, round up to the next whole number.

Nonconsumable Items Per Station

Amounts listed are for one station. If you will have more than one station for this Family Science Challenge, adjust the amounts accordingly.

- box or other container for straws 🛒 ✓
- trash can 🛒 ✓

Nonconsumable Items Per Setup

You may choose to provide more than one setup at each station to allow a number of family teams to work concurrently.

- Styrofoam® tray
  (1 tray per setup) x _____ setups = _____ **Styrofoam trays** 🛒 ✓

- black paper to fit tray
  (1 piece of paper per setup) x _____ setups − _____ **pieces of black paper** 🛒

- cardboard box and (if necessary) white paper for shield
  (1 box per setup) x _____ setups = _____ **boxes** 🛒

- 1-L bottles to make and store bubble solution in
  (1 bottle per setup) x _____ setups = _____ **1-L bottles** 🛒 ✓

Consumable Materials

- drinking straws
  (3 drinking straws per family) x _____ families = _____ **drinking straws** 🛒 ✓

- dishwashing liquid to make bubble solution
  (2 fluid ounces per setup) x _____ setups = _____ **fluid ounces of dishwashing liquid** 🛒

- water to make bubble solution
  enough to fill 1-L bottles listed above

- paper towels
  (1 paper towel per family) x _____ *families =* _____ ***paper towels*** 🛒 ✓

Getting Ready for the Family Science Challenge

Tools or General Supplies Needed for Preparation Only

- 3 sheets of brightly colored cardstock for Table Tent **P**
- adhesive copier labels (template provided) or other materials to make labels
- scissors
- (optional) masking tape

Preparing Materials for Use

- Photocopy the Family Science Challenge handout master to make the number of copies needed.

- Photocopy the Table Tent **P** master onto three sheets of brightly colored cardstock and assemble the table tent.

- Photocopy the label template onto a blank sheet of copier labels to print the labels, or make your own labels.

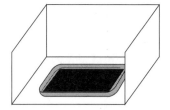

- To make the cardboard shield, remove the top and one side of a cardboard box with a length and width greater than the length and width of the Styrofoam tray. If the inside of the box is white, the shield is finished. Otherwise, tape white paper on the inside walls of the box.

- Prepare the bubble trays by cutting black paper to fit the bottom of the tray and putting it into the tray.

- Prepare 1 L bubble solution for each setup by mixing 2 ounces dishwashing liquid with 1 L water. Cap the bottle and gently shake to mix. Allow the solution to settle so that bubbles subside before use.

- Label the container for the straws and the bottle(s) of bubble solution.

Setting Up the Station

- Place Table Tent **P** at the station in a prominent location.

- Set up the cardboard shields. Place the bubble trays in them. Saturate the black paper on the bottom of the tray, leaving puddles of solution. Use your hands to spread the solution as completely as possible over the entire surface of the paper-lined tray.

- Place a labeled 1-L bottle of bubble solution at each setup.

- Place the labeled container of straws and the paper towels at the station.

- Have a sponge or mop available in case of spills.

Disposal

The Styrofoam trays and cardboard shields can be used again and should be collected after the Family Science event. Rinse any residual soap solution from the trays before storing.

Answers and Observations

❺ *Record your observations in the Observation Table below.*

Answers will vary because of the swirling motion of the soap film. The following table contains some actual observations.

Observation Table		
Trial #	Colors observed (in order if possible)	Color immediately before popping
1	green, red, purple, yellow, blue, yellow	black
2	yellow, green, blue, purple, yellow	black
3	yellow, blue, purple	black
4	pink, yellow, green, blue, purple	black

Answers for Child/Adult Discussion

? *Review your observations. What color do you think indicates that the bubble is ready to pop?*

Observations should show that the bubble appears black just before popping.

Reference

Barber, J., et al. "Predict-A-Pop"; *Bubbleology,* Great Explorations in Math and Science (GEMS); Lawrence Hall of Science: Berkeley, CA, 1986; pp 35–39.

Popping Patterns
Shopping/Gathering List

Use this checklist as a guide to collecting the materials for this Family Science Challenge. Fill in the quantities needed below after doing the calculations called for in the "Calculating Quantities" section.

Total Quantities (from "Planning Notes")

_____ box(es) or other container(s)

_____ Styrofoam® trays*

_____ sheets of black paper

_____ cardboard boxes**

_____ white paper (if necessary)***

_____ 1-L bottles

_____ drinking straws

_____ fluid ounces dishwashing liquid†

_____ liter(s) water

_____ paper towels

_____ sponge(s) or mop

_____ trash can(s)

Tools for Getting Ready

_____ 3 sheets of brightly colored cardstock for Table Tent **P**

_____ adhesive copier labels (template provided) or other materials to make labels††

_____ scissors

_____ (optional) masking tape

---

*   Most grocery stores use rectangular Styrofoam trays in their meat departments. The store may be willing to donate unused trays or charge only a small fee. Styrofoam plates, either circular or rectangular, may also be used as long as they do not have dividers in them.

**   Cardboard boxes of the type that hold 10–12 reams of paper are ideal for making cardboard shields.

*** White paper is necessary to line the cardboard box if the inside is not white.

†   Most dishwashing liquids will produce good bubbles, but the more expensive brands generally work better. Joy® dishwashing liquid has been found to work best for this activity.

††   We have provided a label template that can be photocopied directly onto a blank sheet of copier labels to print all of the labels you need for the activity. Use 1-inch x 2¾-inch copier labels, such as Avery Copier Labels (code 5351). If copier labels are not available, copy the label template onto paper, cut out the labels, and use tape to affix the paper labels. Alternatively, make hand-written labels using permanent marker and masking tape or other similar materials.

Popping Patterns Setup Checklist

The following is a list of items you will need to set up the Family Science Challenge. "Planning Notes" gives step-by-step instructions for setting up the Family Science Challenge.

Items Per Station

The following materials should be left on or near the table for all family teams to use. (A station is a location where family teams work on an activity.)

Material	Total Needed	Notes
☐ Table Tent **P**	_____	Copy master provided
☐ trash can	_____	
☐ sponge or mop	_____	For cleanup
☐ labeled box or other container	_____	For straws

Items Per Setup

The following nonconsumable items will be needed for each setup. You may choose to provide more than one setup at each station to allow a number of family teams to work concurrently.

Material	Total Needed	Notes
☐ Styrofoam® tray lined with black paper	_____	
☐ three-sided cardboard shield	_____	
☐ pencil for recording observations*	_____	

Consumable Materials

The following materials will be used up or taken away by family teams.

Material	Total Needed	Notes
☐ bubble solution in labeled 1-L bottles	_____	
☐ drinking straws	_____	
☐ paper towels	_____	
☐ Family Science Challenge handouts**	_____	Copy master provided

* You may wish to pass out pencils at registration or have families bring their own pencils.

** You may wish to pass out Family Science Challenge handouts as a set at registration rather than at each station.

Popping Patterns
Label Template

 **Straws**
 1 per person; discard after use.

P **Straws**
 1 per person; discard after use.

P **Bubble Solution**
 Please leave at the station.

P **Bubble Solution**
 Please leave at the station.

P **Straws**
 1 per person; discard after use.

P **Straws**
 1 per person; discard after use.

P **Bubble Solution**
 Please leave at the station.

P **Bubble Solution**
 Please leave at the station.

P **Straws**
 1 per person; discard after use.

P **Straws**
 1 per person; discard after use.

P **Bubble Solution**
 Please leave at the station.

P **Bubble Solution**
 Please leave at the station.

P **Straws**
 1 per person; discard after use.

P **Straws**
 1 per person; discard after use.

P **Bubble Solution**
 Please leave at the station.

P **Bubble Solution**
 Please leave at the station.

Quaint Paint

Families study solubility by painting "Paint with Water" pictures with different liquid solvents.

. . . . **Key Science Topics**

- solubility
- solvents

. . . . **Average Time Required**

Performance   10 minutes

Links to *Classroom Science from A to Z*

You can extend this activity into your science curriculum with the following ideas, included in the book *Classroom Science from A to Z*:

- Links to National Science Standards

- Science Activity
  Students investigate the solubility of permanent and water-soluble markers in water and rubbing alcohol.

- Lesson Q Teacher Notes for the Science Activity

- Lesson Q Assessment

- Lesson Q Teacher Notes for the Assessment

- Lesson Q Science Explanation

- Lesson Q Cross-Curricular Integration

Quaint Paint

When you are done...

Throw away	Leave at the table	Take with you
paper towels	liquids	completed handout
	brushes	Paint with Water page
	pencil (if provided at station)	

Quaint Paint
Family Science Challenge

Bring out the hidden colors.

Materials

page from Paint with Water book • a set of the following liquids, each with its own paintbrush: water, vinegar, rubbing alcohol (70% isopropyl alcohol), and oil

Procedure

water	rubbing alcohol
vinegar	oil

Figure 1

❶ Fold your Paint with Water page in half lengthwise and then in half widthwise. Open up and flatten out the page.

❷ Look at the labels on the set of four liquids. Use a pencil to write the name of one solvent in each of the four sections of the paper. (See Figure 1.)

❸ "Paint" the "water" section of the page with water, the "vinegar" section with vinegar, the "rubbing alcohol" section with rubbing alcohol, and the "oil" section with oil. Be sure not to mix up the brushes.

? *What do you observe?*

water section: _____

_____

vinegar section: _____

_____

rubbing alcohol section: _____

_____

oil section: _____

_____

4 Try holding up the paper and looking through it.

? *What do you observe?*

_____

_____

Child/Adult Discussion

? *The Paint with Water books are designed to be used with water. Which other liquids also worked? Which liquid worked best?*

_____

_____

? *What did the oil do that the other liquids did not?*

_____

_____

Explanation

The colored inks on the page of a Paint with Water book are water-soluble, which means they dissolve in water. These water-soluble colors are applied as small dots inside the dark lines outlining the picture. The dark lines are made from water-insoluble inks. When water is painted on, the water dissolves some of the paint and the brush spreads the color across the page. The paint that dissolves in the water does so because it is made up of molecules that are chemically similar to water. As a "rule of thumb," scientists say that like dissolves like. In other words, substances that are chemically similar to water dissolve in it; those that are chemically different do not. In this activity, four solvents are tested; three of these solvents contain water and behave similarly.

Both vinegar and 70% isopropyl alcohol (rubbing alcohol) are mixtures that contain water. (Vinegar is 95 percent water, and rubbing alcohol is 30 percent water.) Both of these liquids dissolve the water-soluble paint to some extent. Oil, on the other hand, has no effect on the water-soluble paint. Oil is chemically very different from water. In fact, oil and water do not mix. You may have noticed this when you've rinsed an oily pan or added oil and water to a recipe.

You may have noticed another interesting phenomenon when you held the paper up to the light. The section you painted with oil appeared almost transparent. The oil interacted with the fibers in the paper to affect the way light interacts with the paper.

Stuff to Try at Home

Try other liquids such as skim milk; clear, colorless soft drink; lemon juice; shampoo; or hand lotion. Try rubbing margarine, butter or lard in a section to see if it behaves similarly to the oil.

Quaint Paint Planning Notes

This section will help you prepare for and carry out your Family Science event.

Calculating Quantities

"Calculating Quantities" contains information to help you calculate how much of each material you will need for your event. Copy values marked with a 🛒 onto the Shopping/Gathering List and those marked with a ✓ onto the Setup Checklist. If any of the calculations result in fractions, round up to the next whole number.

Nonconsumable Items Per Station

Amounts listed are for one station. If you will have more than one station for this Family Science Challenge, adjust amounts accordingly.

- box(es) for Paint with Water pages 🛒 ✓
- sponge(s) 🛒 ✓
- trash can(s) 🛒 ✓

Nonconsumable Items Per Setup

You may choose to provide more than one setup at each station to allow a number of family teams to work concurrently.

- small cups
  (4 cups per setup) x _____ setups = _____ **cups** 🛒 ✓

- tray or cup holder
  (1 tray or cup holder per setup) x _____ setups = _____ **trays or cup holders** 🛒 ✓

- child-sized paintbrushes
  (4 paintbrushes per setup) x _____ setups = _____ **paintbrushes** 🛒 ✓

Consumable Materials

- water in 1- or 2-L plastic soft drink bottles (if a source of running water will not be readily available near the station)
  (0.03 L water per family) x _____ families = _____ **liters of water in 1- or 2-L bottles** 🛒 ✓

- vegetable, baby, or mineral oil
  (1 fluid ounce per family) x _____ families = _____ **fluid ounces of oil** 🛒 ✓

- vinegar
  (1 fluid ounce per family) x _____ families = _____ **fluid ounces of vinegar** 🛒 ✓

- 70% isopropyl alcohol (rubbing alcohol)
  *(1 fluid ounce per family) x _____ families = _____ **fluid ounces of rubbing alcohol*** 🛒 ✓
  Rubbing alcohol is for external use only. Avoid ingestion or contact with the eyes.

- page from a Paint with Water book
  *(1 page per family) x _____ families = _____ **pages*** 🛒 ✓

- paper towels
  *estimate (1 towel per family) x _____ families = _____ **paper towels*** 🛒 ✓

Getting Ready for the Family Science Challenge
Tools or General Supplies Needed for Preparation Only

- 3 sheets of brightly colored cardstock for Table Tent **Q**
- adhesive copier labels (template provided) or other materials to make labels
- staple remover (if necessary)

Preparing Materials for Use

- Photocopy the Family Science Challenge handout master to make the number of copies needed.

- Photocopy the Table Tent **Q** master onto three sheets of brightly colored cardstock and assemble the table tent.

- Photocopy the label template onto a blank sheet of copier labels to print the labels, or make your own labels.

- Leave the oil and other solvents in their original containers. Label the containers. Put water in the 1- or 2-L bottles and label the bottles.

- If the station will not be located near a source of running water (such as a sink or drinking fountain), fill several 1- or 2-L bottles with water to refill the containers of water as needed. Label the bottles appropriately.

- Separate the pages from the Paint with Water books.

- Label the small cups and child-sized paintbrushes for the liquids appropriately. Label the box for the Paint with Water pages.

Setting Up the Station

- Place Table Tent **Q** at the station in a prominent location.

- Place four small cups (one for each liquid) in a tray or cup holder (like those available from fast-food restaurants) at each setup. Pour a small amount of each liquid into its appropriate container. Place the refill bottles where they will be accessible but not in the way. Have a sponge available for cleaning up spills.

- Put the Paint with Water pages in their labeled box. Place the box at the station where it is accessible to all setups but is not in the way.

Disposal

Unused liquids can be saved. If you choose to dispose of them, be sure to dispose of oil with other oil-based wastes.

Answers and Observations

3 *What do you observe?*

Colors appear and spread across the picture. Water works best, but vinegar and rubbing alcohol also work to some extent. Colors do not appear in the section painted with oil.

4 *What do you observe?*

The section painted with oil appears almost transparent.

Answers for Child/Adult Discussion

? *The Paint with Water books are designed to be used with water. Which other liquids also worked? Which liquid worked best?*

Vinegar and rubbing alcohol also worked. Generally water will work best and oil the least well.

? *What did the oil do that the other liquids did not?*

Oil caused the paper to become almost transparent.

Reference

Sarquis, M.; Sarquis, J.; Williams, J. "Paint with Water Books," *Teaching Chemistry with TOYS;* McGraw-Hill: New York, 1995; pp 87–92.

Quaint Paint Shopping/Gathering List

Use this checklist as a guide to collecting the materials for this Family Science Challenge. Fill in the quantities needed below after doing the calculations called for in the "Calculating Quantities" section.

Total Quantities (from "Planning Notes")

_____ pages from Paint with Water book

_____ box(es)*

_____ small cups

_____ tray(s) or cup holder(s)**

_____ child-sized paintbrushes

_____ liter(s) of water

_____ ounces of vegetable, baby, or mineral oil

_____ ounces of vinegar

_____ ounces of 70% isopropyl alcohol (rubbing alcohol)

_____ paper towels

_____ sponge(s)

_____ trash can(s)

Tools for Getting Ready

☐ 3 sheets of brightly colored cardstock for Table Tent **Q**

☐ adhesive copier labels (template provided) or other materials to make labels***

☐ staple remover (if necessary)

* The box must be large enough to hold pages from a Paint with Water book (approximately 8½ inches x 11 inches) without bending them.

** A cardboard cup holder from a fast-food restaurant or a small muffin pan works well.

*** We have provided a label template that can be photocopied directly onto a blank sheet of copier labels to print all of the labels you need for the activity. Use 1-inch x 2¾-inch copier labels, such as Avery Copier Labels (code 5351). If copier labels are not available, copy the label template onto paper, cut out the labels, and use tape to affix the paper labels. Alternatively, make hand-written labels using permanent marker and masking tape or other similar materials.

Quaint Paint Setup Checklist

The following is a list of items you will need to set up the Family Science Challenge. "Planning Notes" gives step-by-step instructions for setting up the Family Science Challenge.

Items Per Station

The following materials should be left on or near the table for all family teams to use. (A station is a location where family teams work on an activity.)

Material	Total Needed	Notes
☐ Table Tent **Q**	_____	Copy master provided
☐ large, labeled box	_____	For Paint with Water pages
☐ sponge	_____	_____
☐ trash can	_____	_____

Items Per Setup

The following nonconsumable items should be placed at each setup. You may choose to provide more than one setup at each station to allow a number of family teams to work concurrently at the station.

Material	Total Needed	Notes
☐ labeled cups	_____	One each for water, oil, vinegar, and alcohol
☐ child-sized paintbrushes	_____	One each for water, oil, vinegar, and alcohol
☐ tray or cup holder	_____	_____
☐ pencil for recording observations*	_____	_____

Consumable Materials

The following materials will be used up or taken away by family teams.

Material	Total Needed	Notes
☐ Paint with Water pages	_____	_____
☐ labeled refill bottle(s) of water	_____	_____
☐ labeled refill bottle(s) of vinegar	_____	_____
☐ labeled refill bottle(s) of rubbing alcohol	_____	_____
☐ labeled refill bottle(s) of oil	_____	_____
☐ paper towels	_____	_____
☐ Family Science Challenge handouts**	_____	Copy master provided

* You may wish to pass out pencils at registration or have families bring their own pencils.

** You may wish to pass out Family Science Challenge handouts as a set at registration rather than at each station.

Quaint Paint
Label Template

Q **Paint with Water pages**
1 per family

Q Water

Q Water
Refill cup as necessary.

Q Water
Paintbrush

Q Oil

Q Oil
Refill cup as necessary.

Q Oil
Paintbrush

Q Vinegar

Q Vinegar
Refill cup as necessary.

Q Vinegar
Paintbrush

Q Rubbing Alcohol

Q Rubbing Alcohol
Refill cup as necessary.

Q Rubbing Alcohol
Paintbrush

Q Oil

Q Vinegar

Q Rubbing Alcohol

 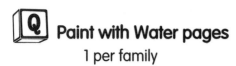

Radical Writing

Family teams determine the color of goldenrod paper painted with several common household chemicals.

. . . . ## Key Science Topics

- acid-base indicators
- acids and bases
- chemical reactions
- household chemistry

. . . . ## Average Time Required

Performance   5–10 minutes

Links to *Classroom Science from A to Z*

You can extend this activity into your science curriculum with the following ideas, included in the book *Classroom Science from A to Z:*

- Links to National Science Standards

- Science Activity 1
  Use goldenrod paper to determine the acidic, basic, or neutral nature of household products.

- Science Activity 2
  Test whether grape juice is an acid-base indicator.

- Lesson R Teacher Notes

- Lesson R Assessment

- Lesson R Science Explanation

- Lesson R Cross-Curricular Integration

Radical Writing

When you are done...

Leave at the table	Take with you
set of four liquids and brushes	used strip of goldenrod paper
tray or cup holder	clean strip of goldenrod paper
pencil (if provided at station)	completed handout

Names _____ _____

_____

Radical Writing
Family Science Challenge

Follow the colorful clues to reveal the secrets from your cupboard.

Materials

strip of goldenrod paper • pencil • set of 4 liquids: baking soda solution, water, vinegar, and dishwashing liquid, each with labeled paintbrush

Procedure

Figure 1

Figure 2

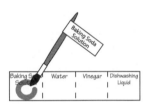

Figure 3

❶ Fold your strip of goldenrod paper into four equal sections as shown in Figure 1. Then unfold the strip to reveal the four sections. Use a pencil to label the four sections as follows: baking soda solution, water, vinegar, dishwashing liquid. (See Figure 2.)

❷ Record the original color of the goldenrod paper at the top of the Observation Table below.

❸ Brush some baking soda solution onto the "baking soda solution" section of the goldenrod paper as shown in Figure 3. Put the paintbrush back in the cup. Record your observations in the Observation Table.

❹ Apply each of the other three test liquids to the appropriate sections of the goldenrod strip. (Be sure to return each paintbrush to the appropriate cup.)

❺ Brush some vinegar over any section that is no longer yellow. Return the paintbrush to the cup. Record your observations.

❻ Brush the baking soda solution over all four sections. Return the paintbrush to the cup. Record your observations.

Observation Table				
Original color of the paper:_____				
	Section 1 baking soda solution, a base	Section 2 water, neutral	Section 3 vinegar, an acid	Section 4 dishwashing liquid
color after liquid was applied (steps ❸ and ❹)				
color after the vinegar (an acid) was applied (step ❺)				
color after the baking soda solution (a base) was applied (step ❻)				

❼ Make sure the paintbrushes are returned to the correct cups. You may take the paper strip with you or discard it in the trash.

Child/Adult Discussion

? *The goldenrod paper contains a chemical that is one color in acid (such as vinegar) and another color in base (such as baking soda). Look at your table. What color is the goldenrod paper when it is in acid?* _____ *What color is it in base?* _____

? *Based on your observations, do you think the dishwashing liquid is an acid or a base? Why?*

_____

_____

Explanation

Some chemicals are one color in an acid and another color in a base. These chemicals are called indicators. The goldenrod paper you used in this activity contains a dye that is yellow in acid (such as vinegar) and red in base (such as baking soda solution or dishwashing liquid). In this Family Science Challenge, you also saw that the indicator in the goldenrod paper can change color more than once—it was yellow originally, turned red when the baking soda solution was rubbed on it, and turned back to yellow when the vinegar was rubbed over the baking soda. This is an example of a reversible chemical reaction. Besides the color change, when the vinegar was rubbed over the baking soda, you also may have seen bubbling. These were bubbles of carbon dioxide gas, which was one of the products of the chemical reaction between vinegar and baking soda.

Stuff to Try at Home

Take a strip of goldenrod paper home with you and try the following: Make a design on the strip of goldenrod paper with clear tape or an old candle (colorless or white ones work best). Make a baking soda solution by dissolving 1 teaspoon baking soda in ¼ cup of water. Paint over and around the design on the goldenrod paper and allow the paper to dry. Why does part turn red and the rest stay yellow?

Radical Writing Planning Notes

This section will help you prepare for and carry out your Family Science event.

Calculating Quantities

"Calculating Quantities" contains information to help you calculate how much of each material you will need for your event. Copy values marked with a 🛒 onto the Shopping/Gathering List and those marked with a ✓ onto the Setup Checklist. If any of the following calculations result in fractions, round up to the next whole number.

Nonconsumable Items Per Station

Amounts listed are for one station. If you will have more than one station for this Family Science Challenge, adjust amounts accordingly.

- small, waterproof container to hold goldenrod strips 🛒 ✓
- sponge or mop and pail 🛒 ✓
- trash can
- (optional) stapler 🛒 ✓

Nonconsumable Items Per Setup

You may choose to provide more than one setup at each station to allow a number of families to work concurrently.

- small plastic containers for test solutions (such as 2-ounce condiment cups or 4- to 8-ounce cups)
  (4 small containers per setup) x _____ *setups =* _____ **small containers** 🛒 ✓

- child-sized paintbrushes
  (4 paintbrushes per setup) x _____ *setups =* _____ **child-sized paintbrushes** 🛒 ✓

- small tray or 4-cup holder
  (1 tray or cup holder per setup) x _____ *setups =* _____ **trays or cup holders** 🛒 ✓

Consumable Materials

- 1-inch x 8½-inch strips of goldenrod paper
  (2 strips per family) x _____ *families =* _____ **strips** ✓
  This allows each family one extra beyond what is required for the activity.
  _____ *strips ÷ (11 strips per sheet) =* _____ **sheets of goldenrod paper** 🛒

- baking soda solution
  How many liters of solution do I need?
  (0.015 L solution per family) x _____ *families =* _____ **liters of solution** ✓

How much baking soda (solid) do I need to make the solution?

_____ *liters of solution x (13 tablespoons baking soda solid per liter of solution) =*

_____ tablespoons of baking soda solid 🛒 **OR**

_____ *tablespoons x (20 grams per tablespoon) =* **_____ grams of baking soda solid** 🛒

How much water do I need to make the solution?

_____ *liters of solution =* **_____ liters of water** 🛒

- water (to use as a test liquid)
  (0.015 L water per family) x _____ *families =* **_____ liters of water** 🛒 ✓

- 1- or 2-L plastic bottles to make and store baking soda solution and water in
  _____ *liters of baking soda solution +* _____ *liters of water =* **_____ 1-L bottles** 🛒 ✓ **OR**
  _____ *1-L bottles ÷ 2 =* **_____ 2-L bottles** 🛒 ✓

- white vinegar
  (½ fluid ounce per family) x _____ *families =* **_____ fluid ounces of vinegar** 🛒 ✓

- dishwashing liquid
  (½ fluid ounce per family) x _____ *families =* **_____ fluid ounces of dishwashing liquid** 🛒 ✓

Getting Ready for the Family Science Challenge
Tools or General Supplies Needed for Preparation Only

- 3 sheets of brightly colored cardstock for Table Tent **R**
- adhesive copier labels (template provided) or other materials to make labels
- Windex® with Ammonia-D
- paper cutter or scissors
- tablespoon measure

Preparing Materials for Use

- Photocopy the Family Science Challenge handout master to make the number of copies needed.

- Photocopy the Table Tent **R** master onto three sheets of brightly colored cardstock and assemble the table tent.

- Photocopy the label template onto a blank sheet of copier labels to print the labels, or make your own labels.

  Do not get ammonia in your eyes—it will cause severe damage. Should contact occur, immediately wash the eyes with large quantities of cool water for at least 15 minutes.
- Test the goldenrod paper. (Since goldenrod paper is dyed in different ways, even paper from the same supplier may not always be the same.) A quick method for testing paper is to spray it with Windex® with Ammonia-D to see if a color change occurs. (The paper should turn dark orange or red.)

- Cut the goldenrod paper into strips approximately 1 inch x 8½ inches.

- For each setup label four small plastic containers (such as 8-ounce cups) with the test liquids to be used: "Baking Soda Solution," "Vinegar," "Dishwashing Liquid," and "Water."

- For each setup label four child-sized paintbrushes by flagging them with labels of the test liquids to be used: "Baking Soda Solution," "Vinegar," "Dishwashing Liquid," and "Water." (See figure.)

- Prepare the baking soda solution in the required number of empty 1-L or 2-L plastic bottles by almost filling each bottle with water and adding 13 tablespoons baking soda for each liter of water used. Cap the bottle(s) and shake well to mix. Some undissolved baking soda will probably remain at the bottom of the bottle; this is okay. Label the bottle(s).

- Fill the required number of 1-L or 2-L plastic bottles with water and label them.

- Label the container for storing goldenrod paper strips. The container could be a "pop beaker," which can be made by cutting off the top of a 2-L bottle.

Setting Up the Station

- Place Table Tent **R** at the station in a prominent location.

- Place the refill bottles of baking soda solution, water, vinegar, and dishwashing liquid at the station but out of the way of the setups. We recommend leaving the vinegar and dishwashing liquid in their original containers.

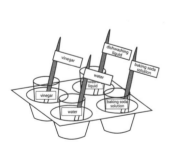

- For each setup, fill a set of the four small, labeled containers about one-quarter full with the appropriate test liquids. Keep the extra liquids in storage bottles on reserve at the station to refill the small containers as needed.

- Set the small containers of test liquids in a small tray or cup holder (like those available from fast-food restaurants) to minimize the chance of spills. Place the appropriate labeled paintbrush in each cup. (See figure.)

- Put the goldenrod paper strips in their labeled pop beaker or other container.

- Have a sponge or mop and pail close by to clean up spills that may occur.

Tips

- You may wish to set up this activity close to a sink to allow disposal of test liquids that become contaminated.
- You may wish to put a stapler at each station so families can staple their test strips to their Family Science Challenge handouts.

Disposal

Unused test liquids can be saved for future use or poured down the drain. Any liquids already poured into dispensing cups should be discarded rather than saved, because contamination is very likely.

Answers and Observations

Observation Table				
Original color of the paper: _____ yellow _____				
	Section 1 baking soda solution, a base	Section 2 water, neutral	Section 3 vinegar, an acid	Section 4 dishwashing liquid
color after liquid was applied (steps ❸ and ❹)	red	yellow	yellow	red
color after the vinegar (an acid) was applied (step ❺)	yellow	yellow	yellow	yellow
color after the baking soda solution (a base) was applied (step ❻)	red	red	red	red

Answers for Child/Adult Discussion

? *Look at your table. What color is the goldenrod paper when it is in acid? What color is it in base?*

The paper is yellow in an acid and red in a base.

? *Based on your observations, do you think the dishwashing liquid is an acid or a base? Why?*

The dishwashing liquid is a base. It turned yellow goldenrod paper red as did the baking soda solution, the known base.

Radical Writing Shopping/Gathering List

Use this checklist as a guide to collecting the materials for this Family Science Challenge. Fill in the quantities needed below after doing the calculations called for in the "Calculating Quantities" section

Total Quantities (from "Planning Notes")

_____ goldenrod paper*

_____ container(s) to hold goldenrod strips

_____ small plastic containers for test solutions (such as 2-ounce condiment cups or 4- to 8-ounce cups)

_____ child-sized paintbrushes

_____ small tray(s) or 4-cup holder(s)**

_____ liters of baking soda solution

_____ tablespoons/grams of baking soda (solid)

_____ liters of water

_____ liters of water

_____ fluid ounces of white vinegar

_____ fluid ounces of dishwashing liquid ***

_____ 1- or 2-L plastic soft-drink bottles

_____ sponge(s) or mop and pail

_____ trash can(s)

_____ (optional) stapler(s)

Tools for Getting Ready

☐ 3 sheets of brightly colored cardstock for Table Tent **R**

☐ adhesive copier labels (template provided) or other materials to make labels†

☐ Windex® with Ammonia-D

☐ paper cutter or pair of scissors

☐ tablespoon measure

*　Not all brands of goldenrod paper contain the indicator dye that is required for this activity. Brands of goldenrod paper that have worked for this activity include Astro Bright's "Galaxy Gold" paper (style #100126) and Mead paper. However, even if using the papers mentioned here or another brand you have used before, test them before using. (See "Getting Ready for the Family Science Challenge.") Goldenrod paper for this activity is available from Terrific Science Books, Kits, & More, 513/727-3269, #GRP01.

**　A cardboard cup holder from a fast-food restaurant or a small muffin pan works well for this.

*** Brands of dishwashing liquid that have worked for this activity include Dawn®, Ultra Joy®, and Ivory®. Other brands may also work; make sure to test whatever brand you will be using before your Family Science event.

†　We have provided a label template that can be photocopied directly onto a blank sheet of copier labels to print all of the labels you need for the activity. Use 1-inch x 2¾-inch copier labels, such as Avery Copier Labels (code 5351). If copier labels are not available, copy the label template onto paper, cut out the labels, and use tape to affix the paper labels.

Radical Writing Setup Checklist

The following is a list of items you will need to set up the Family Science Challenge. "Getting Ready for the Family Science Challenge" gives step-by-step instructions for setting up the Family Science Challenge.

Items Per Station

The following materials should be left on or near the table for all family teams to use. (A station is a location where family teams work on an activity.)

Material	Total Needed	Notes
☐ Table Tent **R**	_____	Copy master provided
☐ labeled container	_____	For goldenrod strips
☐ sponge or mop and pail	_____	_____
☐ trash can	_____	_____
☐ (optional) stapler	_____	_____

Items Per Setup

The following nonconsumable items will be needed for each setup. You may choose to provide more than one setup at each station to allow a number of family teams to work concurrently at the station.

Material	Total Needed	Notes
☐ set of 4 labeled cups	_____	For baking soda solution, vinegar, water, and dishwashing liquid
☐ set of 4 labeled paintbrushes	_____	For baking soda solution, vinegar, water, and dishwashing liquid
☐ small tray or cup holder	_____	_____
☐ pencil for recording observations*	_____	_____

Consumable Materials

The following materials will be used up or taken away by family teams.

Material	Total Needed	Notes
☐ strips of goldenrod paper	_____	_____
☐ refill bottle(s) of baking soda solution	_____	_____
☐ refill bottle(s) of water	_____	_____
☐ refill bottle(s) of white vinegar	_____	Leave in the original container
☐ refill bottle(s) of dishwashing liquid	_____	Leave in the original container
☐ paper towels	_____	_____
☐ Family Science Challenge handouts**	_____	Copy master provided

* You may wish to pass out pencils at registration or have families bring their own pencils.

** You may wish to pass out Family Science Challenge handouts as a set at registration rather than at each station.

Reproduced from *Science Night Family Fun from* Ⓐ *to* Ⓩ

Radical Writing
Label Template

R **Goldenrod Strips**
Use 1. You may take it with you.

R **Vinegar**
Please leave at the station.

R **Baking Soda Solution**
Please leave at the station.

R **Dishwashing Liquid**
Please leave at the station.

R **Water**
Please leave at the station.

R **Goldenrod Strips**
Use 1. You may take it with you.

R **Vinegar**
Please leave at the station.

R **Baking Soda Solution**
Please leave at the station.

R **Dishwashing Liquid**
Please leave at the station.

R **Water**
Please leave at the station.

R **Goldenrod Strips**
Use 1. You may take it with you.

R **Vinegar**
Please leave at the station.

R **Baking Soda Solution**
Please leave at the station.

R **Dishwashing Liquid**
Please leave at the station.

R **Water**
Please leave at the station.

R **Goldenrod Strips**
Use 1. You may take it with you.

Singing Straws

Family teams make their own Singing Straws and use them to explore the production of sound and to investigate the relationship between the length of the straw and the pitch of the sound.

. . . . **Key Science Topics**

- pitch
- sound
- vibrations

. . . . **Average Time Required**

Performance   10 minutes

Links to *Classroom Science from A to Z*

You can extend this activity into your science curriculum with the following ideas, included in the book *Classroom Science from A to Z:*

- Links to National Science Standards

- Science Activity
  See the changes that result when holes are added to a Singing Straw.

- Lesson S Teacher Notes

- Lesson S Assessment

- Lesson S Science Explanation

- Lesson S Cross-Curricular Integration

Singing Straws

When you are done...

Throw away	Leave at the table	Take with you
straw scraps	tape scissors pencil (if provided at station)	Singing Straw completed handout

Singing Straws
Family Science Challenge

Make music and discover that "reeding" is fun.

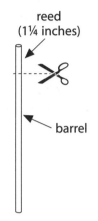

reed
(1¼ inches)

barrel

Figure 2

Materials

2 fat plastic straws • thin plastic straw • scissors • tape

Procedure

❶ Hold one of the fat straws gently between your fingers and blow through it. (For health reasons, do not share straws.)

? *What do you hear? What do you feel?*

_____

_____

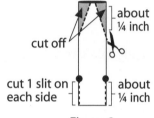

about ¼ inch

cut off

cut 1 slit on each side

about ¼ inch

Figure 3

❷ Make a Singing Straw by doing the following steps:

   a. Cut a 1¼-inch piece (see Figure 1 at right) from one end of one fat straw to serve as the reed. The longer straw piece will be the barrel of the Singing Straw. (See Figure 2.)

   b. Shape the reed by flattening it and cutting both ends as shown in Figure 3.

   c. Slip the square end of the reed over the barrel piece. Slide the end of the barrel up into the reed until it is above the bottom slits of the reed but below the top slits. (See Figure 4.)

   d. Once the pieces are in position, tape the reed to the barrel. (See Figure 5.)

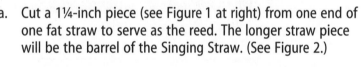

¼ inches

1¼ inches

¼ inches

Figure 1

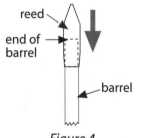

reed

end of barrel

barrel

Figure 4

❸ Press the reed and top of the barrel together with your lips and blow through the reed. Adjust the pressure of your lips until you achieve sound. It may help to moisten the reed and flatten it between your teeth to make a better seal between your lips and the reed.

Only the adult partner should use the scissors in step 4.

❹ Have your adult partner get ready; you will need him or her to carefully but quickly snip small pieces off the bottom of your straw barrel while you "play" your Singing Straw. Now take a breath and blow while your partner cuts the straw barrel. Try to keep producing sound as the straw is cut.

? *How does the sound change?*

_____

_____

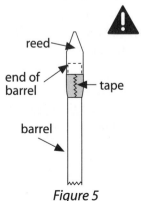

reed

end of barrel

tape

barrel

Figure 5

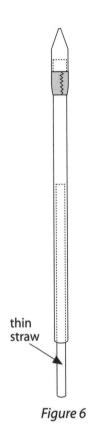

thin
straw

Figure 6

5 Remove the reed and attach it to another fat straw. Slide the thin straw inside the fat straw. (See Figure 6.) Try blowing through the reed into the straw while moving the thin straw in and out of the fat straw.

? *What happens to the sound?*

_____

_____

6 Discard straw scraps in the trash. If you keep your Singing Straws, be sure not to let anyone else blow through them because of the danger of transmitting colds or other more serious diseases. Return the scissors and tape to the station supplies.

Child/Adult Discussion

? *What effect does using a reed have?*

_____

_____

? *Which will make the lower sound, a 3-inch-long Singing Straw or a 7-inch-long Singing Straw?*

_____

_____

Explanation

As you talk, air rushes over special structures in your throat called "vocal cords," which vibrate, producing sound. The sound travels into your mouth, where the positions of your lips and tongue turn these sounds into letters and words. When you put your fingers on your throat as you say your name, the vibrations you feel are caused by air passing over your vocal cords.

The reed of the Singing Straw acts similarly to the way your vocal cords do. When you blow through the straw, the pointed ends of the reed vibrate, producing the sound you hear. The whole straw becomes a vibrating column of air, and the length of this column affects the pitch of the sound. Longer columns produce lower pitches, and shorter columns produce higher pitches. By cutting off pieces of the straw and by moving the thin straw up and down inside the fat straw, you change the length of the column, and thus you change the pitch.

Your Singing Straw belongs to the reed branch of the woodwind family of musical instruments. Reed instruments (like the saxophone, clarinet, and oboe) use a vibrating reed to produce sound, and the player lengthens and shortens the column of vibrating air by opening and closing holes located along the instrument.

Singing Straws Planning Notes

This section will help you prepare for and carry out your Family Science event.

Calculating Quantities

"Calculating Quantities" contains information to help you calculate how much of each material you will need for your event. Copy values marked with a 🛒 onto the Shopping/Gathering List and those marked with a ✓ onto the Setup Checklist. If any of the calculations result in fractions, round up to the next whole number.

Nonconsumable Items Per Station

Amounts listed are for one station. If you will have more than one station for this Family Science Challenge, adjust amounts accordingly.

- container for straws 🛒 ✓
- trash can 🛒 ✓

Nonconsumable Items Per Setup

You may choose to provide more than one setup at each station to allow a number of family teams to work concurrently.

- sharp scissors
  *(1 pair of scissors per setup) x _____ setups = _____ **pairs of scissors*** 🛒 ✓

Consumable Materials

- thin plastic straws
  *(1 thin straw per family) x _____ families + 20 spares = _____ **thin straws*** 🛒 ✓

- fat plastic straws (large enough in diameter to fit over the thin straw)
  *(2 fat straws per family) x _____ families + 20 spares = _____ **fat straws*** 🛒 ✓

- tape
  *estimate (3 linear inches of tape per family) x _____ families = _____ **linear inches of tape*** 🛒 ✓

Getting Ready for the Family Science Challenge
Tools or General Supplies Needed for Preparation Only

- 3 sheets of brightly colored cardstock for Table Tent **S**
- adhesive copier labels (template provided) or other materials to make labels

Preparing Materials for Use

- Photocopy the Family Science Challenge handout master to make the number of copies needed.

- Photocopy the Table Tent **S** master onto three sheets of brightly colored cardstock and assemble the table tent.

- Photocopy the label template onto a blank sheet of copier labels to print the labels, or make your own labels.

- Label one container "fat straws" and one container "thin straws." If you are leaving the straws in their original boxes, label the boxes.

Setting Up the Station

- Place Table Tent **S** at the station in a prominent location.

- If the straws are not being left in their original boxes, place the straws in their appropriately labeled containers. Put the straw containers at the station where they are accessible to all setups but are out of the way.

- Place a pair of scissors and a roll of tape at each setup.

Answers and Observations

❶ *What do you hear? What do you feel?*

We hear air passing through the straw and feel the straw vibrating.

❹ *How does the sound change?*

The pitch of the sound gets higher as the straw gets shorter.

❺ *What happens to the sound?*

The pitch gets higher as the thin straw moves in and lower as it moves out.

Answers for Child/Adult Discussion

? *What effect does using a reed have?*

Blowing through the straw without the reed does not produce the kazoo sounds heard when the reed is in place.

? *Which will make the lower sound, a 3-inch-long Singing Straw or a 7-inch-long Singing Straw?*

The 7-inch-long Singing Straw will make the lower sound.

Singing Straws Shopping/Gathering List

Use this checklist as a guide to collecting the materials for this Family Science Challenge. Fill in the quantities needed below after doing the calculations called for in the "Calculating Quantities" section.

Total Quantities (from "Planning Notes")

_____ thin straws*

_____ fat straws*

_____ containers for straws**

_____ sharp scissors***

_____ inches of tape

_____ trash can(s)

Tools for Getting Ready

☐ 3 sheets of brightly colored cardstock for Table Tent **S**

☐ adhesive copier labels (template provided) or other materials to make labels†

* Drinking straws work well for this activity and may be found in grocery or party supply stores. Coffee stirrers are good thin straws. Some straws do not spring back open when you cut them, which will cause problems when participants are cutting the straws while someone else is blowing into them. Test one fat straw by following the procedure for the Family Science Challenge to make sure this brand of straw will open properly.

** Pop beakers made by cutting off the tops of 2-L plastic soft-drink bottles work well. Alternatively, the straws can be left in their original boxes, if appropriate.

*** The scissors must be sharp enough to cut through plastic and should only be used by the adult partners. Most safety scissors are not sharp enough to cut plastic.

† We have provided a label template that can be photocopied directly onto a blank sheet of copier labels to print all of the labels you need for the activity. Use 1-inch x 2¾-inch copier labels, such as Avery Copier Labels (code 5351). If copier labels are not available, copy the label template onto paper, cut out the labels, and use tape to affix the paper labels. Alternatively, make hand-written labels using permanent marker and masking tape or other similar materials.

Singing Straws
Setup Checklist

The following is a list of items you will need to set up the Family Science Challenge. "Planning Notes" gives step-by-step instructions for setting up the Family Science Challenge.

Items Per Station

The following materials should be left on or near the table for all family teams to use. (A station is a location where family teams work on an activity.)

Material	Total Needed	Notes
☐ Table Tent **S**	_____	Copy master provided
☐ labeled containers	_____	One for thin straws and one for fat straws
☐ trash can	_____	_____

Items Per Setup

The following nonconsumable items should be placed at each setup. You may choose to provide more than one setup at each station to allow a number of family teams to work concurrently.

Material	Total Needed	Notes
☐ sharp scissors	_____	_____
☐ pencil for recording observations*	_____	_____

Consumable Materials

The following materials will be used up or taken away by family teams.

Material	Total Needed	Notes
☐ thin straws	_____	_____
☐ fat straws	_____	_____
☐ tape	_____	_____
☐ Family Science Challenge handouts**	_____	Copy master provided

*   You may wish to pass out pencils at registration or have families bring their own pencils.

** You may wish to pass out Family Science Challenge handouts as a set at registration rather than at each station.

Singing Straws
Label Template

S Thin Straws
Use 1 per family, please.

S Thin Straws
Use 1 per family, please.

S Fat Straws
Use 2 per family, please.

S Fat Straws
Use 2 per family, please.

S Thin Straws
Use 1 per family, please.

S Thin Straws
Use 1 per family, please.

S Fat Straws
Use 2 per family, please.

S Fat Straws
Use 2 per family, please.

S Thin Straws
Use 1 per family, please.

S Thin Straws
Use 1 per family, please.

S Fat Straws
Use 2 per family, please.

S Fat Straws
Use 2 per family, please.

S Thin Straws
Use 1 per family, please.

S Thin Straws
Use 1 per family, please.

S Fat Straws
Use 2 per family, please.

S Fat Straws
Use 2 per family, please.

Tornado in a Bottle

Family teams examine a tornado in a bottle and observe the effect the vortex has on the movement of water from one bottle to another.

Key Science Topics

- circular motion
- soap bubbles
- vortex

Average Time Required

Performance   10–15 minutes

Links to *Classroom Science from A to Z*

You can extend this activity into your science curriculum with the following ideas, included in the book *Classroom Science from A to Z:*

- Links to National Science Standards

- Science Activity
  Investigate how including additives in the water affects the vortex created.

- Lesson T Teacher Notes

- Lesson T Assessment

- Lesson T Science Explanation

- Lesson T Cross-Curricular Integration

Tornado in a Bottle

When you are done...

Leave at the table	Take with you
Tornado in a Bottle toys	completed handout
Glug-Glug Bottle	
clock with second hand	
pencil (if provided at station)	

Tornado in a Bottle
Family Science Challenge

Discover a new twist on emptying a bottle.

Materials

several Tornado in a Bottle toys • Glug-Glug Bottle • clock with second hand

Procedure

To prevent spills, please do not open any of the containers used in this activity.

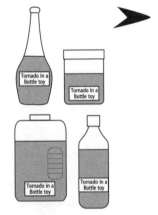

Figure 1

❶ Select one of the Tornado in a Bottle toys from the station. Swirl it continuously in the same direction until you see a tornado-like vortex. If you can't get the vortex to form, ask the station monitor to show you how.

❷ Repeat step 1 using the other Tornado in a Bottle toys that are available. Compare the vortices produced in the different toys.

? *What do you observe?*

_____

_____

❸ Select the Glug-Glug Bottle from the station. (See Figure 2.) Leave the two bottles connected. Turn them over and observe what happens.

? *What do you observe?*

_____

_____

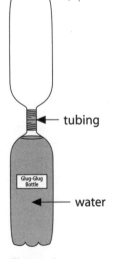

tubing

water

Figure 2

❹ Turn the Glug-Glug Bottle over again, but time how long it takes for all the water to empty from one bottle into the other. If a clock with a second hand is not available, count the seconds by saying "One-Mississippi, two-Mississippi, three-Mississippi," etc.

? *Record the time* _____

❺ Repeat step 4, but this time swirl the Glug-Glug Bottle to make a vortex like you did with the Tornado in a Bottle toys.

? *What happens?*

_____

_____

6 Repeat step 5, but time how long it takes for the water to completely empty from one bottle into the other.

? *How long did it take? Was it slower or faster than when the bottle was not swirled?*

_____

_____

Child/Adult Discussion

? *What was moving in the bottles besides the water?*

_____

_____

? *What were some of the differences between what happened when you transferred the water without swirling (step 4) and with swirling (step 6)?*

_____

_____

? *Did forming a vortex in the Glug-Glug Bottle help speed up the transfer of water? If so, how?*

_____

_____

Explanation

Swirling a bottle of water in a circular motion creates a vortex as the water moves against the sides of the bottle. The Tornado in a Bottle toys contain water with a little salt and soap dissolved in it. This soap causes small bubbles to form when the bottle is swirled. A tornado-like vortex remains visible for several seconds after you stop swirling the bottle because the liquid and the soap bubbles inside are still moving. Different sizes and shapes of bottles typically give different-looking vortices that often follow very different paths.

With the Glug-Glug Bottle, you used the vortex created when you swirled the unit to actually help you empty the water more quickly. The vortex helped because it allowed air to move from the bottom bottle into the top bottle without having to be forced through the water. This simultaneous movement of the air allows the water to move more quickly from the top to the bottom bottle.

Stuff to Try at Home

Fill different shapes and sizes of bottles with water and turn them upside down over a sink to empty. Do the bottles empty faster if you swirl them? Or fill a narrow-mouthed bottle with water and cover the mouth with your thumb. Then invert the bottle over a sink, swirl it, and remove your thumb.

Tornado in a Bottle Planning Notes

This section will help you prepare for and carry out your Family Science event.

Calculating Quantities

"Calculating Quantities" contains information to help you calculate how much of each material you will need for your event. Copy values marked with a 🛒 onto the Shopping/Gathering List and those marked with a ✓ onto the Setup Checklist. If any of the calculations result in fractions, round up to the next whole number.

Nonconsumable Items Per Station

Amounts listed are for one station. If you will have more than one station for this Family Science Challenge, adjust the amounts accordingly.

- 4 or 5 Tornado in a Bottle toys made from the following materials:
  Do not use glass bottles, as they could slip out of someone's hand and shatter.
  - clear, colorless plastic bottles and jars of assorted sizes (not larger than 1-L) and shapes with caps for the Tornado in a Bottle toys
    (1 bottle per setup) x _____ setups + 1 extra bottle = **_____ 1-L or smaller plastic bottles with caps** 🛒

  - water
    enough water to three-quarters-fill the Tornado in a Bottle toys

  - salt
    (½ teaspoon salt per Tornado in a Bottle toy) x _____ Tornado In a Bottle toys = **_____ teaspoons of salt** 🛒

  - dishwashing liquid
    estimate (1 drop per Tornado in a Bottle toy) x _____ Tornado in a Bottle toys = **_____ drops of dishwashing liquid** 🛒

- mop, sponge, and bucket for cleanup of possible spills
- (optional) clock with second hand

Nonconsumable Items Per Setup

You may choose to provide more than one setup at each station to allow a number of family teams to work concurrently.

- Glug-Glug Bottle made from the following:
  - 2, 1- or 2-L clear, colorless plastic soft-drink bottles
    For each setup, you will need two bottles of the same size.
    (2 bottles per setup) x _____ setups = _____ **1- or 2-L soft drink bottles** 🛒
  - water
    enough water to fill one of the soft-drink bottles to within 1–2 inches of the top
  - flexible plastic tubing with an inner diameter of 1 inch and an outer diameter of 1¼ inch
    (1 piece of tubing per setup) x _____ setups = _____ pieces of tubing
    _____ pieces of tubing x (1.75 inches per piece) = _____ **inches of tubing** 🛒

Getting Ready for the Family Science Challenge

Tools or General Supplies Needed for Preparation Only

- 3 sheets of brightly colored cardstock for Table Tent **T**
- adhesive copier labels (template provided) or other materials to make labels
- scissors or utility knife
- bottle of red, blue, or green food color
- teaspoon measure
- toothpick
- (optional) waterproof tape

Preparing Materials for Use

- Photocopy the Family Science Challenge handout master to make the number of copies needed.

- Photocopy the Table Tent **T** master onto three sheets of brightly colored cardstock and assemble the table tent.

- Photocopy the label template onto a blank sheet of copier labels to print the labels, or make your own labels.

- Prepare the Tornado in a Bottle toys by filling the bottles and jars about three-quarters full with water. (Use clear, colorless plastic bottles of assorted sizes but none larger than 1 L.) Add a drop of food color to lightly color the water. Add ½ teaspoon salt to each container. Cap the container and gently shake it to dissolve the salt. Open the container, dip a toothpick into the dishwashing liquid, and lightly touch the toothpick to the salt solution to add a very small amount of dishwashing liquid. Cap the container again and swirl the bottle in a circular motion until you observe the vortex. If the vortex is not clearly visible, add just a bit more liquid detergent, using the toothpick method described above. Do not repeat this addition more than three times, as it is very easy to add too much soap, which will lead to excessive sudsing. If too many suds form, hold the bottle over a sink, completely fill the bottle with water so that the bubbles spill out the top, and then pour off the excess water. Label the Tornado in a Bottle toys appropriately.

- Prepare each Glug-Glug Bottle by filling one 1- or 2-L clear, colorless plastic soft-drink bottle with water to within 1–2 inches of the top. Add several drops of food color. Use scissors or a utility knife to cut a 1¾-inch-long piece of 1-inch-diameter flexible plastic tubing. Put the piece of tubing over the neck of the bottle. Invert the second empty bottle (same size as the first bottle) and attach it to the other end of the tubing. Push to be sure the seal is tight. Hold the connected bottles over a sink and invert the unit several times to make sure it doesn't leak. If it does leak, try pushing the bottles into the tubing more firmly, using different bottles, or wrapping the ends of the tubing (where the tubing meets the bottle) with waterproof tape. Label the Glug-Glug Bottle appropriately.

Setting Up the Station

- Place Table Tent **T** at the station in a prominent location.

- Set the assorted Tornado in a Bottle toys at the station where they will be accessible from all setups.

- Put a Glug-Glug Bottle at each setup.

- Have a mop, sponge, and bucket handy in case someone tries to open the containers and spills the water.

Answers and Observations

❷ *What do you observe?*

All of the toys should produce vortices that differ slightly depending on the size and shape of the container.

❸ *What do you observe?*

The water flows from the top bottle to the bottom bottle, pausing occasionally while a big bubble of air moves upward.

❺ *What happens?*

The water flows more smoothly from the top bottle to the bottom bottle.

❻ *How long did it take? Was it slower or faster than when the bottle was not swirled?*

This time should be shorter than the time measured in step 4.

Planning Notes

Answers for Child/Adult Discussion

? *What was moving in the bottles besides the water?*

Air was also moving in the bottles.

? *What were some of the differences between what happened when you transferred the water without swirling (step 4) and with swirling (step 6)?*

Transferring the water between bottles took longer when the bottles were not swirled.

? *Did forming a vortex in the Glug-Glug Bottle help speed up the transfer of water? If so, how?*

Yes, it allowed the air to move easily into the top bottle without having to be forced through the water.

Tornado in a Bottle Shopping/Gathering List

Use this checklist as a guide to collecting the materials for this Family Science Challenge. Fill in the quantities needed below after doing the calculations called for in the "Calculating Quantities" section.

Total Quantities (from "Planning Notes")

_____ 1-L or smaller clear, colorless plastic bottles or jars with caps (for Tornado in a Bottle toys)*

_____ 1- or 2-L plastic soft-drink bottles (for Glug-Glug Bottles)**

_____ water to make both the Tornado in a Bottle toys and the Glug-Glug Bottles

_____ teaspoons of salt

_____ teaspoons of dishwashing liquid***

_____ flexible plastic tubing with an inner diameter of 1 inch and an outer diameter of 1¼ inch[†]

_____ mop, sponge, and bucket for cleanup

_____ (optional) clock with second hand[††]

Tools for Getting Ready

☐ 3 sheets of brightly colored cardstock for Table Tent **T**

☐ adhesive copier labels (template provided) or other materials to make labels[†††]

☐ scissors or utility knife

☐ bottle of red, blue, or green food color

☐ teaspoon measure

☐ toothpick

☐ (optional) waterproof tape

*   Use assorted sizes and shapes. Examples of clear, colorless plastic bottles and jars that are smaller than 1 L include 20-ounce soft-drink bottles, juice bottles, cooking oil bottles, peanut butter jars, and some dishwashing liquid bottles.

**   If you use both 1- and 2-L bottles, be sure you have an even number of each type of bottle.

***   As the amount of dishwashing liquid needed is very small, you may want to bring a small amount from home or ask another teacher or parent to provide it instead of buying an entire bottle.

[†]   Flexible plastic tubing is available at most large hardware stores. As you will need only a 1¾-inch piece, buy the smallest length of tubing possible. Alternatively, you could check with other people to see whether they have a small piece of tubing they would be willing to donate.

[††]   If the room in which you will be holding the Family Science event has a clock with a second hand on the wall, you may want to set up the station near the clock and alert family teams to the location of the clock.

[†††]   We have provided a label template that can be photocopied directly onto a blank sheet of copier labels to print all of the labels you need for the activity. Use 1-inch x 2¾-inch copier labels, such as Avery Copier Labels (code 5351). If copier labels are not available, copy the label template onto paper, cut out the labels, and use tape to affix the paper labels. Alternatively, make hand-written labels using permanent marker and masking tape or other similar materials.

Tornado in a Bottle
Setup Checklist

The following is a list of items you will need to set up the Family Science Challenge. "Planning Notes" gives step-by-step instructions for setting up the Family Science Challenge.

Items Per Station

The following materials should be left on or near the table for all family teams to use. (A station is a location where family teams work on an activity.)

Material	Total Needed	Notes
☐ Tornado in a Bottle toy	_____	Make according to the directions provided
☐ Table Tent **T**	_____	Copy master provided
☐ mop, sponge, and bucket	_____	For cleanup
☐ (optional) clock with second hand	_____	

Items Per Setup

The following nonconsumable items will be needed for each setup. You may choose to provide more than one setup at each station to allow a number of family teams to work concurrently.

Material	Total Needed	Notes
☐ Glug-Glug Bottle	_____	Make according to the directions provided
☐ pencil for recording observations*	_____	

Consumable Materials

The following materials will be used up or taken away by family teams.

Material	Total Needed	Notes
☐ Family Science Challenge handouts**	_____	Copy master provided

* You may wish to pass out pencils at registration or have families bring their own pencils.

** You may wish to pass out Family Science Challenge handouts as a set at registration rather than at each station.

Tornado in a Bottle
Label Template

T **Tornado in a Bottle toy**
Please leave at the station.

T **Glug-Glug Bottle**
Please leave at the station.

T **Tornado in a Bottle toy**
Please leave at the station.

T **Glug-Glug Bottle**
Please leave at the station.

T **Tornado in a Bottle toy**
Please leave at the station.

T **Glug-Glug Bottle**
Please leave at the station.

T **Tornado in a Bottle toy**
Please leave at the station.

T **Glug-Glug Bottle**
Please leave at the station.

T **Tornado in a Bottle toy**
Please leave at the station.

T **Glug-Glug Bottle**
Please leave at the station.

T **Tornado in a Bottle toy**
Please leave at the station.

T **Glug-Glug Bottle**
Please leave at the station.

T **Tornado in a Bottle toy**
Please leave at the station.

T **Glug-Glug Bottle**
Please leave at the station.

T **Tornado in a Bottle toy**
Please leave at the station.

T **Glug-Glug Bottle**
Please leave at the station.

Under Construction

Family teams become engineers as they design paper bridges and learn how shape affects strength.

Key Science Topics

- engineering
- design
- geometric shapes

Average Time Required

Performance   15–20 minutes

Links to *Classroom Science from A to Z*

You can extend this activity into your science curriculum with the following ideas, included in the book *Classroom Science from A to Z*:

- Links to National Science Standards

- Science Activity
  Investigate the strength of various geometric shapes.

- Lesson U Teacher Notes

- Lesson U Assessment

- Lesson U Science Explanation

- Lesson U Cross-Curricular Integration

Under Construction

When you are done…

Leave at the table	Take with you
blocks	your paper bridges
pennies	completed handout
cardboard	
pencil (if provided at station)	

Under Construction
Family Science Challenge

Build a better bridge.

Materials

2 blocks • Block Template • 4 strips of paper 2¼ inches x 11 inches • about 100 pennies • piece of corrugated cardboard

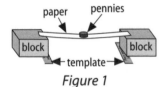

Figure 1

Procedure

❶ Place two blocks on the template on the table. Put one strip of paper on the blocks like a bridge.

❷ Without using pennies or your fingers to anchor the ends of the paper, place pennies on the suspended part of the bridge as shown in Figure 1. Continue adding pennies until the bridge collapses or you run out of pennies.

? *How many pennies did the bridge hold?* _____

❸ The stacking arrangement of the pennies on the strip makes a difference in how many it will hold. Try some different arrangements.

? *Draw the stacking arrangement that gave the best results in the space to the left.*

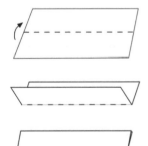

❹ Try folding the paper strip in half lengthwise as shown in Figure 2. Lay this folded strip on the blocks like you did in step 1, and see how many pennies it will hold.

? *How many pennies did the bridge hold?* _____

❺ Examine the piece of corrugated cardboard carefully, especially from the side. How many pennies do you think it will hold? Place it on the books and test it to find out the number it will actually hold. (Stop when you run out of pennies.)

Figure 2

? *How many pennies did the cardboard bridge hold?* _____

❻ Try folding three new strips of paper in different ways and see how many pennies each bridge can hold. Draw a picture of each of the bridges you tried in the Observation Chart on the next page, and record how many pennies each bridge held. (If you would like a hint, look at Figure 3 on the next page.)

❼ Clean up the station. It's okay to take the bridges you've made. Please leave the pennies, cardboard, and blocks for others to use.

Observation Chart		
drawing of bridge	drawing of bridge	drawing of bridge
# of pennies held:	# of pennies held:	# of pennies held:

Child/Adult Discussion

? *Which paper bridge design held the most pennies?*

_____

_____

? *Why could the corrugated cardboard hold more pennies than any of the paper bridges?*

_____

_____

_____

Explanation

The unfolded paper bridge holds very few pennies before it collapses because the unfolded paper is rather flimsy. When pennies are added to it, their mass exerts a downward force directly beneath the pennies which causes the paper to be pushed down. Folding the bridge lengthwise helps reinforce the bridge and make it more rigid. This in turn helps to distribute the weight of the pennies more along the length of the bridge and allows it to hold more pennies. A variety of folds can be used to increase the paper's strength even more. These include folding the sides of the paper up to make a trough shape and pleating the paper lengthwise. (See Figure 3.) The corrugated cardboard applies the ideas of folding and multiple layers to add strength and reinforce its structure and also is constructed of a stronger material than the office paper.

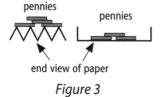

end view of paper

Figure 3

Under Construction Planning Notes

This section will help you prepare for and carry out your Family Science event.

Calculating Quantities

"Calculating Quantities" contains information to help you calculate how much of each material you will need for your event. Copy values marked with a 🛒 onto the Shopping/Gathering List and those marked with a ✓ onto the Setup Checklist. If any of the calculations result in fractions, round up to the next whole number.

Nonconsumable Items Per Station

Amounts listed are for one station. If you will have more than one station for this Family Science Challenge, adjust amounts accordingly.

- 2 containers for pennies and paper strips 🛒 ✓
- trash can or recycling bin 🛒 ✓
- (optional) stapler 🛒 ✓

Nonconsumable Items Per Setup

You may choose to provide more than one setup at each station to allow a number of family teams to work concurrently.

- 2 wooden blocks of about equal thickness
  (2 blocks per setup) x _____ setups = **_____ blocks** 🛒 ✓

- Block Template (provided)
  (1 template per setup) x _____ setups = **_____ Block Templates** 🛒 ✓

- 100 pennies
  (100 pennies per setup) x _____ setups = **_____ pennies** 🛒 ✓

- 2¼-inch x 11-inch pieces of corrugated cardboard
  (1 piece per setup) x _____ setups = **_____ pieces of corrugated cardboard** 🛒 ✓

Consumable Materials

- 2¼-inch x11-inch strips of office paper
  (4 strips per family) x _____ families = **_____ strips of office paper** ✓
  _____ strips of office paper ÷ (4 strips per sheet of office paper) = **_____ sheets of office paper 8½ inches x 11 inches** 🛒

Getting Ready for the Family Science Challenge

Tools or General Supplies Needed for Preparation Only

- 3 sheets of brightly colored cardstock for Table Tent **U**
- adhesive copier labels (template provided) or other materials to make labels
- scissors or paper cutter
- ruler
- utility knife
- masking tape

Preparing Materials for Use

Use caution when working with the utility knife.

- Photocopy the Family Science Challenge handout master to make the number of copies needed.

- Photocopy the Block Template master to make the number of copies needed. Cut each sheet in half.

- Photocopy the Table Tent **U** master onto three sheets of brightly colored cardstock and assemble.

- Photocopy the label template onto a blank sheet of copier labels to print the labels, or make your own labels.

- Use a utility knife to cut the cardboard into 2¼-inch x 11-inch pieces. Make sure that at least one cross-section of each piece shows the corrugation of the cardboard clearly.

- Cut the sheets of office paper into 2¼-inch x 11-inch strips. Each sheet of office paper should yield eight strips.

- Label a container, such as a plastic cup or "pop beaker" made by cutting off the top of a 2-liter bottle, to hold the pennies.

- Label a container, such as a shoe box, pencil box, or plastic bag to hold the paper strips so they will not get bent or crumpled before use.

Setting Up the Station

- Place Table Tent **U** at the station in a prominent location.

- Place a Block Template at each setup. The template will serve as a guide for families to place the wooden blocks at the appropriate distance.

- Place a trash can or recycling bin at the station so family teams can discard their paper bridges if they wish.

- Put the pennies and paper strips into their respective containers and set the containers where they will be accessible to family teams.

- You may wish to put a stapler at the station so families can staple their bridges to their Family Science Challenge handouts.

Disposal

The paper can be recycled.

Answers and Observations

2 *How many pennies did the bridge hold?*

Answers will vary, but the paper will not hold many pennies.

4 *How many pennies did the bridge hold?*

Answers will vary, but the folded paper should hold more pennies than the unfolded paper.

5 *How many pennies did the cardboard bridge hold?*

Answers will vary, but the corrugated cardboard should hold more pennies than the paper bridges.

Answers for Child/Adult Discussion

? *Which paper bridge design held the most pennies?*

Answers will vary, but the records set during our testing were 63 pennies for the trough design and 45 pennies for the pleated design. How the pennies are added will also influence the results.

? *Why could the corrugated cardboard hold more pennies than any of the paper bridges?*

The cardboard applies two strengthening techniques—folding and multiple layers—and therefore holds more pennies than any bridge made from a single strip of paper. It is also constructed of a stronger material than office paper.

Under Construction Shopping/Gathering List

Use this checklist as a guide to collecting the materials for this Family Science Challenge. Fill in the quantities needed below after doing the calculations called for in the "Calculating Quantities" section.

Total Quantities (from "Planning Notes")

_____ wooden blocks*

_____ sheets of office paper for Block Template

_____ sheets of office paper for strips (standard size, 8½ inches x 11 inches)**

_____ pennies***

_____ piece(s) of corrugated cardboard†

_____ containers

_____ trash can(s) or recycling bin(s)

_____ (optional) stapler(s)

Tools for Getting Ready

☐ 3 sheets of brightly colored cardstock for Table Tent **U**

☐ adhesive copier labels (template provided) or other materials to make labels††

☐ scissors or paper cutter

☐ ruler

☐ utility knife

☐ masking tape

* The blocks should be of about equal thickness.

** You can recycle previously printed paper for this use.

*** All pennies used should be from 1983 or later, because at that time pennies changed in composition and became lighter.

† The piece of corrugated cardboard will be cut to 2¼ inches x 11 inches.

†† We have provided a label template that can be photocopied directly onto a blank sheet of copier labels to print all of the labels you need for the activity. Use 1-inch x 2¾-inch copier labels, such as Avery Copier Labels (code 5351). If copier labels are not available, copy the label template onto paper, cut out the labels, and use tape to affix the paper labels. Alternatively, make hand-written labels using permanent marker and masking tape or other similar materials.

Reproduced from *Science Night Family Fun from* Ⓐ *to* Ⓩ

Under Construction
Setup Checklist

The following is a list of items you will need to set up the Family Science Challenge. "Planning Notes" gives step-by-step instructions for setting up the Family Science Challenge.

Items Per Station

The following materials should be left on or near the table for all family teams to use. (A station is a location where family teams work on an activity.)

Material	Total Needed	Notes
☐ large trash can or recycling bin	_____	_____
☐ Table Tent **U**	_____	Copy master provided
☐ 100 pennies	_____	_____
☐ 2 labeled containers	_____	For pennies and paper strips
☐ (optional) stapler	_____	_____

Items Per Setup

The following nonconsumable items will be needed for each setup. You may choose to provide more than one setup at each station to allow a number of family teams to work concurrently at the station.

Material	Total Needed	Notes
☐ 2 wooden blocks	_____	_____
☐ piece of cardboard	_____	_____
☐ Block Template	_____	Copy master provided
☐ pencil for recording observations*	_____	_____

Consumable Materials

The following materials will be used up or taken away by family teams.

Material	Total Needed	Notes
☐ paper strips	_____	_____
☐ Family Science Challenge handouts**	_____	Copy master provided

* You may wish to pass out pencils at registration or have families bring their own pencils.

** You may wish to pass out Family Science Challenge handouts as a set of registration rather than at each station.

Place wooden block here.

Place wooden block here.

U **Block Template**

Please leave at the station.

U **Block Template**

Please leave at the station.

Place wooden block here.

Place wooden block here.

Under Construction
Label Template

Paper Strips for Bridges
Use 3 or 4 per family.

Wooden Block

Pennies
Please leave at the station.

Wooden Block

Cardboard
Please leave at the station.

Paper Strips for Bridges
Use 3 or 4 per family.

Wooden Block

Pennies
Please leave at the station.

Wooden Block

Cardboard
Please leave at the station.

Paper Strips for Bridges
Use 3 or 4 per family.

Wooden Block

Pennies
Please leave at the station.

Wooden Block

Cardboard
Please leave at the station.

Wooden Block

Vertically Challenged

Family teams test their aim as they try to drop coins into a cup that is submerged in water.

Key Science Topics

• gravity   • resistance

Average Time Required

Performance   15 minutes

Links to *Classroom Science from A to Z*

You can extend this activity into your science curriculum with the following ideas, included in the book *Classroom Science from A to Z:*

• Links to National Science Standards

• Science Activity
  Students use inertia and gravity to perform simple tricks.

• Lesson V Teacher Notes

• Lesson V Assessment

• Lesson V Science Explanation

• Lesson V Cross-Curricular Integration

Vertically Challenged

When you are done...

Leave at the table	Take with you
pennies	completed handout
Dry Target	
Submerged Target	
pencil (if provided at station)	

Vertically Challenged Family Science Challenge

Ready, aim… hit the target?

Materials

10 pennies • Dry and Submerged Targets

Procedure

❶ Try dropping the pennies one by one into the Dry Target from different heights. How successful are you at hitting the target?

❷ Now try dropping a penny into the Submerged Target.

? *What happens?*

_____

_____

❸ Try dropping the coins at different angles, such as edge downward or flat side downward.

? *Does one angle work best? If so, what angle?*

_____

_____

❹ Once you decide on a height and style of release that you think works best for you, try dropping 10 pennies into the Submerged Target this way and see how successful you are.

? *How many coins made it into the Submerged Target?*

_____

Child/Adult Discussion

? *Was it easier to drop the coins into the Dry Target or to drop them into the Submerged Target?*

_____

_____

Explanation

Gravity is an important factor in this Family Science Challenge. It causes the pennies to fall when you release them. You probably had a very easy time dropping pennies into the Dry Target but found it harder to hit the Submerged Target. When the pennies hit the water, they slowed down and typically veered in one direction or another. This veering occurred because water resistance is greater than air resistance. When the pennies hit the water, it absorbed some of the kinetic energy the pennies had. The water helped to break the pennies' fall, slow them down, and cause them to veer off a straight path.

Stuff to Try at Home

Investigate the effect of dropping pennies from a consistent height off the ground but varying the depth of water the pennies must fall through. Try some tossing-type games like horseshoes or ring toss. If you have a small children's pool, try some of these games in water as well. See how your results compare.

Vertically Challenged Planning Notes

This section will help you prepare for and carry out your Family Science event.

Calculating Quantities

"Calculating Quantities" contains information to help you calculate how much of each material you will need for your event. Copy values marked with a 🛒 onto the Shopping/Gathering List and those marked with a ✓ onto the Setup Checklist. If any of the calculations result in fractions, round up to the next whole number.

Nonconsumable Items Per Station

Amounts listed are for one station. If you will have more than one station for this Family Science Challenge, adjust amounts accordingly.

- box or other container for pennies 🛒 ✓
- sponge 🛒 ✓
- trash can 🛒 ✓

Nonconsumable Items Per Setup

You may choose to provide more than one setup at each station to allow a number of family teams to work concurrently.

- pennies
  (10 pennies per setup) x _____ setups = _____ **pennies** 🛒 ✓

- 2 clear plastic jars, or pop beakers made from 1-L bottles
  (2 jars or pop beakers per setup) x _____ setups = _____ **jars or pop beakers** 🛒 ✓

- small rocks or marbles
  (2–3 small rocks or marbles per setup) x _____ setups = _____ **small rocks or marbles** 🛒 ✓

- 10-gallon aquarium or clear plastic tub
  (1 aquarium or tub per setup) x _____ setups = _____ **aquariums or clear plastic tubs** 🛒 ✓

- water
  enough to fill each aquarium or tub 🛒 ✓

- rubber mat or towel
  (1 mat or towel per setup) x _____ setups = _____ **rubber mats or towels** 🛒 ✓

Consumable Materials

- paper towels

  estimate (2 towels per family) X _____ *families =* **_____ paper towels** 🛒 ✓

Getting Ready for the Family Science Challenge

Tools or General Supplies Needed for Preparation Only

- 3 sheets of brightly colored cardstock for Table Tent **V**
- adhesive copier labels (master provided) or other materials to make labels
- clear tape

Preparing Materials for Use

- Photocopy the Family Science Challenge handout master to make the number of copies needed.

- Photocopy the Table Tent **V** master onto three sheets of brightly colored cardstock and assemble the table tent.

- Photocopy the label template onto a blank sheet of copier labels to print the labels, or make your own labels.

- Label one plastic jar or pop beaker "Dry Target" and one "Submerged Target." Apply clear tape over the Submerged Target's label to protect it from water when the container is submerged. We have suggested that wide-mouthed plastic containers be used for the Dry Target to prevent any possibility of glass breakage.

- Label the penny container.

Setting Up the Station

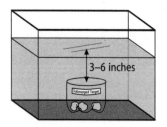

- For each setup, place the 10-gallon aquarium or clear plastic tub on a rubber mat or towel on the floor and fill it about three-quarters full with water. Carefully place the Submerged Target in the aquarium or tub. Add a few small rocks or marbles to weight the target down so it will stay submerged during the activity. The water level should be 3–6 inches above the rim of the Submerged Target.

- Set the plastic Dry Target on the floor at least 1 foot away from the aquarium or tub containing the Submerged Target.

- Put the pennies in their labeled container. Set out a sponge to wipe up spills.

Tips

- To prevent people from tripping over or kicking the items on the floor, make a barrier of chairs or other items on either side of each setup.

Answers and Observations

❷ *What happens?*

The penny probably slows down and veers to one side, probably missing the target.

❸ *Does one angle work best? If so, what angle?*

Dropping the pennies edge downward probably works best consistently.

Answers for Child/Adult Discussion

? *Was it easier to drop the pennies into the Dry Target or to drop them into the Submerged Target?*

Dropping the pennies into the Dry Target was much easier.

Reference

Sarquis, M. "Penny Dropping," *Community Approach to Science in Elementary Schools (CASES).* Unpublished work, 1983.

Vertically Challenged Shopping/Gathering List

Use this checklist as a guide to collecting the materials for this Family Science Challenge. Fill in the quantities needed below after doing the calculations called for in the "Calculating Quantities" section.

Total Quantities (from "Planning Notes")

_____ pennies

_____ box(es) or other container(s) for pennies

_____ clear plastic jars or pop beakers

_____ small rocks or marbles

_____ 10-gallon aquarium or clear plastic tub*

_____ water to fill aquarium or tub

_____ rubber mat(s) or towel(s)

_____ paper towels

_____ sponge(s)

_____ trash can(s)

Tools for Getting Ready

☐ 3 sheets of brightly colored cardstock for Table Tent **V**

☐ adhesive copier labels (template provided) or other materials to make labels**

☐ clear tape

* The aquarium or clear plastic tub must be deep enough to allow a plastic jar or pop beaker to be submerged under 3–6 inches of water.

** We have provided a label template that can be photocopied directly onto a blank sheet of copier labels to print all of the labels you need for the activity. Use 1-inch x 2¾-inch copier labels, such as Avery Copier Labels (code 5351). If copier labels are not available, copy the label template onto paper, cut out the labels, and use tape to affix the paper labels. Alternatively, make hand-written labels using permanent marker and masking tape or other similar materials.

Vertically Challenged Setup Checklist

The following is a list of items you will need to set up the Family Science Challenge. "Planning Notes" gives step-by-step instructions for setting up the Family Science Challenge.

Items Per Station

The following materials should be left on or near the table for all family teams to use. (A station is a location where family teams work on an activity.)

Material	Total Needed	Notes
☐ Table Tent **V**	_____	Copy master provided
☐ pennies in a labeled container	_____	_____
☐ sponge	_____	_____
☐ trash can	_____	_____

Items Per Setup

The following nonconsumable items should be placed at each setup. You may choose to provide more than one setup at each station to allow a number of family teams to work concurrently at the station.

Material	Total Needed	Notes
☐ labeled Dry Target	_____	Clear plastic jar or pop beaker
☐ labeled Submerged Target	_____	Jar or beaker submerged in aquarium or tub
☐ rubber mat or towel	_____	_____
☐ pencil for recording observations*	_____	_____

Consumable Materials

The following materials will be used up or taken away by family teams.

Material	Total Needed	Notes
☐ paper towels	_____	_____
☐ Family Science Challenge handouts**	_____	Copy master provided

* You may wish to pass out pencils at registration or have families bring their own pencils.

** You may wish to pass out Family Science Challenge handouts as a set at registration rather than at each station.

Vertically Challenged
Label Template

 Pennies
Use 10. Please leave at the station.

 Submerged Target
Please leave at the station.

 Dry Target
Please leave at the station.

 Pennies
Use 10. Please leave at the station.

 Submerged Target
Please leave at the station.

 Dry Target
Please leave at the station.

 Pennies
Use 10. Please leave at the station.

 Submerged Target
Please leave at the station.

 Dry Target
Please leave at the station.

 Pennies
Use 10. Please leave at the station.

 Submerged Target
Please leave at the station.

 Dry Target
Please leave at the station.

 Pennies
Use 10. Please leave at the station.

 Submerged Target
Please leave at the station.

 Dry Target
Please leave at the station.

 Pennies
Use 10. Please leave at the station.

Wow! Pop This

Family teams discover the effect of gas being produced in a film canister.

············· ## Key Science Topics

- carbon dioxide gas
- chemical reactions

············· ## Average Time Required

Performance   5–10 minutes

Links to *Classroom Science from A to Z*

You can extend this activity into your science curriculum with the following ideas, included in the book *Classroom Science from A to Z*:

- Links to National Science Standards

- Science Activity
  Students use a chemical reaction to reveal the treasures inside "treasure rocks" made of flour and baking soda.

- Lesson W Teacher Notes

- Lesson W Assessment

- Lesson W Science Explanation

- Lesson W Cross-Curricular Integration

Wow! Pop This

When you are done...

Throw away	Leave at the table	Take with you
paper towels	film canister and lid	completed handout
	cups	
	pencil (if provide at station)	

Wow! Pop This
Family Science Challenge

Pop your top… no hands allowed.

Materials

Alka-Seltzer® tablet • clear plastic cup • water • film canister with matching lid • Target Box • paper towels • waste bucket

Procedure

❶ Open an Alka-Seltzer® package and remove one tablet. Return the package with any other tablets to the original container for others to use. Break your tablet into quarters. Keep these away from water until instructed to use them.

❷ Half fill a clear, plastic cup with water. Drop a one-quarter piece of the Alka-Seltzer tablet into the cup and observe for a few moments.

? *What do you observe?*

_____

_____

❸ Empty the contents of the cup into the waste bucket and return the cup to the station supplies.

❹ Select a film canister and its matching lid. (The numbers should match.) Half-fill the canister with water.

❺ Have your adult partner hold the open film canister away from anyone's face and be ready to snap the lid on the canister and aim the canister into the Target Box when asked to do so in the next step.

❻ Drop a one-quarter piece of the Alka-Seltzer tablet into the water in the canister. Your adult partner should immediately snap the lid on the canister and aim the canister into the Target Box as shown in Figure 1.

? *What happens?*

_____

_____

_____

Figure 1

7 Retrieve the top of the canister. Leave any remaining liquid in the canister, adding water if necessary so it is half full. Repeat steps 5 and 6 with another one-quarter piece of the Alka-Seltzer tablet.

? *What do you observe?*

_____

_____

8 Repeat step 7 with the last one-quarter piece of the Alka-Seltzer tablet.

? *What do you observe?*

_____

_____

9 Pour the contents of the film canister into the waste water bucket and wipe up any spilled water. Leave the canister and its lid for others to use.

Child/Adult Discussion

? *What do you think caused the film canister lid to pop off?*

_____

_____

Explanation

The fizzing and bubbling you saw in the plastic cup were caused by a chemical reaction. Alka-Seltzer is a mixture of solids, including sodium bicarbonate (commonly known as baking soda), acetylsalicylic acid (aspirin), and citric acid. When added to water, these solids react with each other to form bubbles of carbon dioxide gas, as you observed in step 2. When the Alka-Seltzer and water are mixed in the closed film canister, the carbon dioxide gas is trapped. As the amount of trapped carbon dioxide gas increases, the pressure inside the canister increases. Eventually the pressure becomes great enough to cause the lid to pop off.

Stuff to Try at Home

Try the activity using ice water and hot tap water. Can you tell any difference in how fast the lid pops off?

Wow! Pop This
Planning Notes

This section will help you prepare for and carry out your Family Science event.

Calculating Quantities

"Calculating Quantities" contains information to help you calculate how much of each material you will need for your event. Copy values marked with a 🛒 onto the Shopping/Gathering List and those marked with a ✓ onto the Setup Checklist. If any of the calculations result in fractions, round up to the next whole number.

Nonconsumable Items Per Station

Amounts listed are for one station. If you will have more than one station for this Family Science Challenge, adjust amounts accordingly.

- container to hold packaged Alka-Seltzer tablets 🛒 ✓
- sponge 🛒 ✓
- bucket for waste water 🛒 ✓
- trash can 🛒 ✓

Nonconsumable Items Per Setup

You may choose to provide more than one setup at each station to allow a number of family teams to work concurrently.

- 4- to 8-ounce clear plastic cup
  (1 cup per setup) x _____ setups = _____ **4- to 8-ounce clear plastic cups** 🛒 ✓

- film canister with matching lid
  (1 canister per setup) x _____ setups = _____ **film canisters with lids** 🛒 ✓

- cardboard box approximately 1 foot x 1 foot x 1 foot
  (1 box per setup) x _____ setups = _____ **cardboard boxes** 🛒 ✓

Consumable Materials

- Alka-Seltzer tablets
  (1 tablet per family) x _____ families = _____ **tablets** 🛒 ✓

- water in 1- or 2-L plastic soft-drink bottles (if a source of running water will not be readily available near the station)
  estimate (0.015 L water per family) x _____ families = _____ **liters** 🛒 ✓
  _____ liters of water = _____ **1-L bottles** 🛒 ✓; OR
  _____ liters of water ÷ 2 = _____ **2-L bottles** 🛒 ✓

- paper towels
  (estimate 1 towel per family) x _____ families = _____ **paper towels** 🛒 ✓

Getting Ready for the Family Science Challenge

Tools or General Supplies Needed for Preparation Only

- 3 sheets of brightly colored cardstock for Table Tent **W**
- adhesive copier labels (template provided) or other materials to make labels

Preparing Materials for Use

- Photocopy the Family Science Challenge handout master to make the number of copies needed.

- Photocopy the Table Tent **W** master onto three sheets of brightly colored cardstock and assemble the table tent.

- Photocopy the label template onto a blank sheet of copier labels to print the labels, or make your own labels.

- To get the desired results, it is important that you match film canisters with tightly fitting lids. Test pairs of film canisters and lids by doing steps 4–6 of the Family Science Challenge and making sure the desired pop results. Once appropriate matches are found, label the cap and canister with the same numbers. (Use the labels provided or permanent markers.)

- Label the plastic cups, bottles for water, bucket for waste water, and container for packages of Alka-Seltzer tablets.

- For each setup, remove the lid or cut the flaps off a cardboard box and label it "Target Box."

- If the station will not be located near a source of running water (such as a sink or drinking fountain), fill several 1- or 2-L bottles with water to refill the containers of water as needed. Label the bottles appropriately.

Setting Up the Station

- Place Table Tent **W** at the station in a prominent location.

- Place the packaged Alka-Seltzer tablets in their labeled container or in their original boxes at the station.

- Place the bucket for waste water and a sponge to wipe up spills in a central location at the station.

- Place a plastic cup, a film canister with its matching lid, and a Target Box at each setup.

Disposal

Pour liquids down the drain. Rinse the film canisters and caps with water and save them for reuse.

Answers and Observations

❷ *What do you observe?*

Bubbling and fizzing occur, and the Alka-Seltzer tablet disappears as the reaction proceeds.

❻ *What happens?*

The lid pops off.

❼ *What happens?*

The lid pops off.

❽ *What happens?*

The lid pops off.

Answers for Child/Adult Discussion

? *What do you think caused the film canister lid to pop off?*

The canister lid pops off because bubbles form when the Alka-Seltzer tablet is added to water. This increases the pressure inside the canister.

References

Sarquis, A.M.; Woodward, L.M. "Chinese New Year Poppers," *Science Projects for Holidays Throughout the Year;* McGraw-Hill: New York, 1999.

Sarquis, A.M.; Woodward, L.M. "Alka-Seltzer Poppers: An Interactive Exploration," *Journal of Chemical Education, 76,* March 1999, pp 385–386.

Wow! Pop This Shopping/Gathering List

Use the checklist as a guide to collecting the materials for this Family Science Challenge. Fill in the quantities needed below after doing the calculations called for in the "Calculating Quantities" section.

Total Quantities (from "Planning Notes")

_____ Alka-Seltzer® tablets

_____ wide-mouthed container(s)*

_____ 4- to 8-ounce clear plastic cups

_____ film canisters with matching lids**

_____ cardboard boxes approximately 1 foot x 1 foot x 1 foot

_____ water

_____ 1- or 2-L plastic soft-drink bottles

_____ paper towels

_____ sponge(s)

_____ bucket(s) for waste water

_____ trash can(s)

Tools for Getting Ready

☐ 3 sheets of brightly colored cardstock for Table Tent **W**

☐ adhesive copier labels (template provided) or other materials to make labels***

* A pop beaker made by cutting off the top of a 2-L bottle works well.

** If possible, use black or gray film canisters with lids that fit over the top as shown in the figure. Translucent white canisters with lids that fit inside the canister top (like a plug) build up much more pressure and pop with much more force. Thus, the process takes longer and could present a hazard.

*** We have provided a label template that can be photocopied directly onto a blank sheet of copier labels to print all of the labels you need for the activity. Use 1-inch x 2¾-inch copier labels, such as Avery Copier Labels (code 5351). If copier labels are not available, copy the label template onto paper, cut out the labels, and use tape to affix the paper labels. Alternatively, make hand-written labels using permanent marker and masking tape or other similar materials.

Wow! Pop This Setup Checklist

The following is a list of items you will need to set up the Family Science Challenge. "Planning Notes" gives step-by-step instructions for setting up the Family Science Challenge.

Items Per Station

The following materials should be left on or near the table for all family teams to use. (A station is a location where family teams work on an activity.)

Material	Total Needed	Notes
☐ Table Tent **W**	_____	Copy master provided
☐ labeled container	_____	For the packaged Alka-Seltzer tablets
☐ sponge	_____	_____
☐ labeled bucket for waste water	_____	_____
☐ trash can	_____	_____

Items Per Setup

The following nonconsumable items should be placed at each setup. You may choose to provide more than one setup at each station to allow a number of family teams to work concurrently.

Material	Total Needed	Notes
☐ labeled plastic cup	_____	_____
☐ film canister with matching lid	_____	_____
☐ Target Box	_____	_____
☐ pencil for recording observations*	_____	_____

Consumable Materials

The following materials will be used up or taken away by family teams.

Material	Total Needed	Notes
☐ Alka-Seltzer tablets	_____	_____
☐ bottles of water	_____	_____
☐ paper towels	_____	_____
☐ Family Science Challenge handouts**	_____	Copy master provided

* You may wish to pass out pencils at registration or have families bring their own pencils.

** You may wish to pass out Family Science Challenge handouts as a set at registration rather than at each station.

Wow! Pop This Label Template

 Alka-Seltzer Tablets
1 tablet per family

 Alka-Seltzer Tablets
1 tablet per family

 Cup for Use in Step 2
Please leave at the station.

 Cup for Use in Step 2
Please leave at the station.

 Film Canister #____
Please leave at the station.

 Film Canister #____
Please leave at the station.

 Lid #___
Return to station.

 Lid #___
Return to station.

 Target Box
Please leave at the station.

 Target Box
Please leave at the station.

 Water

 Water

 Water

 Water

 Waste Water

 Waste Water

X Marks the Spot

Family teams explore some interesting properties of water as they move a drop through a maze.

Key Science Topics

- absorbency
- adhesion
- cohesion
- properties of water

Average Time Required

Performance   10 minutes

Links to *Classroom Science from A to Z*

You can extend this activity into your science curriculum with the following ideas, included in the book *Classroom Science from A to Z:*

- Links to National Science Standards

- Science Activity
  Students investigate the effect that the slope of a surface has on a water drop's motion and speed.

- Lesson X Teacher Notes

- Lesson X Assessment

- Lesson X Science Explanation

- Lesson X Cross-Curricular Integration

X Marks the Spot

Start →

Finish

When you are done...

Throw away	Leave at the table	Take with you
paper towels	cardboard	Straight Path sheet
	waxed paper	X Marks the Spot Maze sheet
	acetate sheet	completed handout
	paper clips	
	pencil (if provided at station)	

X Marks the Spot
Family Science Challenge

Maneuver the water drop through the maze.

Materials

Straight Path sheet • X Marks the Spot Maze sheet • 4 paper clips • cardboard • dropper bottle or squeeze bottle of colored water • waxed paper • acetate sheet • paper towels

Procedure

Figure 1

❶ Paper-clip a Straight Path sheet to a piece of cardboard as shown in Figure 1. Place a drop of colored water at "START" and hold the cardboard straight up and down. Watch the movement of the water for about 10–15 seconds.

? *What do you observe?*

_____

_____

❷ Wipe off the Straight Path with a paper towel and place a piece of waxed paper over it. Refasten the paper clips to hold the waxed paper in place as shown in Figure 2. Repeat the experiment.

? *What do you observe?*

_____

_____

Figure 2

❸ Try step 2 again using an acetate sheet in place of the waxed paper.

? *What do you observe?*

_____

_____

❹ Repeat steps 2 and 3 and time how long it takes the drop to reach the "X" finish mark. If a watch with a second hand is not available, you can count "One Mississippi, two Mississippi, etc." to count the number of seconds.

waxed paper (seconds) _____

acetate (seconds) _____

Figure 3

5 Paper clip the Maze sheet to a piece of cardboard. (See Figure 3.)

? *What do you think would happen if you tried to move a water drop through the paper maze? What if you covered the maze with waxed paper or an acetate sheet?*

_____

_____

_____

6 Test your hypothesis. Try not to let the water drop cross any lines or fall off the paper.

? *Describe what happens to the water drop.*

_____

_____

_____

7 To clean up, return the waxed paper, acetate sheet, cardboard, and paper clips to the station. You may keep the Maze sheet and Straight Path sheet.

Child/Adult Discussion

? *Why do you think the water drop behaved as it did?*

_____

_____

Explanation

A single drop of water contains trillions and trillions of water molecules. Water molecules have a strong attraction for other water molecules because of a force we call cohesion (co HEE zhun). This force is responsible for the shape of the water drop as well as the drop's ability to stay together as it rolls on the waxed paper or the acetate sheet.

In the activity, you observed another interesting property of water—it is absorbed by paper but not by the waxed paper or the acetate sheet. These differences result from the fact that water is attracted to the paper due to a force called adhesion. Adhesion is weak, however, between water and the waxed paper or acetate, which explains why the water drop is not absorbed by either one. So, placing the waxed paper or acetate sheet over the paper creates a barrier over which the water drop can slide more easily.

Marks the Spot Planning Notes

This section will help you prepare for and carry out your Family Science event.

Calculating Quantities

"Calculating Quantities" contains information to help you calculate how much of each material you will need for your event. Copy values marked with a 🛒 onto the Shopping/Gathering List and those marked with a ✓ onto the Setup Checklist. If any of the calculations result in fractions, round up to the next whole number.

Nonconsumable Items Per Station

Amounts listed are for one station. If you will have more than one station for this Family Science Challenge, adjust amounts accordingly.

- bottle of food color 🛒 ✓
- boxes or other containers to hold Straight Path sheets and Maze sheets 🛒 ✓
- trash can 🛒 ✓

Nonconsumable Items Per Setup

You may choose to provide more than one setup at each station to allow a number of family teams to work concurrently.

- piece of cardboard approximately 8½ inches x 11 inches
  (1 piece per setup) x _____ setups = _____ **pieces of cardboard** 🛒 ✓

- piece of waxed paper approximately 8½ inches x 11 inches
  (1 piece per setup) x _____ setups = _____ **pieces of waxed paper** 🛒 ✓

- 8½-inch x 11-inch acetate sheets
  (1 sheet per setup) x _____ setups = _____ **acetate sheets** 🛒 ✓

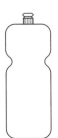

- paper clips
  (4 paper clips per setup) x _____ setups = _____ **paper clips** 🛒 ✓

- dropper bottles or squeeze bottles
  (1 bottle per setup) x _____ setups = _____ **bottles** 🛒 ✓

Consumable Materials

- water
  (enough to fill dropper bottles or squeeze bottles listed above)

- Straight Path sheets (master provided)
  (1 sheet per family) x _____ families = _____ **Straight Path sheets** 🛒 ✓

- Maze sheets (master provided)
  (1 maze sheet per family) x _____ families = _____ **Maze sheets** 🛒 ✓
- paper towels 🛒 ✓
  estimate (2 towels per family) x _____ families = _____ **paper towels** 🛒 ✓

Getting Ready for the Family Science Challenge
Tools or General Supplies Needed for Preparation Only

- 3 sheets of brightly colored cardstock for Table Tent **X**
- adhesive copier labels (template provided) or other materials to make labels
- scissors

Preparing Materials for Use

- Photocopy the Family Science Challenge handout master to make the number of copies needed.

- Photocopy the Table Tent **X** master onto three sheets of brightly colored cardstock and assemble the table tent.

- Photocopy the label template onto a blank sheet of copier labels to print the labels, or make your own labels.

- Photocopy the Straight Path Template (provided) to make the number of copies needed.

- Photocopy the Maze Template (provided) to make the number of copies needed.

- Fill the dropper bottles or squeeze bottles with water and add a few drops of food color to each.

- Cut cardboard into 8½-inch x 11-inch pieces.

- Cut waxed paper into 8½-inch x 11-inch pieces.

- Label the acetate sheets and pieces of waxed paper. (Place each label in a corner so it will be out of the way.)

- Label the dropper bottles or squeeze bottles and the boxes or containers for the Straight Path sheets and Maze sheets.

Setting Up the Station

- Place Table Tent **X** at the station in a prominent location.

- Put the Straight Path sheets and the Maze sheets in their labeled boxes. Place the boxes at the station.

- At each setup, place 1 piece of cardboard, 1 piece of waxed paper, 4 paper clips, 1 acetate sheet, and a labeled dropper bottle or squeeze bottle of colored water.

Answers and Observations

❶ *What do you observe?*

The water drop will probably be absorbed into the paper as it moves along the sheet and typically leaves a color trail on the path. (See figure.)

❷ *What do you observe?*

The water drop will move faster but may need a nudge to get started. It is not absorbed by the waxed paper.

❸ *What do you observe?*

As with the waxed paper, the water drop is not absorbed by the acetate sheet, and it moves faster than it did on the paper.

❻ *Describe what happens to the water drop.*

The water is not absorbed by the waxed paper or acetate but instead moves through the maze as the maze is tilted.

Answers for Child/Adult Discussion

? *Why do you think the water drop behaved as it did?*

The paper is porous and can absorb the water. The waxed paper and acetate sheet are not porous and cannot absorb the water.

X Marks the Spot
Shopping/Gathering List

Use this checklist as a guide to collecting the materials for this Family Science Challenge. Fill in the quantities needed below after doing the calculations called for in the "Calculating Quantities" section.

Total Quantities (from "Planning Notes")

_____ 8½-inch x 11-inch pieces of cardboard*

_____ 8½-inch x 11-inch pieces of waxed paper

_____ 8½-inch x 11-inch acetate sheets**

_____ boxes or other containers

_____ paper clips

_____ dropper bottles or squeeze bottles

_____ water

_____ food color

_____ paper towels

_____ Straight Path sheets

_____ Maze sheets

_____ trash can(s)

Tools for Getting Ready

☐ 3 sheets of brightly colored cardstock for Table Tent **X**

☐ adhesive copier labels (template provided) or other materials to make labels ***

☐ scissors

*   The cardboard can come from cereal boxes or other boxes.

**   This type of sheet is commonly used with overhead projectors.

*** We have provided a label template that can be photocopied directly onto a blank sheet of copier labels to print all of the labels you need for the activity. Use 1-inch x 2¾-inch copier labels, such as Avery Copier Labels (code 5351). If copier labels are not available, copy the label template onto paper, cut out the labels, and use tape to affix the paper labels. Alternatively, make hand-written labels using permanent marker and masking tape or other similar materials.

Marks the Spot Setup Checklist

The following is a list of items you will need to set up the Family Science Challenge. "Planning Notes" gives step-by-step instructions for setting up the Family Science Challenge.

Items Per Station

The following materials should be left on or near the table for all family teams to use. (A station is a location where family teams work on an activity.)

Material	Total Needed	Notes
☐ Table Tent **X**	_____	Copy master provided
☐ labeled containers	_____	To hold Straight Path sheets and Maze sheets
☐ trash can	_____	

Items Per Setup

The following nonconsumable items should be placed at each setup. You may choose to provide more than one setup at each station to allow a number of family teams to work concurrently.

Material	Total Needed	Notes
☐ 8½-inch x 11-inch piece of cardboard	_____	
☐ 8½-inch x 11-inch piece of waxed paper	_____	
☐ 8½-inch x 11-inch acetate sheet	_____	
☐ 4 paper clips	_____	4 per setup
☐ colored water in a labeled dropper bottle or squeeze bottle	_____	
☐ pencil for recording observations*	_____	

Consumable Materials

The following materials will be used up or taken away by family teams.

Material	Total Needed	Notes
☐ Straight Path sheets	_____	Copy master provided
☐ X Marks the Spot Maze sheets	_____	Copy master provided
☐ paper towels	_____	
☐ Family Science Challenge handouts**	_____	Copy master provided

*   You may wish to pass out pencils at registration or have families bring their own pencils.

** You may wish to pass out Family Science Challenge handouts as a set at registration rather than at each station.

Straight Path Straight Path

Start

Start

X
Finish

X
Finish

Marks the Spot Maze

Start

Finish

Marks the Spot
Label Template

X **Straight Path Sheets**
1 per family. You may keep it.

X **Acetate Sheet**
Please leave at the station.

X **Maze Sheets**
1 per family. You may keep it.

X **Waxed Paper**
Please leave at the station.

X **Colored Water**

X **Straight Path Sheets**
1 per family. You may keep it.

X **Acetate Sheet**
Please leave at the station.

X **Maze Sheets**
1 per family. You may keep it.

X **Waxed Paper**
Please leave at the station.

X **Colored Water**

X **Straight Path Sheets**
1 per family. You may keep it.

X **Acetate Sheet**
Please leave at the station.

X **Maze Sheets**
1 per family. You may keep it.

X **Waxed Paper**
Please leave at the station.

X **Colored Water**

X **Straight Path Sheets**
1 per family. You may keep it.

Yellow Submarine

Can an object be made to float, sink, and float again in a sealed plastic bottle? Family teams learn how and why this is possible in this investigation.

Key Science Topics

- buoyancy
- gases
- mass
- pressure
- relative density
- volume

Average Time Required

Performance   10 minutes

Links to *Classroom Science from A to Z*

You can extend this activity into your science curriculum with the following ideas, included in the book *Classroom Science from A to Z*:

- Links to National Science Standards

- Science Activity
  Students investigate various designs for twirling divers.

- Lesson Y Teacher Notes

- Lesson Y Assessment

- Lesson Y Science Explanation

- Lesson Y Cross-Curricular Integration

Yellow Submarine

When you are done...

Leave at the table	Take with you
Yellow Submarine toy	your straw diver
bottle of water	completed handout
Test Container	
Retriever Hook	
pencil (if provided at station)	

Yellow Submarine Family Science Challenge

Dive in and take command—make your sub sink and float.

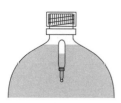

Figure 1

Materials

Yellow Submarine toy • half of a drinking straw • bobby pin • paper clips • capped plastic bottle filled with water • Retriever Hook • paper towels • "Test Container" filled with water

Procedure

❶ Observe the Yellow Submarine toy. (See Figure 1.) Try squeezing the sides of the bottle very firmly until you see a change in the position of the submarine. Watch closely.

❷ Stop squeezing the sides of the bottle. What does the Yellow Submarine toy do when you stop squeezing the sides?

❸ Squeeze and release several more times. Pay particular attention to the sides of the diver.

? *What did you observe?*

_____

_____

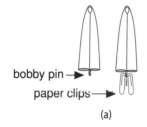

bobby pin →

paper clips →

(a)

(b)

Figure 2

❹ Return the Yellow Submarine toy to the station supplies.

❺ Make your own diver by bending a half straw piece in half and hooking the open ends together with a bobby pin as shown in Figure 2a. Attach two paper clips to the end of the bobby pin. Lower your diver, paper clips first, into the Test Container. It should float with just a small amount of the straw bend above the water level as shown in Figure 2b. If this is not the case, adjust the amount of water in the diver and/or the number of paper clips on the diver as needed.

   a. If it sinks, remove one of the paper clips and try again.

   b. If it floats too high, try squeezing the straw while it is out of the water and then holding the open ends under the water while releasing the squeeze to allow water to rise into the straw. If it fills with too much water, squeeze out some of the water.

   c. If it lies on its side on the water, readjust the bobby pin and add more paper clips.

Draw water level in diver
before squeezing.

(a)

6 Remove the cap from one of the unused 1- or 2-L bottles that is filled to the cap with water. Carefully move your diver from the Test Container into the bottle of water. Try not to allow the water level inside the straw diver to change during the process. Your diver should float. If it does not, use the Retriever Hook to remove it from the bottle and repeat step 5. Once the straw diver is floating in the bottle, twist the cap on tightly. On Figure 3a, draw a line in the straw diver to indicate the water level.

7 With the cap tightly closed, squeeze the sides of the bottle.

? *What happens to the diver? What happens to the water level inside the straw diver when you squeeze the bottle? Use Figure 3b to draw what you saw.*

_____

_____

8 Retrieve your straw diver from the bottle using the Retriever Hook. Wipe up any spills. Return the bottle of water and Retriever Hook to the station. You may keep your straw diver.

Child/Adult Discussion

? *In what ways were the Yellow Submarine toy and the straw diver similar and different?*

_____

_____

Draw position of diver
and water level in diver
when it's squeezed.

(b)

Figure 3

Explanation

Objects either sink or float in water because of their density. Objects more dense than water sink, but objects less dense than water float. The two divers in this activity are multipart "systems." While some of the individual parts alone are more dense than water and thus would sink in it, when assembled to include air the resulting system is less dense than water and floats.

The divers used in this activity can move up and down in water depending on the pressure applied to the bottle. When you squeezed the bottle of the Yellow Submarine toy, the sides of the submarine were pushed in and the air trapped in the diver was compressed. The volume of the diver decreased but its mass did not change. This caused its density to increase. As a result, the diver sank.

The straw divers worked a little differently. Squeezing the bottle pushed more water into the straw. This additional amount of water caused the diver's mass and density to increase, and the diver sank.

In both cases, when you released the bottle, the air trapped in the diver expanded to its original volume. In the straw diver, this forced out the extra water. This resulted in a decrease in the diver's mass and density so that the system was once again less dense than water and floated to the top.

Yellow Submarine Planning Notes

This section will help you prepare for and carry out your Family Science event.

Calculating Quantities

"Calculating Quantities" contains information to help you calculate how much of each material you will need for your event. Copy values marked with a 🛒 onto the Shopping/Gathering List and those marked with a ✓ onto the Setup Checklist. If any of the calculations result in fractions, round up to the next whole number.

Nonconsumable Items Per Station

Amounts listed are for one station. If you will have more than one station for the Family Science Challenge, adjust amounts accordingly.

- 3 boxes or other containers for straws, paper clips, and bobby pins 🛒 ✓
- sponge 🛒 ✓
- trash can 🛒 ✓

Nonconsumable Items Per Setup

You may choose to provide more than one setup at each station to allow a number of family teams to work concurrently.

- disposable Beral graduated pipets
  (1 pipet per setup) x _____ *setups =* _____ ***Beral pipets*** 🛒 ✓

- brass, stainless steel, or galvanized $^{12}/_{24}$ hex nuts
  (1 hex nut per setup) x _____ *setups =* _____ ***hex nuts*** 🛒 ✓

- clear, colorless 1-L soft-drink bottles with caps for Yellow Submarine and straw diver
  (2 bottles per setup) x _____ *setups =* _____ ***1-L bottles*** 🛒 ✓

- water to fill diver setups and Test Containers

- tall, transparent containers, such as pop beakers
  (1 container per setup) x _____ *setups =* _____ ***containers*** 🛒 ✓

- 22-gauge wire for Retriever Hooks
  (1 hook per setup) x _____ *setups =* _____ ***Retriever Hooks*** ✓
  (15 inches of wire per hook) x _____ *setups =* _____ ***inches of 22-gauge wire*** 🛒

Consumable Materials

- drinking straw halves

  (1 straw half per family) x _____ *families =* _____ **straw halves** ✓

  _____ *straw halves ÷ (2 halves per straw) =* _____ **whole straws** 🛒

- bobby pins

  (1 bobby pin per family) x _____ *families =* _____ **bobby pins** 🛒 ✓

- paper clips

  estimate (3 paper clips per family) x _____ *families =* _____ **paper clips** 🛒 ✓

- paper towels

  estimate (1 towel per family) x _____ *families =* _____ **paper towels** 🛒 ✓

Getting Ready for the Family Science Challenge

Tools or General Supplies Needed for Preparation Only

- 3 sheets of brightly colored cardstock for Table Tent **Y**
- adhesive copier labels (template provided) or other materials to make labels
- scissors
- plastic cup
- water
- yellow food color
- hot-melt glue gun and glue

Preparing Materials for Use

- Photocopy the Family Science Challenge handout master to make the number of copies needed.

- Photocopy the Table Tent **Y** master onto three sheets of brightly colored cardstock and assemble the table tent.

- Photocopy the label template onto a blank sheet of copier labels to print the labels, or make your own labels.

- Cut the drinking straws in half. Each family will use one straw half.

- Wash out the 1-L bottles for the straw divers and remove the labels. Fill the bottles with water almost to the cap and cap them. Label them appropriately. Label the pop beaker or other container as the "Test Container."

- Make the Retriever Hooks for families to use in steps 6 and 8 of the Family Science Challenge (to get the diver out of the bottle): Cut the 22-gauge wire into 15-inch pieces with scissors. Bend one end of each length of wire into a hook. Label the hooks.

- Label the boxes for the straws, paper clips, and bobby pins.

- Prepare the Yellow Submarine toy as follows:

  - Using the ruler at left as a guide, use the scissors to clip off the stem of the pipet approximately 14–15 mm (⅝ inch) below the bulb. (See figure below.) Screw a hex nut onto a pipet stem up to the bulb. (See figure below.) The hex nut should cut grooves, or "threads," into the plastic.

⅝ inch

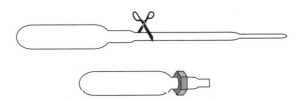

  - About half-fill a diver with brightly colored yellow water. You'll probably have to do this by squeezing the bulb and putting the open end in the yellow water, then relaxing the squeeze to draw the liquid into the bulb.

  - Place this diver in a cup of water to see if it floats. If it sinks, squeeze out a little of the liquid and try again. Adjust the amount of liquid in the diver so that the top of the bulb floats about ½ cm above the surface of the water. (See figure at left.)

  - Carefully remove the diver from the cup without losing any of the water inside the diver. Seal the end of the diver using one of the following methods:
    Method 1: Apply a little chewed chewing gum or sticky-tack to the open end. (No one else will be touching the diver, so chewed gum would not represent a health hazard.)
    Method 2: Apply oil-based clay or silicone caulking to the open end.
    Method 3: Use hot-melt glue to seal the pipet with a small amount of glue. (See figure at left.) Be carefully not to apply too big a glob of glue. Once the glue has cooled, gently squeeze the diver to check the seal. Apply more glue if necessary, but don't overdo it.

  - Test each diver to see if it still floats in water. If it doesn't, you'll need to remove some of the mass, either by using less sealing material or by removing some water from the diver. Make the necessary adjustments and repeat the float test.

- Wash the 1-L bottles for the Yellow Submarine and remove the labels. Fill the bottles almost to the top with water. Place one diver, stem side down, in the water. It should float near the top. (See figure at left.) If it doesn't, remove the diver and adjust the amount of water as before.

- Once the diver is inside the bottle and is floating at the proper level, screw the cap onto the bottle securely. Squeeze the bottle and watch the diver descend. When you release the squeeze, the diver should return to its original position. Label each bottle "Yellow Submarine toy."

Setting Up the Station

- Place Table Tent **Y** at the station in a prominent location.

- Place a Yellow Submarine toy, a capped 2-L bottle filled with water, a Test Container, and a Retriever Hook at each setup. Fill the Test Containers about three-quarters full with water.

- Place the straws, paper clips, and bobby pins in their appropriate boxes. Put the boxes at the station where they are accessible to all setups but are not in the way. Have a sponge handy to clean up spills.

Answers and Observations

Figure 3b should show a diver position and water level similar to this.

❸ *What did you observe?*

When the bottle is squeezed, the sides of the submarine are pushed in, and the submarine sinks. When the squeeze is released, the sides of the submarine expand, and the submarine rises.

❼ *What happens to the diver? What happens to the water level inside the straw diver when you squeeze the bottle? Use Figure 3b to draw what you saw.*

The diver sinks and the water level in the straw rises because squeezing the bottle forces more water into the straw diver.

Answers for Child/Adult Discussion

? *In what ways were the Yellow Submarine toy and the straw diver similar and different?*

Both divers sank when the bottle was squeezed, but the way they looked when sunk differed. The Yellow Submarine's sides appeared pushed in, while the straw diver's water level changed.

Yellow Submarine Shopping/Gathering List

Use this checklist as a guide to collecting the materials for this Family Science Challenge. Fill in the quantities needed below after doing the calculations called for in the "Calculating Quantities" section.

Total Quantities (from "Planning Notes")

_____ disposable Beral™ graduated pipets*

_____ brass, stainless steel, or galvanized $^{12}/_{24}$ hex nuts**

_____ clear, colorless plastic 1-L soft-drink bottles with caps***

_____ tall, transparent plastic containers†

_____ liters of water

_____ inches of 22-gauge wire

_____ drinking straws

_____ bobby pins

_____ paper clips

_____ boxes or other containers

_____ paper towels

_____ sponge(s)

_____ trash can(s)

Tools for Getting Ready

☐ 3 sheets of brightly colored cardstock for Table Tent **Y**

☐ adhesive copier labels (template provided) or other materials to make labels††

☐ scissors

☐ plastic cup

☐ water

☐ yellow food color

☐ chewed chewing gum or sticky-tack, oil-based clay or silicone caulking, or hot-melt glue gun and glue

---

* Beral graduated pipets come in many models and sizes. Model number B78-400 from Micro Mole Scientific, 1312 N. 15th Street, Pasco, WA, 99301, 509/545-4904, is used and illustrated in this lesson.

** Pipet manufacturers sometimes change the design and specifications of the pipets. You may want to wait to purchase the hex nuts until after the pipets have arrived, then use these pipets to select the appropriate hex nuts. The nuts should be just smaller than the pipet stem so that the nut cuts grooves, or threads, into the stem. Hex nuts can be purchased from a hardware store. If you cannot find hex nuts of the right size, you can wrap clear tape around the pipet stem to make it bigger and allow the nuts to fit tightly.

*** 2-L bottles work well but may be difficult for small hands to squeeze. Twelve-ounce bottles also work.

† The plastic container must be tall enough so that the straw, bobby pin, and paper clip will float without touching the bottom. A pop beaker made from a cut-off 2-L soft-drink bottle works well. Alternatively, you can use an aquarium, which is not as easily tipped over as a pop beaker or cup.

†† We have provided a label template that can be photocopied directly onto a blank sheet of copier labels to print all of the labels you need for the activity. Use 1-inch x 2¾-inch copier labels, such as Avery Copier Labels (code 5351). If copier labels are not available, copy the label template onto paper, cut out the labels, and use tape to affix the paper labels. Alternatively, make hand-written labels using permanent marker and masking tape or other similar materials.

Yellow Submarine Setup Checklist

The following is a list of items you will need to set up the Family Science Challenge. "Planning Notes" gives step-by-step instructions for setting up the Family Science Challenge.

Items Per Station

The following materials should be left on or near the table for all family teams to use. (A station is a location where family teams work on an activity.)

Material	Total Needed	Notes
☐ Table Tent **Y**	_____	Copy master provided
☐ 3 labeled boxes	_____	For straws, paper clips, and bobby pins
☐ trash can	_____	_____
☐ (optional) sponge	_____	_____

Items Per Setup

The following nonconsumable items should be placed at each setup. You may choose to provide more than one setup at each station to allow a number of family teams to work concurrently.

Material	Total Needed	Notes
☐ Yellow Submarine Toy	_____	A diver inside a capped 2-L bottle filled with water
☐ capped 2-L plastic soft drink bottle filled with water	_____	_____
☐ labeled Test Container	_____	_____
☐ Retriever Hook	_____	_____
☐ pencil for recording observations*	_____	_____

Consumable Materials

The following materials will be used up or taken away by family teams.

Material	Total Needed	Notes
☐ straw halves	_____	_____
☐ bobby pins	_____	_____
☐ paper clips	_____	_____
☐ paper towels	_____	_____
☐ Family Science Challenge handouts**	_____	Copy master provided

* You may wish to pass out pencils at registration or have families bring their own pencils.

** You may wish to pass out Family Science Challenge handouts as a set at registration rather than at each station.

Yellow Submarine Label Template

Y Yellow Submarine Toy
Leave the cap on.
Please leave at the station.

Y Yellow Submarine Toy
Leave the cap on.
Please leave at the station.

Y Test Container
Please leave at the station.

Y Test Container
Please leave at the station.

Y Straws
1 per family.

Y Straws
1 per family.

Y Paper Clips
2–3 per family.

Y Paper Clips
2–3 per family.

Y Bobby Pins
1 per family.

Y Bobby Pins
1 per family.

Y 2-L bottle of water
Use for your straw diver.

Y 2-L bottle of water
Use for your straw diver.

Y Retriever Hook
Please leave at the station.

Y Retriever Hook
Please leave at the station.

Y Straws
1 per family.

Y Straws
1 per family.

Zap

Students and their families produce light by pulling open the wrapper from an adhesive bandage.

.... ## Key Science Topics

- light
- triboluminescence

.... ## Average Time Required

Performance   10 minutes

Links to *Classroom Science from A to Z*

You can extend this activity into your science curriculum with the following ideas, included in the book *Classroom Science from A to Z:*

- Links to National Science Standards

- Science Activity
  Students make their own glow-in-the-dark paint.

- Lesson Z Teacher Notes

- Lesson Z Assessment

- Lesson Z Science Explanation

- Lesson Z Cross-Curricular Integration

Zap

When you are done…

Throw away	Leave at the table	Take with you
bandage	viewing box	completed handout
wrapper	pencil (if provided at station)	
adhesive tape		

Names _____   _____

_____   _____

Zap
Family Science Challenge

Discover what's so "a-peeling" about the wrapper.

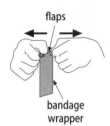

flaps

bandage
wrapper

Figure 1

Materials

Curad® adhesive bandage in its wrapper • viewing box or access to dark room • adhesive tape • scissors

Procedure

1. Have your adult partner use both hands to hold the adhesive bandage wrapper by the two flaps with the rest of the wrapper and adhesive bandage hanging down. (See Figure 1.) Have your adult partner keep his or her hands in the same position and, without tugging on the wrapper, reach under the fabric flap into the viewing box. (See Figure 2.)

2. Look through the view hole and make sure the top of the wrapper is directly below the viewing hole. Adjust the fabric flap to cover the back of the box as completely as possible. Then cover the sides of your eyes with your hands as shown in Figure 3.

3. Allow your eyes to adjust to the dark as you look directly at the top of the bandage wrapper. When you are ready, tell your adult partner to quickly pull apart the two flaps of the wrapper. The event you are observing happens fast, so be ready!

? *What do you observe?*

_____

_____

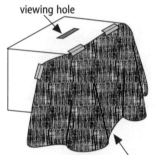

viewing hole

Put your hands inside
the viewing box.

Figure 2

4. Try reassembling the original wrapper (without the bandage strip) and repeating the procedure.

? *What do you observe?*

_____

_____

Figure 3

5. Cut two pieces of adhesive tape to about the same length as the bandage wrapper. Stick the sticky sides of the tape pieces together except for about half an inch at the top to make something that resembles the bandage wrapper. Now repeat steps 1–3.

? *What do you observe?*

_____

_____

❻ If either a darkened room or a walk-in cardboard "darkroom" is available, repeat the activity there using a new Curad® bandage wrapper but without the viewing box.

❼ Discard all used materials, including the bandage, in the trash.

Child/Adult Discussion

? *Discuss the similarities of the three trials and the differences in the three results.*

_____

_____

_____

_____

Explanation

The light given off when the adhesive bandage wrapper is pulled apart results from a process called triboluminescence. Triboluminescence occurs when light is given off as a result of the shearing, breaking, or crushing of a chemical.

The light you see with the Curad® adhesive bandage wrappers is a result of the shearing of a chemical in the glue that was used to hold the wrapper together. When you quickly pull the two sides of the wrapper apart, the mechanical energy you apply is transformed into light energy. It is sometimes possible to produce light a second time by reassembling and pulling apart the same wrapper. However, the intensity of the glow is often less. The adhesive tape doesn't produce the sparks of light because its adhesive does not contain the special chemical used in the bandage wrapper's glue.

Why does the bandage wrapper glue contain a chemical that produces triboluminescence? The manufacturer adds the chemical for a completely different reason. This same chemical also glows when ultraviolet light (black light) shines on it. This effect is called fluorescence. The manufacturer adds the chemical so that the placement of the glue on the paper wrappers can be monitored under ultraviolet light while the wrappers are being made.

Stuff to Try at Home

Place one or two Wint-O-Green® Life Savers® in a plastic bag. In a darkened room, use a pair of pliers to crush the candy and watch for sparks of light in the candy. This is the same phenomenon that was seen with the bandage wrapper.

Zap

Planning Notes

This section will help you prepare for and carry out your Family Science event.

Calculating Quantities

"Calculating Quantities" contains information to help you calculate how much of each material you will need for your event. Copy values marked with a 🛒 onto the Shopping/Gathering List and those marked with a ✓ onto the Setup Checklist. If any of the calculations result in fractions, round up to the next whole number.

Nonconsumable Items Per Station

Amounts listed are for one station. If you will have more than one station for this Family Science Challenge, adjust amounts accordingly.

- box or other container for bandages 🛒 ✓
- trash can 🛒 ✓

Nonconsumable Items Per Setup

You may choose to provide more than one setup at each station to allow a number of family teams to work concurrently.

- viewing box

  (1 viewing box per setup) x _____ setups = _____ **viewing boxes** ✓

  How many cardboard boxes do I need?
  (1 box per setup) x _____ setups = _____ **cardboard boxes** 🛒

  How many pieces of dark cloth do I need?
  (1 piece per setup) x _____ setups = _____ **pieces of dark cloth** 🛒

- pair of scissors
  (1 pair of scissors per setup) x _____ setups = _____ **pairs of scissors** 🛒 ✓

Consumable Materials

- Curad® adhesive bandages in wrappers
  (2 bandages per family) x _____ families = _____ **bandages** 🛒 ✓

- adhesive tape, about 1-inch- to 1½-inch-wide
  (estimate 8 linear inches per family) x _____ families = _____ **linear inches of adhesive tape** 🛒 ✓

Getting Ready for the Family Science Challenge

Tools or General Supplies Needed for Preparation Only

- 3 sheets of brightly colored cardstock for Table Tent **Z**
- adhesive copier labels (template provided) or other materials to make labels
- scissors or utility knife (if necessary)
- masking tape

Preparing Materials for Use

- Photocopy the Family Science Challenge handout master to make the number of copies needed.

- Photocopy the Table Tent **Z** master onto three sheets of brightly colored cardstock and assemble the table tent.

- Photocopy the label template onto a blank sheet of copier labels to print the labels, or make your own labels.

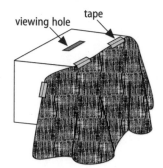

- Prepare the viewing box as follows:
  - Cut the top flaps, if any, off the box.
  - Lay the box on its side with the open end facing you. The open end becomes the front of the viewing box.
  - In the middle of the top of the viewing box, cut out a rectangle approximately 4 inches long and 1 inch wide. This is the viewing hole.
  - Carefully tape the dark cloth close to the top edge of the box and halfway down the sides. The cloth should drape over the front of the box. Leave the bottom untaped so participants can reach in and out of the box easily.
  - Test the box to be sure it is dark enough to see the light emitted from the wrappers.
  - Label the viewing box.

- Label the box for the bandages.

Setting Up the Station

- Place Table Tent **Z** at the station in a prominent location.

- Put the bandages in their labeled box at the station. Place the tape at the station.

- Put one labeled viewing box and a pair of scissors at each setup.

Tips

You may wish to make a child-sized walk-in "darkroom" from an appliance carton by cutting a doorway and adding a black curtain, as shown to the left. This "darkroom" can be used in step 6 of the Family Science Challenge.

Disposal

The adhesive bandages will no longer be sterile after the activity is completed; do not allow them to be saved for later use.

Answers and Observations

3 *What do you observe?*

Light is given off as the glued sides of the wrapper are pulled apart.

4 *What do you observe?*

About 30–40% of the people who have tried this activity report seeing light again when reusing the same wrapper, but typically the light is less intense. The remaining 60–70% don't see light a second time.

5 *What do you see?*

Pulling apart the adhesive tape produces no light.

Answers for Child/Adult Discussion

? *Discuss the similarities of the three trials and the differences in the three results.*

Each trial involves pulling apart two sticky things. Trials with the bandage wrapper produce light, while trials with the adhesive tape do not.

Zap
Shopping/Gathering List

Use this checklist as a guide to collecting the materials for this Family Science Challenge. Fill in the quantities needed below after doing the calculations called for in the "Calculating Quantities" section.

Total Quantities (from "Planning Notes")

_____ Curad® adhesive bandages*

_____ inches of 1-inch- to 1½-inch-wide adhesive tape

_____ pairs of scissors

_____ cardboard box(es)**

_____ dark cloth(s)**

_____ box(es) or other container(s)

_____ trash can(s)

Tools for Getting Ready

☐ 3 sheets of brightly colored cardstock for Table Tent **Z**

☐ adhesive copier labels (template provided) or other materials to make labels***

☐ scissors**

☐ masking tape**

* Other brands of adhesive bandage wrappers also work but not nearly as well as Curad.

** These materials are needed to make a viewing box. The cardboard box should be large enough for you to put your hands inside and open a bandage wrapper. The dark cloth should be 12–16 inches greater in length and width than the open end of the box.

*** We have provided a label template that can be photocopied directly onto a blank sheet of copier labels to print all of the labels you need for the activity. Use 1-inch x 2¾-inch copier labels, such as Avery® Copier Labels (code 5351). If copier labels are not available, copy the label template onto paper, cut out the labels, and use tape to affix the paper labels. Alternatively, make hand-written labels using permanent marker and masking tape or other similar materials.

Zap
Setup Checklist

The following is a list of items you will need to set up the Family Science Challenge. "Planning Notes" gives step-by-step instructions for setting up the Family Science Challenge.

Items Per Station

The following materials should be left on or near the table for all family teams to use. (A station is a location where family teams work on a challenge.)

Material	Total Needed	Notes
☐ Table Tent **Z**	_____	Copy master provided
☐ labeled box or other container	_____	For the bandages
☐ trash can	_____	

Items Per Setup

The following nonconsumable items should be placed at each setup. You may choose to provide more than one setup at each station to allow a number of family teams to work concurrently.

Material	Total Needed	Notes
☐ pencil for recording observations*	_____	
☐ labeled viewing box	_____	The dark cloth should already be attached.
☐ pair of scissors	_____	

Consumable Materials

The following materials will be used up or taken away by family teams.

Material	Total Needed	Notes
☐ Curad® adhesive bandages	_____	
☐ adhesive tape	_____	
☐ Family Science Challenge handouts**	_____	Copy master provided

* You may wish to pass out pencils at registration or have families bring their own pencils.

** You may wish to pass out Family Science Challenge handouts as a set at registration rather than at each station.

Zap
Label Template

Z Curad® bandages
Use 2 per family, please.

Z Curad® bandages
Use 2 per family, please.

Z Viewing Box

Z Viewing Box

Z Curad® bandages
Use 2 per family, please.

Z Curad® bandages
Use 2 per family, please.

Z Viewing Box

Z Viewing Box

Z Curad® bandages
Use 2 per family, please.

Z Curad® bandages
Use 2 per family, please.

Z Viewing Box

Z Viewing Box

Z Curad® bandages
Use 2 per family, please.

Z Curad® bandages
Use 2 per family, please.

Z Viewing Box

Z Viewing Box

Index of Science Topics